S0-ADD-589

27 September 2000

To Tom and Becky,

with deep appreciation
for your commitment to community
and to justice and to integrity
and living the WORD — all
aspects of John's implications
contained within—

with love, Anna

*Medieval Arts Doctrines on Ambiguity and
Their Place in Langland's Poetics*

In this far-ranging yet concise study, John Chamberlin helps readers
of *Piers Plowman* understand some of the most characteristic and
inventive elements of Langland's work. Using an interdisciplinary
approach, Chamberlin brings together an examination of Langland's
poetic practices, a discussion of the historical development of the
arts-of-discourse doctrines from which they derive, and some broad
considerations of the implications of these doctrines for language
theory.

Chamberlin's focal point for this synthesis is the concept of ambiguity, which has played an important role in the liberal arts tradition
and in medieval discourses regarding reading and preaching – discourses that are fundamental to Langland's poetic ways with words.
He deals with lexical ambiguity and the ambiguity of words-as-words
– in which words themselves are taken as objects – offering linguistic, philosophical, and historical perspectives on these subjects.
Chamberlin's work takes its place among other recent attempts to
retrieve medieval literary theory, allowing it to inform the reading
of medieval literature, but he places this theory within a particularly
wide context. He claims that the excess of meaning that ambiguity
gives language is at least as important as allegory to the understanding of *Piers Plowman* and other medieval texts.

Chamberlin shows how ambiguity works in Langland's poetry
in his close analysis of a number of passages from the poem. His
overview of the historical development of the concept of ambiguity
pays special attention to the doctrines of Augustine and the twelfth-
century masters. He elucidates these by reference to similar ideas
from romantic and twentieth-century theorists, providing a coherent
view of language that stands as an alternative to structuralist and
poststructuralist views.

JOHN CHAMBERLIN taught in the English Department at Wilfrid
Laurier University and had published two previous books, as well as an
article in *Style* entitled "What Makes *Piers Plowman* So Hard to Read?"

Medieval Arts Doctrines on Ambiguity and Their Place in Langland's Poetics

JOHN CHAMBERLIN

McGill-Queen's University Press
Montreal & Kingston · London · Ithaca

© McGill-Queen's University Press 2000
ISBN 0-7735-2073-2

Legal deposit third quarter 2000
Bibliothèque nationale du Québec

Printed in Canada on acid-free paper

This book has been published with the help of a grant
from the Humanities and Social Sciences Federation of
Canada, using funds provided by the Social Sciences
and Humanities Research Council of Canada.

McGill-Queen's University Press acknowledges the
financial support of the Government of Canada
through the Book Publishing Industry Development
Program (BPIDP) for its publishing activities. It also
acknowledges the support of the Canada Council for
the Arts for its publishing program.

Funds for the indexing of this book were provided by
the Wilfrid Laurier University SSHRC General
Research Grant.

Canadian Cataloguing in Publication Data

Chamberlin, John, 1942–1999
    Medieval arts doctrines on ambiguity and their place in
    Langland's poetics
    Includes bibliographical references and index.
    ISBN 0-7735-2073-2
    1. Langland, William, 1330?–1400?. Piers the
    Plowman. 2. Ambiguity in literature. 3. Poetics –
    History – To 1500. I. Title.
    PR2017.L35C43 2000   821'.1   C00-900082-8

Typeset in New Baskerville 10.5/13
by Caractéra inc.

The scholarship of integration means interpretation, fitting one's own research – or the research of others – into larger intellectual patterns ... The distinction ... between "discovery" and "integration" can be best understood, perhaps, by the questions posed. Those engaged in discovery ask, "What is to be known, what is yet to be found?" Those engaged in integration ask, "What do the findings *mean*? Is it possible to interpret what's been discovered in ways that provide a larger, more comprehensive understanding?" Questions such as these call for the power of critical analysis and interpretation. They have a legitimacy of their own and if carefully pursued can lead the scholar from information to knowledge and even, perhaps, to wisdom.

Ernest L. Boyer, *Scholarship Reconsidered*, 19–20

Creating and moving in a medium which presents the absent, the poetic language is a language of cognition – but a cognition which subverts the positive ... Naming the "things that are absent" is the ingression of a different order of things into the established one – "le commencement d'un monde." (Valéry)

For the expression of this other order, which is transcendence within the one world, the poetic language depends on the transcendent elements in ordinary language.

Herbert Marcuse, *One-Dimensional Man*, 67–8

Contents

Preface   ix

Acknowledgments   xi

Introduction   3

PART ONE   LEXICAL AMBIGUITY
IN THE ARTS OF DISCOURSE AND
IN *PIERS PLOWMAN*

1   Lexical Ambiguity: Context, Ground,
    and Overview   13

2   Augustine on Ambiguity   24

3   The Twelfth Century and Arts of
    Discourse   45

4   *Piers Plowman*: The Resources of
    Ambiguity in the Samaritan's Sermon   60

    Transition   73

PART TWO   THE AMBIGUITY
OF WORDS-AS-WORDS IN THE ARTS
OF DISCOURSE AND IN *PIERS PLOWMAN*

5   Words-as-Words: Context, Ground, and
    Overview   81

6   Augustine on Words-as-Words   93

7   The Twelfth Century and
    Words-as-Words   108

8   *Piers Plowman* and the Ambiguity of
    Words-as-Words   139

    Conclusion   157

    Works Cited   161

    Index   177

Preface

This project was in progress for a good long time. I think it was the "shaking down" of my subject that took so long. The process of reading and deciding what not to include was almost as time-consuming as deciding what to include and getting that down on paper. The patterns of development that would accommodate what I wanted to say emerged only slowly.

The reader will notice that I've used neither footnotes nor endnotes but have followed the MLA expediency of sending my reader as clearly and simply as possible back to the bibliography for references. I resisted temptations to expatiate or found ways to wiggle an interesting aside into the text.

Failing health has kept me from doing all that I would have liked to have done in the final preparation stages of my manuscript. I hope my reader will not be too impatient with details.

John Chamberlin
14 December 1999

Acknowledgments

My first expression of appreciation must go to my friend and colleague in Wilfrid Laurier University's Philosophy Department, Dr Leo Groarke. His encouragement, his continued interest in my work, and his belief that my book could be worthwhile helped me to overcome setbacks that I might very well have succumbed to had it not been for his support.

Derek Pearsall made a significant contribution to the project's inception by receiving me as an honorary visiting fellow at the Centre for Medieval Studies, University of York, England, in the winter term of 1983. I'm sure Derek Pearsall has helped out many young scholars, as I was then, by sharing so generously his wide-ranging knowledge, his contacts with other senior scholars, and his ability to put the inexperienced at ease. I'm grateful also to James Simpson for sponsoring me as a visiting scholar at Cambridge University for several weeks in the winter of 1992.

Librarians and their personnel are indispensable to scholarly work. I am especially grateful for permission to consult works in certain special collections. I thank the librarian of Corpus Christi College, Cambridge; the authorities at the Cambridge University Library; Canon Iain Mackenzie, the librarian at Worcester Cathedral; and the library staff at Wilfrid Laurier University.

McGill-Queen's University Press has been uncommonly generous in accommodating itself to my circumstances. I appreciate the flexibility and sensitivity that it has shown.

ADDENDUM: Had my husband lived to oversee the final stages of publication, he would no doubt have added words of appreciation and gratitude to those individuals who generously helped in the final preparation of the manuscript: to Joanne Buehler-Buchan, for putting the manuscript on disc, to Lorne Ellaschuk and Jane Campbell, for kindly checking references when John was too ill to do so; to Liz Graham, for helping check citations in Works Cited; to Peter Erb, for graciously and meticulously editing Works Cited; to Elaine Auerback, for her gift of laboriously proof reading the manuscript; and to John and Anna Parry – to John, for his sensitive copy editing of the text, and to Anna, for her careful preparation of the index. My husband's original work has been greatly enhanced by the generous contributions of all these colleagues and friends.

Anna Hemmendinger
17 March 2000

Medieval Arts Doctrines on Ambiguity and Their Place in Langland's Poetics

Introduction

I wrote this book in the midst of the theory wars; inevitably my ideas received direction from that turmoil. In reaction to the outbreak of hostilities in literature departments, and in response to the new developments, we medievalists (lest we lose ground within academic institutions, if for no other reason) have sought to become more self-aware about theoretical assumptions in approaching texts. To this end, renewed efforts have taken place, with considerable success, to retrieve medieval notions about what is involved in the rhetoric of texts and to apply those ideas to deepen our reading of medieval literature.

In such a project of retrieval, current theoretical ideas, implicit or not, inevitably mediate the historical scholarship involved; completely objective archaeologizing is impossible, even if it were desirable. In sum, we must be aware of the vantage point from which we proceed and make a deliberate choice among possible theoretical perspectives on the past. I have taken up a standpoint that I believe is both valid and not antithetical to the medieval ideas that I am attempting to grasp. My epigraph from Marcuse gives some indication of my approach.

My attempt to give attention both to language theory on the one hand and to literary and historical criticism of Langland on the other is a consequence of my own new theoretical self-consciousness. I have sought theoretical ideas relevant to a reading of Langland in the medieval traditions of the art of grammar and in the practices of medieval preaching. I have proposed a few points of contact between the retrieved ideas and contemporary theory in order to situate and mediate difficult concepts and to argue for their reasonableness, because it is possible that it may be our conception of the world that needs modifying. This is the approach taken also by Samuel Levin in his book *Metaphoric Worlds*. There he takes seriously the implication of the poetic language of the romantics; he accepts their imaginative statements literally rather than regarding them as mere figures of speech. We are meant to "conceive of" the reality of the indicated state of affairs, even of such a statement as "the sea is laughing": "We must try to conceive of the possibility that a state of affairs which exceeds anything that our experience has acquainted us with and which in fact transcends what we know the world to be like might yet somehow obtain" (17–18).

In the case of *Piers Plowman*, in my attempt to take seriously the poet's assumptions about language and the implicit underlying arts-of-discourse doctrines, I regard the language itself as having the potential to serve as a resource for knowledge. Language has this potential for excess signification, what I call "hypersemiosis." This superabundance of meaning is neither a deviation from the surface meaning of the text nor an allegorical level extrinsic to its plain sense. This is why (unlike Irvine in *The Making of Textual Culture*) I do not make allegory a central concept in my consideration of grammatical doctrine. I believe my analysis is in line with medieval writers' own conceptions of the teaching of the discourse arts. Discussing Augustine's *De doctrina christiana* in particular, Irvine notes the "'allegory' *sees itself* [my emphasis] as recovering the polysemy of what is encoded" (246); in his sermons on the Psalms, Augustine finds, remarks Irvine, "an overplus of signification to be drawn out in exegesis" (261). This suggests that, for Augustine, the surplus of meaning is not something separate or added on, but an ordinary and to-be-expected depth of significance in language itself. Interpretation is only the drawing out of an implicit potentiality that is not an exceptional but is a normal component of discourse. I adduce briefly several romantic and contemporary theoretical ideas that make this understanding of the nature of language seem reasonable.

I concentrate on two points of doctrine in the arts-of-discourse tradition in this effort at retrieval: lexical ambiguity and the ambiguity of words-as-words. Both topics have attracted the interest of literary critics, linguists, and philosophers of language in the twentieth century. We can say, as preliminary definitions, that "ambiguity" refers to the feature of some words of being open to being understood as having more than one meaning (typified by homonymy) and that the ambiguity of words-as-words denotes the way in which the make-up of a word or patterns of the language system match some aspect of what is designated (typified by onomatopoeia).

Twentieth-century Russian formalists, new critics, and deconstructionists have stressed their particular relevance to poetic language. But even earlier, ambiguity had been the object of long-standing theoretical interest in the arts tradition, back even to classical antiquity. Attention to the ambiguity in language has tended to lead to speculation about the relation between language and reality: if the same word can mean more than one thing, then how reliable can words be as indicators of things in the world? Some have said that Langland's century was, like ours, an age beset by anxiety over this unreliability of language – a "crisis of signs" (Cerquiglini, 172). Whether or not the fourteenth century seriously challenged the prevailing "logocentrism" of antiquity and the Middle Ages (which postmodernism now sees itself has having disposed of), we should reconsider its grounds and its implications for medieval poetics.

The two studies offered here are my attempts at what Ernest Boyer has called "the scholarship of integration" – i.e., "serious, disciplined work that seeks to interpret, draw together, and bring new insight to bear on original research" (*Scholarship Reconsidered*, 19). To that end, I have set out to integrate the results of work from several disciplines. My aim is to pull together a comprehensive view of two sharply defined ideas crucial to our present understanding both of the nature of language and of our reading of Langland's poem.

This book consists of two studies, semi-independent from each other, yet parallel. But also, I try in both of them to achieve two interdisciplinary purposes, one of them proper to literary criticism, the other to the philosophy of language. First, I try to give an account of what modern readers have found so perplexing and difficult in the experience of reading *Piers Plowman*; I assume that such an explanation will deepen our appreciation and understanding of the poem on rereading. Second, I explore the space that lies between the poles of the two schools sometimes called realism and nominalism in search of positions where intermediary literary theories and philosophies of language might locate.

The doctrines of the arts of discourse, medieval and modern, provide the common basis for these explorations. The reader encounters discussion of Langland only in the first and last chapters of parts I and II, except for the mention in between of some key points of contact; the poem and Langland criticism received extended treatment in these first and last chapters only. Exposition of my arts-of-discourse contexts I am trying to construct makes up the greater part of the book. Nor do I intend those readings to be the only justification for the investigation of the arts doctrines. I mean for my attention to the arts of discourse to stand in its own right as a contribution to the task of clarifying underlying theoretical questions.

This project follows on a previous one of mine that tried to characterize the particular difficulties that Langland's readers are faced with and to describe in psycho-linguistic terms the reasons for them (Chamberlin, 1989). There I showed that the multiplicity of lexico-semantic interconnections at the level of surface structure makes for a "combinatorial explosion" that severely taxes the reader's powers of comprehension (40). I then tried to show that certain assumptions on the part of the poet and his literary culture about language contributed to this feature of the poem's texture, particularly the assumption that words, in the richness and multiplicity of their concatenations in the network of language, have a unique power to reveal reality, that language itself can be a resource for knowing about the world. This assumption goes a long way to explaining the reader's frequent impression that the poet, as Manly remarked, seems helplessly subject to "the suggestions of the words he happens to use" (quoted in Chamberlin, 1989, 42); the words themselves drive the poem because, in Langland's poetics, exploration of the resources of language is a way of finding out the truth about things. The present work pursues that point by sketching out rather fully certain arts-of-discourse doctrines that serve as the context or ground that throws into relief and explains the multiplicities and infigurations of Langland's poem.

Thus part of my purpose is to offer, in this integrative, interdisciplinary way, an account of some particularly characteristic and important features of *Piers Plowman*. My claim is that these features, constitutive as they are of the poem, lie in the various sorts of ambiguities embedded in the textual surface of the poem's language, rather than in the narrative line. So much of *Piers Plowman* does not seem to me to be accounted for by the story that it tells. What the Russian formalist Boris Eichenbaum argued in the case of Gogol holds true also, I believe, for Langland: the plot does not have central significance, for "the real dynamism, and thence also the composition of his things, lies ... in playing with language" ("The Structure," 382). And, in addition, I am keen to clarify the serious assumptions, both historically and theoretically understood, that underlie that play with and exploration of language. Accordingly, another and complementary part of my purpose is to inquire into these assumptions as topics of theoretical significance in their own right by investigating the medieval arts of grammar and of preaching at certain key moments in their historical development.

The relevance of the arts doctrines to the reading of medieval English poetry, which I am here taking for granted, has been disputed (although even a sceptic might be willing to grant the case for Langland, who shows such an obvious interest in language). N.F. Blake, in *The English Language in Medieval Literature* (1979), warned that we should not take the sophisticated theoretical self-awareness about language embodied in the arts tradition as pertaining to the reading of literature in the vernaculars; only the Latin language was regarded as worthy of learned attention, while "English words were insubstantial things" (100; see also 51, 97). But others besides me have disagreed. John Alford in his 1982 *Speculum* article concludes by remarking that the grammatical metaphor is "an important clue to the medieval mentality," with broad implications for medieval philosophy and literatures (760). Eugene Vance, in *Marvelous Signals* (1986), stresses that medieval grammarians professed the arts doctrines to hold universally, for the vernaculars as well as for Latin (261–2). Suzanne Reynolds in her *Medieval Reading* (1996) shows that the pedagogy of the grammar schools shaped the literacy of medieval readers generally; she argues for the influence of the theoretical assumptions of the arts doctrines on the procedures of glossing and expounding literary texts of all kinds (see 3, 52). And Martin Irvine, as well, in *The Making of Textual Culture* (1994), substantiates the view that the art of grammar defines the doctrines and practices of medieval literary composition in general, including the vernaculars. It is his conviction, and mine, that we should take a comprehensive, long view of the historical tradition of the arts of discourse, including grammar especially, and that Augustine is a pivotal figure for the adaptation of those arts for the Christian Middle Ages. Irvine relates this grammatical tradition to Old English poetry, but he concludes: "In English literature, the works of Chaucer, Langland, and Gower continually reflect on the assumptions and values of grammatical culture" (466).

As well, I try to argue for the likelihood of Langland's having had contact with and being especially influenced by the twelfth-century traditions of the arts of discourse. One can exaggerate the differences between twelfth-century thought and later scholasticism (Minnis, 3), but we can distinguish the grammatical art as understood by the Paris Masters from later, speculative grammar, and also the verbally oriented sermon of the beginnings of the urban preaching revival from the theologically elaborated school sermon. While there is both older and more recent scholarship that suggests ways in which late medieval university learning influenced vernacular literature, and Chaucer and Langland in particular (Schmidt, "Langland and Scholastic Philosophy"; Coleman, *Piers Plowman*; Minnis, *Medieval Theory*; and see Bowers, *Crisis of Will*, n. 52; Spencer, *English Preaching*, 86, 151, 268), it has recently been shown that the fourteenth-century vernacular English sermon, closely linked with those features of *Piers Plowman* that I am pursuing here, owed more to the idiom of twelfth-century preaching than to the school sermon that developed later.

And other readers of *Piers Plowman* have argued that the range of interests and learning shown by Langland suggests a culture other than that of the contemporary scholasticism at the universities. Bloomfield writes that attributing to Langland "a knowledge of monastic philosophy" is essential to understanding his poem (75). Davlin makes the point that the view of language implied in *Piers Plowman* seems out of step with the prevailing nominalistic scholasticism of the time (115). And Bowers proposes that Langland, rather than having been educated at the universities, probably attended a program of lectures at Worcester Cathedral and had access to its significant collection of manuscripts (21–2). My own claim that twelfth-century arts doctrines help explain Langland's poem is in keeping with these opinions.

I place the part on lexical ambiguity first in the book because it deals with a phenomenon that points to the more philosophical issues raised by the second part, which examines the ambiguity of

words-as-words: if language does not simply match up straightforwardly with the items of our experience but seems to "have ideas
of its own" (Culler, "The Call," 15), then how can we conceive of
words-as-words as relating to the world?

I arrange the two parts in a somewhat parallel way; the chapters'
headings correspond, but their contents differ. Chapters 1 and 5
begin with a review of Langland criticism on my particular topic,
lay down a theoretical basis for the inquiry that follows, and outline
the argument for that part by touching on relevant twelfth-century
arts-of-discourse doctrines. In chapters 2 and 6 I then go back
further in time to take up arts doctrines on the different kinds of
ambiguity from the classical period on. Both parts focus on two
pivotal moments in the history of the arts-of-discourse tradition:
that of St Augustine (chapters 2 and 6), seen in relation to his
classical antecedents, and that of the twelfth-century renaissance
(chapters 3 and 7). I attempt as well to bring the ideas of Augustine
and the Paris Masters into an encounter with a few of today's
theorists of language and literature at certain crucial points. A
comprehensive treatment of the relation of contemporary theory
to the historical and theoretical ideas that I raise is not among my
principal purposes, but I situate briefly some key ideas from the
history of the theory of ambiguity and language ontology in relation to current theoretical issues. I then attempt to show how these
historical and theoretical contexts can deepen our reading of
passages in Langland's poem. It is only in the first section of
chapters 1 and 5 and in chapters 4 and 8 that I deal at length with
Piers Plowman and Langland criticism.

This structure reflects this study's being a project of interdisciplinary integration. By bringing together the topics of the two
studies (lexical ambiguity and the ambiguity of words-as-words),
the approaches of two disciplines (language theory and literary and
historical criticism), and two eras (the ancient and medieval past
and the present), I link broad perspectives that benefit from the
light that they shed on each other. Contemporary ideas make it
possible for us to bring the past into our realm of experience and
understanding, but just as important are the ways in which the past
might mediate the present (as Marcuse says), so that new possibilities may come to light for us. After all, it may be our own conception of the world that needs modifying.

PART ONE

Lexical Ambiguity in the Arts of Discourse and in Piers Plowman

Lexical Ambiguity: Context, Ground, and Overview

PREACHING AND WORDPLAY IN THE SECONDARY LITERATURE

Langland's *The Vision of Piers Plowman* baffles the reader's expectations by the complexities of the ways in which it develops. Putting the poem in certain contexts of medieval discourse can help one understand how it proceeds and what it means. Although Langland's poem is certainly not a sermon, readers have thought it helpful to situate it in the discourse context of preaching. I wish to argue that one particular way of developing a sermon assisted the writer in "spinning out" the stuff of the poem: development by ambiguity – i.e., the invention of multiple significances from certain words. Wordplay is one such technique. This strategy for exploring the resources of the meaning of ambiguous words, especially those in Scripture, implies certain assumptions about language and about how we can elicit its surpluses of meaning that, for Langland in particular, have their roots in the twelfth-century doctrine of the arts of discourse. Their original sources lie further back in classical and Augustinian ideas about language.

Past readers of *Piers Plowman* have suggested ways to explain at least in part much of what is perplexing about the poem by noting its affinities with medieval exegetical preaching (see Wenzel's overview in "Medieval Sermons"). Over fifty years ago, Owst showed that many of the recurring themes in *Piers Plowman* appear also in the sermon literature of the time: "the messages of the preacher and poet [Langland] are fundamentally the same" (*Literature and*

Pulpit, 575). Owst argues that the portraits of the Deadly Sins in passus v of the B text (B.v) in particular are but the rather incomplete narrativizations of homiletic commonplaces (278–9, 371, 434–41, 450, 489), saying, for example, in the case of Accidia, that "the imagination of the artist is not yet freed from the formal didactic procedure of the homily book, which he thus clumsily adopts" (89). For Owst, Langland writes very much in the homiletic idiom, though unsuccessfully.

Later readers have looked to the artistic principles of homiletic purpose and technique to exonerate this apparent "clumsiness" in the structure and style of Langland's poem. Elizabeth Salter proposes that we can better appreciate the art of the poem if we relate it to *ars praedicandi* doctrines (*Introduction*, 6). She shows that the purposes and procedures of the medieval art of preaching help to account for one particularly characteristic feature of *Piers Plowman* – the way in which the poem develops through "a loose-knit, linking system of repetitions, correspondences and cross-references" (48). A.C. Spearing also makes the association between preaching and Langland's stylistic device of frequent repetition ("Art," 112, 127; "Repetition," 722). Such repetition foregrounds certain words, charging them with a potential for surplus significance.

The repetitiousness and complexity of the poem's textual surface manifest themselves in the interaction of sameness and difference in repeated words and meanings. This interaction is the subject of a key article by Huppé on wordplay in *Piers Plowman*. He takes the idea of the pun as a witty but seriously religious poetic expression from Walter Ong's earlier article on wordplay in medieval Latin hymns ("Wit and Mystery"). Huppé sees such interplay of sound and sense as an important feature in the poetic structuring of Langland's work. The homonym is the defining instance here: it is a single word that has more than one meaning (as phonetically, though not graphically, "eye" and "I"). In wordplay these several meanings are somehow associated in their significance; their sharing the same lexical representation in sound or writing indicates and reinforces this thematic connection among different meanings.

Huppé gives many examples from Langland's poem, including the following instance of double or interlocking homonymy (Grace is entrusting Piers with his responsibilities as plowman in B.xix): "And for to *tilie* truthe a *teeme* shal he have" (B.xix.263). *To tilie* means both "to till" and "to tell"; *a teeme*, both "a theme" and "a team" (Huppé, 168). These two senses of both homonyms connect up across the statement to give, with surprising consistency, the two sides of a fairly common similitude from Scripture: the metaphor of the plowman or sower as preacher (see Barney, "The Plowshare of the Tongue"). In the syntax of the statement understood in its two parallel senses, ME "to tilie" signifies the activity; ME "a teeme," the instrument with which it is done: the plowman tills with a team, the preacher tells with a theme. That the two homonyms link up as they do brings out further the richness and force of their meanings. Huppé argues (179) that Langland's poem as a whole is structured particularly by the wordplays inaugurated in the Prologue.

Putting the several meanings of a homonym in a tension of sameness and difference by relating them in wordplay has the effect of plumbing the semantic depths of a word or of extending the reach of its meaning beyond the grasp of ordinary understanding. There is something mysterious about the unexpected wealth of the disclosed significance and about the way in which the complex holds together. Sister Mary Davlin, in *A Game of Heuene: Word Play and the Meaning of "Piers Plowman" B*, writes of this effect as an opening up of unrealized possibilities of meaning (3), "an expanding fullness of meaning, as if one meaning were inside another by analogy, etymology, sound or logical implication" (43). This rich plenitude of signification seems to be a resource that language itself offers. By exploring it, the poet draws the reader into an experiential realization of God's immanence in the world (113).

Editors of *Piers Plowman*, faced with an uncertain textual tradition, have had to give particularly close attention to its alliteration and the wordplay. These two features of the text are often interrelated, as they were in Huppé's example above of "to tilie" and "a teeme" (Schmidt, "Lele Wordes," 141; Lawton, 237–41). Schmidt's interest in Langland's puns apparently emerged from his editorial work ("Lele Wordes," 149). For him, the poem's wordplay releases the spiritual meaning of a figure, often supported by the themes of Scripture or by the very words of the Latin Vulgate itself (142, 147; also his *Clerkly Maker*, 90–1). James Halm also stresses that it is Scripture, particularly the biblical message of the Incarnation, that ultimately underlies the poem's "kinetic word play" ("The Word Made Flesh," 124, 318). Halm places this feature of Langland's style in a larger context of the theology of the Word and of a "logolog-ical" view of language that owes much to Augustine and something as well to twelfth-century arts of discourse (74–159). Halm's argu-ment is here broadly similar to my own.

In order to discern in Langland's wordplay the several possible meanings for a biblical expression, Halm (179ff.) consults one of the most remarkable accomplishments of the arts of the twelfth century – a scriptural dictionary of homonyms and synonyms – the *Distinctiones dictionum theologicalium* of Alanus de Insulis (died 1202). Robertson and Huppé had suggested some time earlier that Langland might have made use of reference works for preachers, particularly concordances and such *distinctiones* dictionaries as Ala-nus's, in composing his poem (*Piers Plowman and Scriptural Tradi-tion*, 5). John Alford showed how the consultation of concordances seems to have contributed to the structuring of *Piers Plowman* ("Role," 86), and Judson Allen showed much the same for *distinc-tiones* dictionaries ("Langland's Reading," 343, 353; *Ethical Poetic*, 276–8). These investigations make it clear that the repetition and wordplay of Langland's poem in many instances draw in and become implicated in scriptural texts and the interpretation of those texts according to the reading practices of exegetical preach-ing. This also was the case in Huppé's examples above of "to tilie" and "a teeme," where the wordplay involved a metaphor from Scripture – the plowman/sower.

In addition to the *distinctiones* dictionaries, there are other achievements especially characteristic of twelfth- century learning with which *Piers Plowman* has striking affinities. Sister Mary Davlin has remarked on how much the ideas of "Kynde" and "kynde knowing," so key to major sections of the poem, owe to the twelfth-century understanding of Nature ("Kynde Knowyng," 8; and see Schmidt's editorial note to B.xi. 320, '95 ed. 453.) Schmidt has shown that a number of passages in *Piers* echo allegories in the poetic works of Alanus de Insulis ("Langland and Alanus," 484[a]). And James Simpson has pointed out that Dame Study's educational program in Passus x has its parallel in twelfth-century formulations of the arts rather than in the university curricula of the thirteenth and fourteenth centuries ("Varieties of Ambiguity," 58–9). The learning, including arts-of-discourse doctrines regarding ambiguity, that was being assimilated into new forms during this century, seems to have particular significance for Langland's poem.

THE THEORETICAL GROUND:
SEMANTICIST POETICS

In what follows in chapters 2 and 3, I explore key developments in the history of the medieval arts-of-discourse doctrines regarding ambiguity that underlie the procedures for developing multiple meaning in medieval exegetical preaching, as they figure into the wordplay of Langland's poem. Some theoretical basis for this exploration is in order; I offer a model for the concept of ambiguity that draws on linguistics semantics, a schema particularly useful in clarifying Augustine's exposition of scriptural multivocity, which I take to be central to the medieval preaching tradition and *Piers Plowman*.

Language is shot through with ambiguity in all its contextual dimensions – lexical, syntactic, pragmatic. This study takes a primarily lexical perspective as being most relevant to the sort of ambiguity to be found in medieval preaching and *Piers Plowman*, although I note the other dimensions if they are pertinent.

Lexical ambiguity has its basis in the excess of meaning (or hypersemiosis) that a word carries, whether used or not in any single occurrence within a context. Certain contexts have the capability of bringing out of a word two or more viable significations, distinct both from each other and in their clarity of meaning. Ambiguity is the result (definition in Su, 59, 113, 116). Various kinds of repetition seem to play a key role in contexts that show this capability. The rhetorical language of sermons and the highly patterned language of poetic verse are especially replete with repetitions that provide contexts capable of realizing this potential that words have for hypersemiosis.

Greg Simpson observes that "all words [seem to] have associated with them more information than is typically needed in a single instance" (15). Thus, no single occurrence of the word in a particular context uses all the resources of a word's meaning. Words with the potential for ambiguity have a certain configuration of significations that concentrates meaning around more than one focal point (Cruse's term is "pre-existing bundle of semantic properties," 60). Thus the written word "eye" has (at least) these two focal points of signification: the organ of sight and the leaf-bud of a potato. The first is more central to the word's overall semantic field than the second. These senses, though not unconnected, do not seem very close in meaning; there is a certain similarity of appearance in what they designate, but non-metaphorical relations of meaning are possible, such as relation by association (metonymy). Focal points of meaning for a word that are fairly close to each other are *polysemous*; if the distances make the meanings appear unconnected, they are *homonymous*. Thus the spoken sound for the first-person pronoun "I" designates meanings graphically represented as "I," but also as "eye." The meanings of "I" and "eye" seem wholly unrelated; these words are phonic homonyms. The line between polysemy and homonymy lies somewhere along a continuum (the range of distances between focal points of meaning), and thus is difficult to draw definitively. But it is the distance between semantic focal points that makes possible a potential for ambiguity.

There is a certain mirror-image symmetry between homonymy and metaphor, and polysemy is where they join. If the relation between polysemous meanings ("eye" as organ of sight, "eye" as leaf-bud of a potato) is taken in the direction of likeness of words but divergence of meanings, homonymy results (in terms of sound, "eye" as organ of sight, "I" as first-person pronoun). If, however, the relation between polysemous meanings is taken in the opposite direction (i.e., towards some semantic connection between focal points of meaning configured in the fields of the two words), metaphor results (the eye is like a window – "eye" as organ of sight, "window" as opening in a wall) (see Su, 135–7, and 160 n. 4). Looked at this way, metaphor becomes not so much a "way of speaking" – a rhetorical figure that involves an externally imposed level of overlaid significance ("window" lifted out and carried over to mean "eye" as organ of sight) – but rather a development of a potential that lies in the rich configuration of literal meanings inherent in the word (137–8, 161 n. 8). The more unique – i.e., the less reasonable – the connection between focal points of meaning made by the metaphor, however, the more the reader responds with surprise and appreciation of rhetorical ingenuity; the more believable the metaphorical connection, the more one can gain knowledge of the resources of meaning implicit in the word's literal range and insight into that to which the word refers.

Words with potential for ambiguity (such as "eye") may not have that hypersemiosis invoked by a particular context that deals straightforwardly with a single topic. A paragraph on planting potatoes is not likely to call forth a reading of the word "eye" in

the sense "organ of sight" as well as the sense "leaf-bud of a potato."
Nor is a paragraph in an optometry text likely to evoke potatoes.
If we contrast these two polysemous senses of the word "eye" we
can call them "disjunctive" (Kaplan and Kris, 417; see also Cruse,
52–3, which uses the term "contextual selection"). In such contexts,
the popping up of the intrusive sense would not help us understand planting potatoes or improving sight. In the arts-of-discourse
tradition, logic takes up the task of sorting out disjunctive ambiguous meanings to prevent obscurity and misunderstanding.

But there is also an ambiguity that aids understanding, more the
concern of the grammarian in the arts tradition, where the hypersemiosis makes for an often-astonishing plenitude of meaning and
increase of knowledge. In this so-called conjunctive ambiguity,
more than one distinct possibility for a word's significance registers
conjointly in a given context in such a way that the multiple meanings do not inhibit but rather enrich or reinforce one another
(Kaplin and Kris, 419). Contexts that bring out this conjunctive
ambiguity are such that they provide alternative meaning structures
which accommodate the multiple focal points of signification in
the word. The contexts facilitate relevant interconnections, which
incorporate the word's multiple senses into lines of meaning that
develop at least sporadically alongside each other. Contextual
constraints, or "stringencies," rather than excluding a potential
hypersemiosis (as in disjunctive ambiguity), call forth alternate,
conjunctive patterns of coherence that draw together the different
meanings (Su, 80–1, Kaplin and Kris, 431–2).

These alternate lines of development, which have in common a
polysemous or homonymous word, produce a sort of duplication
of each other, making the same line of thought over again but
different. The writer indicates this duplication either explicitly, by
repetition in the text, or implicitly, by getting readers to respond
to some invitation to supply the repetition themselves. The explicit
form could consist of the occurrence of a synonym for one of the
senses or the repetition of the ambiguous word itself in such a way
as to shift from one of its meanings to another (Su, 126–7). The
latter shift constitutes the rhetorical figure of antanaclasis, defined
by Fontanier as "the proximity of two occurrences of a homonymous word, the two occurrences having different meanings" (348).
Many of the numerous repetitions in *Piers Plowman*, which Salter
and Spearing have noted, are of this sort. If not explicitly stated,

then the doubling up of meaning depends solely on implication (Su, 50–2). This can happen, as Su notes, "where the ambiguity in the given expression is 'reflected' from allusion to another context" (126). Whether explicitly or implicitly, then, repetition is integral to ambiguity.

Frequently in *Piers Plowman* the ambiguous doubling of meaning derives from the "reflection" by allusion to another context – namely, Scripture. This is the case in Huppé's example of wordplay from Passus xix (263) of the B version: "And for to tilie truthe a teeme shal he have." Just before this line, Grace says that he has chosen Piers for his plowman; just after it the oxen of the "*teeme*" are named – the four Evangelists. The context for the line thus invokes two alternate and conjunctive concatenations of meaning, the one agricultural, the other evangelistic. "*To tilie*" is accordingly repeated by this reflection, made relevant in both lines of development. The distance between the two focal points of signification ("to till," "to tell") appears great enough for this to be a case of homonymy: ME "*to tillen*" (MnE "to till"), ME "*to tillen*" (one way of spelling ME "*to tellen*," MnE "to tell"). Empson remarks that the lack of standardization in spelling and punctuation in the writing practices of earlier periods gives a greater scope to ambiguity (83). These two patterns of coherence, running alongside each other, overlap again in the homonymy of "*teeme*"; this additional implied repetition seems to reinforce the duplication of meaning – same, yet different. In this way words seem to disclose a greater abundance of meaning than expected: to till with a team is also (but with a difference) to tell with a theme. This discovery of the surplus meaning of words reveals language to be a resource of knowledge in its own right; it is a means of finding out things. Jonathan Culler has referred to this implied assumption as the premises that "homonyms know something" (15).

"Semanticist critics" is Ducrot and Todorov's term (275) for those twentieth-century literary theorists who regard ambiguity as essential to poetic language. They mention particularly William Empson (*Seven Types of Ambiguity*, 1930) and Yuri Tynianov (*The Problem of Verse Language*, 1924). Empson writes that "the machinations of ambiguity are among the very roots of poetry" (3). The formal structures of poetry – for example, the metrical scheme – "impose a sort of intensity of interpretation upon the grammar," inviting the reader to find a more abundant significance, a greater richness of implication, than is expected in prose discourse (28). Similarly, Tynianov argues that the words of poetic texts are particularly ambiguous, "chameleon-like," capable of taking on multiple semantic colourings under the pressure of poetic structures, such as meter and stanzaic configuration, themselves repetitions of various kinds. For Langland's poetry, we need to add here the alliterative line as another device of repetition. The formal patterns of poetic contexts offer especially intricate opportunities to "destabilize" meaning and to give meaning simultaneous multiple senses, which oscillate or criss-cross among themselves, now diverging in meaning, now converging again (Tynianov, 64–71). As Tynianov says elsewhere, "If you will line up in [poetic] formation disparate, but like-sounding words, they will become cognates" – i.e., homonyms will come to seem related in meaning (quoted by Erlich, 228).

More recent critics carry much further this view of the potential of word meanings in literary texts to become "destabilized." Roland Barthes sees the reader as savouring the liberties that can be taken with hypersemiosis (*Criticism and Truth*, 37–40). As becomes apparent below, structuralist and poststructuralist understandings of Augustine's theory of ambiguity reveal something of the ranges of opinions regarding what factors constrain the proliferation of multiple meaning.

The insights of the semanticist-critics have particular relevance to the way in which Langland's verses, by their repetitions of various sorts, provide formal and semantic contexts that bring out the surplus meanings of ambiguous words. As David Lawton has noted, thematic patterning and lexical recurrence come together in Langland's alliterative line ("Alliterating Style," 240). It is in such a way that Langland releases hypersemiosis, expanding lexical meaning, thereby exploring the resources of signification inherent in language. The ideas of the semanticist-critics, the Paris Masters, and Augustine illumine Langland's poetic practice in this regard.

TWELFTH-CENTURY ARTS TRADITION

For the theologians of the twelfth century, language constituted a complex system of signs that mirrored the meanings of nature and of Scripture in an abundance of interrelated significations. They took language itself to be a resource for learning about the world and its Creator. The richness of the networks of signification afforded the preacher many possible interpretations to develop, all for the purpose of teaching and moral edification. M.-D. Chenu has remarked that the twelfth century was an age of "symbolic density," of "multiform truth" (*Théologie*, 161–2). The interest in patterns of unity in plurality and of plurality in unity, as displayed in synonyms and homonyms, is clear in the title of Adelard of Bath's major theological work: *De eodem et diverso* (On the Same and the Different).

Both dialecticians and grammarians sought to sort out the multiplicity and complexity of the interrelations between words and things. Hugh of St Victor, in his exegetical writings, and Abelard in *Sic et non*, for instance, set out to overcome apparent contradictions in Scripture by distinguishing several senses for the same word used in different contexts (Evans, *Language: Earlier*, 54, 78, 82, 136). John of Salisbury explored in *Policraticus* the ambiguity of various kinds of signs, both in texts and in the heavens. The study of language to further the interpretation of the richness of moral significance in the Bible and the world received particular impetus and direction from the period's evangelical awakening and the ensuing explosion of popular preaching. A renewed commitment to trying to follow the apostolic ideal in day-to-day life focused attention on the literal sense and on the contexts and applications of meanings. Both the Victorines and the Paris Masters pursued studies along such lines.

Peter the Chanter was one of the most prolific and influential of the Paris Masters. His wide-ranging and popular work of moral theology as it applies to practical issues, *Verbum abbreviatum* (*not* a "brief word" on his chosen topics at all, as it turns out), seemed already to Skeat a likely source for several of Langland's Latin quotations; see Early English Text Society (EETS) edition, ed. Skeat (1869), Part IV, section 1 [Notes], notes to B.ix.91 (p. 223), to B.xiv.76 (p. 324), to B.xv.336 (p. 356), and to B.xvii.297 (p. 393). A more recent study of Langland's sources (Quick) has concluded that "it seems extremely likely that Langland knew the Verbum Abbreviatum of Peter the Chanter ... More of Langland's quotations, both Biblical and non-Biblical, can be found in the Verbum Abbreviatum than in any other source" (32). In much of his work Peter follows the standard classroom procedure of taking up the *Glossa ordinaria* or its elaborations, exegetical commentaries compiled ultimately from patristic sources, first put together by Anselm of Laon and his school (Smalley, *Study*, 64, and *Gospels*, 3, 7, 29–30; Baldwin, *Masters*, 92, 151). Lecturing on Scripture in this way was the basis for the academic pursuit of theology in the twelfth century. The commentary format engaged many of the procedures of the arts of discourse, including the doctrines of ambiguity. This learning supported and enriched the practice of preaching.

Early in his life, shortly after his conversion, Augustine very deliberately and self-consciously began to reconstruct the classical cultural legacy for the new Christian era, which effort remained pivotal for the next thousand years. He composed several treatises on individual arts (a *De dialectica* and a *De musica*) and a bit later in *De doctrina christiana* set out procedures for using the arts in exegetical preaching (Rist, *Augustine*, 141, 300). The doctrines that Augustine there takes up, qualifies, and applies to the reading of Scripture relate to all three of the arts of the trivium – grammar, logic, and rhetoric – but most of all to grammar (Marrou, *Augustine*, 15, 247, 530). His understanding of how to sort out the multiple senses of ambiguous words and his procedure for taking up the scriptural text in sermons have their roots back in the literary and philosophical pursuits of classical antiquity – as we see in chapter 2 – so remarkably conservative was ancient pedagogical tradition.

CHAPTER TWO

Augustine on Ambiguity

SOURCES OF THE
AUGUSTINIAN SYNTHESIS:
CLASSICAL ARTS DOCTRINES
ON LEXICAL AMBIGUITY

Near the end of the classical period, Augustine reformulated, in a definitive way for the Middle Ages that followed, the classical arts of discourse for Christian uses. The long and rich tradition on the theory and practice of verbal expression on which Augustine drew had already had much to say about lexical ambiguity, a tradition that reached back to Plato and to the Sophists to whom Plato in so many ways reacted philosophically. It was they who first made close scrutiny of the various meanings of words in literary texts the basis of an education for participation in the *polis* (Marrou, *Education*, 89). Whereas archaic pedagogy had emphasized athletic exercises and musical accomplishments, the Sophists placed language at the centre of their teaching, both in their exposition of key cultural texts, such as Homer, and in their instruction on avoiding obscurity in public speaking (Ebbesen, 16). The fifth-century Sophist Antisthenes stated: "the investigation of words is the beginning of education" (quoted and discussed by Pfeiffer, 36–7; Pfeiffer's reference is to *Artium scriptores*, ed. L. Radermacher, B.xix.6).

A passage in Plato's dialogue *Protagoras* (335^a9–348^b8) illustrates well how the Sophists might have used a poetic text to teach students about language as well as about ethical and philosophical matters. The Sophist Protagoras, pursuing the topic of virtue by putting questions to Socrates regarding a poem by Simonides, remarks: "I think that the most important part of a person's education is to be skilled in the poets" (338°6–339ª1). Protagoras then examines in detail the words of Simonides' verses, the sort of investigation that evidently led him at some time to distinguish various grammatical classes of words, as he is said by later writers to have done (Pfeiffer, 37–8).

Socrates calls on Prodicus, another Sophist present at the discussion in the dialogue, to contribute the skill for which he is particularly renowned – the ability to make fine distinctions among synonyms and the various senses of words: "I call on you [Prodicus]," says Socrates, "for that art, to determine whether 'to wish' and 'to desire' are different or the same" (340ª7–340ᵇ2). Prodicus's interest in the precise differences and similarities among words seems to have led him to draw up lists of related words in specialized glossaries (Pfeiffer, 41). Socrates, in responding to Protagoras's questions about the poem, shows his own adroitness at the idiom, but he ends by rejecting a pursuit of learning based on literary texts and proceeding by the investigation of words (347°1–348ª1). However, the many centuries of continuous tradition of classical education to come concentrated on the Sophists' ideas and procedures rather than on Plato's, especially on the careful differentiation of word meanings. These pursuits come to constitute part of the art of grammar and have particular significance for Augustine.

The most important theoretical insights regarding ambiguity took place in the fourth and third centuries BC and were subsequently passed on and worked over by later Greek and Latin writers in the arts tradition (Ebbesen, 15). Both Aristotelian and Stoic philosophers regarded the multiple meanings of words as a problem needing careful dialectical analysis so that the confusions that it caused could be avoided. They regarded the investigation of ambiguity not as a resource for the exploration of meaning so much as a way of avoiding misunderstanding – i.e., they took a disjunctive perspective. Aristotle remarks in *Rhetoric* that ambiguity is a transgression against good Greek (3.5, 1407ª). And worse, homonyms are a type of word apt only for the deceits of Sophists, although synonyms do have poetic uses (3.2, 1404ᵇ).

In his *On Sophistical Refutations*, Aristotle treats of ambiguity disjunctively in the course of analysing and sorting out the confusions of expression that give rise to misleading arguments. He observes that there are inevitably more things than names, so that there cannot be a one-to-one relationship between verbal expressions and what they signify; since one word must cover many cases, the same word may designate quite different things, thus opening the way to possible confusion (165ª11–14; see also 169ª30–3; quoted and discussed by McKeon, part II, 30ª–31ª, and Kretzmann, 362ᵇ–363ª; see also Atherton, Appendix I, 505–6). The emphasis here is on the careful distinctions in word use necessary in constructing and evaluating arguments; accurate deductions require reliable lexical meanings.

Artistotle goes on in *On Sophistical Refutations* to distinguish three sorts of fallacy involving ambiguity. First, in homonymy, three different things can be designated by one word, as κύων can mean dog, dog-star, or Cynic philosopher (166ª15–17; see also Rhetoric, 1401ª15–20). Second, in polysemy, one word can cover several associated senses, as, for instance, μανθα´νειν means both "to understand" and "to learn from" (165ᵇ30–3, 166ª17). Third, one word can be construed differently within the context of a phrase, as in "knowing letters," which can mean either letters-in-the-know or the letters that someone is knowing (166ª18–19). This last example involves looking at the source of fallacy from a syntactic rather than from a lexical perspective. Equivocation is an important concept for Aristotle in other contexts as well, and he treats it at some length also in *Categories*, in *On Interpretation*, and in *Topics*.

Like Aristotle, the Stoics attributed real philosophical value to the study of language (Pfeiffer, 243–4). Attention to the multiple meanings of words was a crucial part of dialectic for them. Augustine was familiar with their doctrines and drew on them in his own formulations of the discourse arts. Diogenes Laertius, one of the major sources for what we know of Stoic logic, attributes some half-dozen works on ambiguity to the great Stoic logician Chrysippus (Diogenes Laertius, *Lives*, VII.193). Diogenes does preserve what must be a major Stoic definition of ambiguity (VII.62), but, because a number of terms that figure into it and which seem crucial to Stoic philosophy of language are of uncertain significance, the import of the statement is much disputed (Atherton, 131–74).

Also useful among the few remains that we have of Stoic doctrine on ambiguity are two lists of kinds of "amphibolia" (texts from Galen and from Theon of Alexandria, in Atherton, 180–3, 188–91; discussed 215–406). These lists suggest a subtle teaching on ambiguity, implying some understanding of the relevance of context to meaning and postulating three perspectives of analysis – lexis (polysemy and homonymy), construing of word complexes (such as matters of pronoun reference or the function grouping of words – something like Aristotle's "knowing letters" example), and sequence (for example, word division). The example given for this last sort of ambiguity (Αυλη-τρις πέπτωκε, which can mean either "the flute girl has fallen" or "the house three times has fallen") is given also by Diogenes to illustrate his definition of ambiguity, suggesting that this was the first category under that definition in a standard list of types.

Aulus Gellius records as a curiosity the opinion of Chrysippus that "every word is naturally ambiguous, since from the same word two or even more things can be understood" (text given by Atherton, 298, discussed on 298–310). This statement might seem to approach the insight of modern semantic theory – that every word in a given context potentially carries with it a surplus of signification – but passages in Augustine suggest that Chrysippus means that a word, besides having its usual sense in usage, can figure in grammatical study as a word in itself, a word-as-word (Atherton, 290–1).

Grammar as a coherent subject in its own right emerged in the first century BC (Daniel B. Taylor, 13). On the one hand, grammar continued to play its key role in education, perpetuating the pedagogical methods of the Sophists. It was poetic texts in particular that the grammarians took up, much in the manner of the Sophists Protagoras and Prodicus in their commenting on the Simonides poem. Having once established the canon of great writers of the past, the art of grammar prescribed study and teaching of their texts by the procedures of ἐξήγησις (*enarratio* in Latin – i.e., grammatical commentary, or glossing), taking up the words and phrases of the text one by one in succession, according to a method that one could characterize as "compositional" (Marrou, *Education*, 223–42, especially 231–4; Ebbesen, 31). The Latin grammarians followed closely the methods of their Hellenistic predecessors, except of course that Latin authors replaced Greek and Virgil replaced Homer. On the other hand, at the same time, grammar developed into a science in its own right, with both a descriptive and a theoretical side owing much to the dialectical doctrines of the Aristotelians and the Stoics (Marrou, *Education*, 236). Again, Greek treatises on the fundamentals of the art of grammar gave way to their Latin counterparts. The major classical Latin treatises on the subject for the Middle Ages were the *Ars grammatica* of Donatus (fl. 350), teacher of Jerome, and the *Institutiones* of Priscian (fl. 500), who first analysed syntax.

These grammarians deal with the doctrine of the ambiguity and polysemy of words in their treatises on grammar and also apply it in their *enarratio* on texts. Donatus in his *Ars grammatica* considers ambiguity ("amphibolia") among other defects of style as a deviation from straightforward usage (Desbordes, 86). One reason why it occurs, Donatus explains, is "on account of homonyms, as someone would say '*aciem*,' and not clarify whether they mean 'keen glance' or 'battle line' or 'knife!'" (*Ars grammatica*, 399, 20–5). This is the disjunctive perspective of Aristotle and the Stoics; both dialecticians and grammarians see ambiguity mainly as a problem, not as a resource for exploring the knowledge inherent in language.

However, elsewhere in his treatise, Donatus pairs homonyms with synonyms, mentioning both merely as classes of the noun (373, 21–3). Since rhetoricians sometimes include synonyms as ornaments of amplification, this pairing suggests ambiguity as being something other than just a stylistic fault (Desbordes, 90). Also, grammarians treat polysemous senses originating in conceptual associations such as metaphor indirectly in their discussion of the rhetorical tropes, in terms of proper and transferred senses. They have in mind unique uses of similitudes and other figures in poetic language, but their terminology can cover more established usages. Thus, to repeat our example, the word "eye," as in a potato, is a use of the word transferred from its usual, proper meaning of organ of sight (399). The grammarians regard tropes as obvious instances of deliberate ornament and so do not condemn the figures as deviations from clear expression.

Grammatical doctrines on ambiguity did have their usefulness in glossing texts. Donatus, in his commentary on the plays of Terence, praises the astuteness of his author by pointing out two words that are different but of the same or very similar meaning (synonyms) and two meanings that are different but of the same or very similar words (homonyms). These are grammatical procedures that Augustine will adopt and systematize for the reading of Scripture. Thus Donatus comments that the poet has with good reason chosen the word *duriter* over the near-synonym *dure*, because *duriter*, appropriately here (*Andria*, line 74), suggests exertion rather than the inappropriate brutality of *dure*, and he reveals how cunningly Terence has avoided ambiguity (*amphibolia*) (at line 156) by choosing a construction with *ab illo* rather than the more usual but ambiguous *ejus*.

Servius on Virgil also demonstrates his author's greatness by showing the appropriateness of the poet's diction, doing so by carefully differentiating the various possible senses for words. He comments on one of the first words of the *Aeneid* – "*cano*," "I sing of" ("I sing of arms and the man ... ") – that it can mean three things: to praise, to prophesy, and to sing about (Servius, *In Vergilik*, Bk i.1). This last sense is the apt one here, particularly since poetic works (and this is a poem) are meant to be performed melodiously. But Servius notes that Vergil uses the other two senses as well later in the *Aeneid*, and he distinguishes meanings and cites instances for them, just as Augustine in *De doctrina christiana* and the Paris Masters in their *distinctiones* collections will do for biblical words. Servius (Bk i.51) makes distinctions among polysemous senses of the same word also when he remarks that *fetus* ("full") can by itself mean either "fruitful" or "fraught," just as *venenum* ("drug") can signify either "medicine" or "poison" ("*bonum* venenum et *malum* venenum"). This distinction between opposed polysemous senses (*in malo, in bono*) will later be important for Augustine and for the twelfth-century compilers.

Sometimes, though infrequently, the commentators praise the poets for their skilful use of ambiguities rather than for their avoidance of them (Atherton, *Stoics*, 484–5). Thus Donatus notes the deliberate wordplay (at line 564) by his author on the near-homonyms *perpetuo* and *perpeti*. But Augustine will go very much further than this in celebrating the ambiguities of Scripture. As we see below, he takes in the sacred text what might elsewhere be regarded as an infelicity as a mystery instead; the dialecticians' concern with clarity of understanding loses ground to the devout reader's search for complex meanings on which to meditate. In this endeavour, grammatical doctrines regarding ambiguity are readily turned to account.

Attention to the words of texts inevitably led to the compilation of lists of "hard" words, glossaries such as those that Prodicus's interests in differentiating meanings would have produced. Just as today a glossarial supplement is often appended to a composition handbook, so in antiquity such word lists frequently accompanied grammar textbooks (Della Casa, 38). Smaragdus of St Mihiel, a ninth-century Carolingian grammarian remarkable for adding scriptural examples to those from classical sources in his *Expositio super Donatum* (Leclerq, "Smaragde," 20), deals with homonyms, as Donatus had done only very briefly, as a class of nouns worthy of collection in a specialized list or glossary (19–21). For homonyms, in addition to Donatus's example, *acies*, but very much in the same manner, he cites (20) examples from Scripture in which the word *cornu* (horn) has a whole range of various polysemous or figurative senses available for wordplay: "'Horn' is said of an animal, if an ox gore with its horn [*cornu*]" (Ex. 21:28); or of an army, "Bachides was in the right wing [*cornu*]" (1 Macc. 7:12), or of pride, "I have said to the hurtful, do not wish to act unjustly, and to transgressors, do not wish to raise the horn [*cornu*], do not wish to lift your horn [*cornu*] on high" (Ps. 4:5–6). A fifth-century bishop of Lyons had already compiled just such a list of differentiated meanings for scriptural words, clearly following the principles of Augustine's *De doctrina christiana*; this was Eucherius's *Formulae spiritualis intelligentiae*. Its similarity to Smaragdus's exposition shows the essentially grammatical basis of Augustine's explanation of scriptural signs and attests to the continuation and reworking of his exegetical procedures into the Middle Ages. The lists of scriptural homonyms drawn up by Eucherius and Smaragdus culminate in the twelfth-century *distinctiones* compilations by Peter the Chanter and others.

While the classical arts traditions made grammatical practices the central activity of education and provided the essential doctrines and procedures for glossing texts (including doctrines regarding ambiguity), Augustine's adaptation of these traditions put a new emphasis on ambiguity as a resource of meditative richness in reading Scripture. These classical traditions – those of the grammarians, of Aristotle and his commentators, of the Stoics – are also the earliest sources of the twelfth-century reformulation of the arts, following Augustine, with its consequences for the preaching mode of *Piers Plowman* and for Langland's use of ambiguity for his poetic purposes of wordplay. Thus Langland has Conscience proceed in the manner of the ancient dialecticians in clarifying for the King the meaning of "Mede" by distinguishing disjunctively two different senses for the word (in B.iii). But Langland also, more in the Augustinian manner, explores the resource of richly complex conjunctive

meanings that the hypersemiosis of ambiguous words can supply –
for instance, in the case of "for to tile truthe a teeme shal he have."
Augustinian theory informs the approach of both Langland and the
twelfth-century Paris Masters to this understanding of ambiguity.

AUGUSTINE ON THE ARTS
AND AMBIGUITY

Thus Hellenistic culture, now Latinized, furnished the arts-of-
discourse theories of ambiguity and the practices of reading appropriate to disclosing the abundant signification of words that are
key to Augustine's reconstruction, in *De doctrina christiana*, of the
arts of trivium (grammar, logic, rhetoric) for the Christian purposes of reading and preaching from Scripture. The methods of
scriptural interpretation that he proposes are essentially those of
the grammatical *enarratio*, adapted to the reading of a sacred text
for which certain assumptions were pre-conditions. For this reason,
Martin Irvine has called *De doctrina* "a Christian *ars grammatica*"
(*Making*, 178). In particular, Augustine's consideration of multiple
meanings, literal and metaphorical, owes much both to grammarians on homonyms and synonyms and to dialecticians on ambiguity. But Augustine gave a profound philosophical and religious
dimension to the doctrines of the Hellenistic grammarians and
dialecticians (Marrou, *Saint-Augustin*, 241, 223, 291). This new
dimension entailed a crucial difference of emphasis in his view of
ambiguity: ambiguous words are no longer a problem to be cleared
up nor merely a figurative ornament so much as a resource for
learning about the Creator and the created world.

In his *De dialectica*, Augustine sorts out, preliminary to *De doctrina
christiana* and still within the Hellenistic paradigm, some of the
classical doctrines about ambiguity. (*De dialectica* has generally been
regarded as an authentic work of Augustine's since the 1975 edition, used here, by B. Darrell Jackson and Jan Pinborg [see p. 71].)
Its arts-of-discourse doctrines seem to derive from Stoic logic in
particular (Jackson, "Theory," 123, and Pinborg "Classical Antiquity," 98) but with little or no attention paid to verbal sequences
beyond the single word; the approach is primarily lexical. Augustine treats ambiguity in the chapters that deal with the force (*vis*)
of words (100–1). The force of words, their significative import, is
either effective or ineffective – i.e., made ineffective or deprived

of force by certain hindrances. These hindrances are of two kinds – *obscuritas* and *ambiguitas* (102). Obscurity runs the spectrum from the indistinct and easily mistaken to the impenetrable. Augustine's approach seems to be a logical one, disjunctive, aimed at clarifying the interpretation of words in texts and documents.

Ambiguity (*ambiguitas*) further breaks down into a bewildering array of subdivisions, unnecessarily complicated partly because Augustine is mingling incompatible categories taken from Aristotelian dialectic and Stoic semantics (Atherton, 292). Thus he divides ambiguity into univocals and equivocals, terminology that goes back to Aristotle's *Categories* (110–11, and see Jackson's note 7, 131–2). Ambiguous univocals (an apparent contradiction) receive dialectical, even ontological, treatment in terms of definition and predication involving concepts of genus, species, and instance (111). By contrast, ambiguous equivocals are treated more grammatically; they are divided further into "art" and "use" (112–13). Attention to ambiguous equivocals in "art" takes up words as objects of grammatical study in themselves, words-as-words (this is the way in which there comes to be a universal ambiguity of words that Chrysippus seems to have identified; see Atherton, 298), while attention to ambiguous equivocals in "use" takes up words in so far as they function to convey meaning. There turn out to be two sorts of ambiguous-equivocals-in-use: homonyms as such, words with the same form but different, unrelated meanings (Augustine gives the grammarians' stock example of *acies* here; 108–9); and the same words showing different meanings but related to the same source, whether that source be the word (*homo* can take different forms, accidentals, such as vocative or nominative, and so on) or whether that source be the thing (Tullius Cicero the orator, a statue of him, a book of his writings all are called "Tullius" in some sense [114–15]; it is characteristic of the Stoics to regard proper names as showing the properties of common nouns – Ebbesen, 28). In analysing those ambiguous-equivocals-in-use, which are related to the same source, that source being a thing, Augustine is identifying some of the kinds of relationships possible among polysemous focal points of meaning – by likeness, by association, and so on (116–17).

Augustine will carry this distinction between obscurity and ambiguity into *De doctrina christiana* as his fundamental distinction between unknown and ambiguous signs. Also central to his categories there are both sorts of ambiguous equivocals-in-use as identified in *De dialectica*: homonyms such as *acies* and polysemous senses such as *Tullius*. But this second instance requires qualification – Augustine regards the derived polysemous senses in *De doctrina* as "transferred" from literal to metaphorical meanings, a distinction that goes back to the grammarians' treatment of the rhetorical figures. In his work on scriptural intepretation and preaching, Augustine appropriates concepts from dialectic and rhetoric and assimilates them into a theory of ambiguity suitable to grounding a grammatical procedure of exegesis (Copeland, 158 – although Copeland in my view overemphasizes rhetorical theory's contribution.) This theory will enable Augustine to find in Scripture a rich depth of significance in the hypersemiosis of conjunctive ambiguities and polysemous similitudes.

At the end of the Prologue to *De doctrina christiana*, Augustine explains that "one who offers guidance on how a text is to be interpreted is like one who teaches the abc's of reading," for the grammarian in performing both roles instils certain rules: the teacher, rules about construing letters into words and sentences; the exegete, rules about dealing with textual obscurities and ambiguities (prol. 9, trans. 7). In *De utilitate credendi*, Augustine mentions Donatus's commentary on Terence – just as a reader of Terence would probably consult a grammatical commentator to appreciate the poet, even more so a reader of Scripture would probably consult a knowledgeable interpreter (7.17, CSEL vol. 25, sec. 6, part 1, 21–2). The scriptural exegete is in a position analogous to that of the scholiast on Virgil or Terence, making similar assumptions while applying much the same body of theory about language and following a more or less common method (Marrou, *Augustin*, 423).

Two assumptions of the grammatical commentator in particular set the course of Augustine's program for interpreting Scripture. First, he or she encounters the text as a succession of discrete words or phrases rather than a coherent whole that encompasses linguistic units of several types and levels – an incremental approach to language analysis that has been called "compositionality." Second, everything mentioned is significant and charged with profitable teaching, which means that nothing is merely incidental (Marrou, *Augustin*, 428–30). Apparent obscurities and ambiguities allow the interpreter of Scripture to explore the revelation of God through the resource of language. Drawing surplus meaning out of the richness of words is itself discovery and devotion. Augustine proposes as well that what is turned up by the procedures of grammatical commentary is the stuff of Christian preaching; *enarratio* serves as rhetorical invention for the sermon (Marrou, *Augustin*, 530, especially n. 2).

Books II and III of *De doctrina christiana* offer advice for guiding interpretation and for generating homiletic material – for solving problematic readings and for exploring the richness of scriptural language. The schema that organizes those strategies is a four-celled matrix produced by multipying together two sets of two different kinds of signs to give a sort of compounded ambiguity: along one co-ordinate lie the categories of (1) obscure or unknown signs and of (2) ambiguous signs (2.6.7, trans. 37) – a distinction made also in *De dialectica*. Along the other co-ordinate lie (3) literal or proper signs and (4) figurative or translated signs (2.10.15, trans. 43), a distinction that Augustine has taken from the theory of tropes, territory shared by rhetoric and grammar. This schema offers a much simpler taxonomy than *De dialectica*, though covering some of the same phenomena.

This four-part heuristic applies particularly to Scripture. First, it depends on the interpreted text having parallels by other texts – the Latin Bible always has running alongside it the original Hebrew or Greek, as well as other Latin versions, to which the reader can resort for clarity and elaboration. This duplication or repetition is crucial to releasing the potential ambiguity of scriptural words and revealing their meaning(s). Second, it takes for granted that in this unique text one sort of surplus meaning of words occurs in particular abundance: viz., similitudes, focal points of meaning that bridge over to metaphor – a sort of representation that seems to bestow meaning on the very things of creation. Third, the schema's validity relies on the axiom that the verbal field of the scriptural text is circumscribed. That there are limits to the text's significance and language guarantees a consistency of doctrine and finite range to the variation of its signifying.

The strategy for discerning a valid interpretation for category 1 – obscure or unknown expressions of simple, literal meaning – helps establish the entire heuristic, for it makes two assumptions that hold for the whole system. First, there are parallel networks of signification, a kind of duplication or repetition, which can help the reader determine a meaning for the problematic signifier – in this case, the texts in the original biblical languages and other Latin translations. Second, readers should avail themselves of additional meanings gathered from the parallel networks if these meanings are in keeping with both the immediate and the general context of the Bible – its overall, summative meaning. As Augustine says, "a text of the prophet Isaias reads, 'If you will not believe, you shall not understand,' and in another translation: 'If you will not believe, you shall not continue.' Which of these is to be followed is uncertain unless the text is read in the original language. But both of them nevertheless contain something of great value for the discerning reader" (2.12.17, trans. 45). The parallel translations release meanings in each other; the several possible interpretations gain their validity from increasing the overall coherence of scriptural meaning. These two assumptions extend in different ways to dealing with the other classes of difficult scriptural signs.

Augustine considers a second category of word in Scripture that poses somewhat different complexities: words that are polysemous because of metaphorical significations. Paul in one of his epistles (1 Cor. 9:9) shows by his own reading of an Old Testament passage that biblical language lends itself to revealing this kind of surplus meaning. Paul quotes Deut. 25:4, "Thou shalt not muzzle the ox that treadeth out the corn" and understands "ox" here to mean "apostle." As Su comments (B5–8) such figurative transferences depend on relations of meaning that link connotations, which are usually located at the periphery of a word's overall semantic make-up. That being so, the core, the central sense of "ox," and its various possible concentrations of figurative meaning (such as "apostle" – both have a role to play in the harvest), are usually polysemous rather than homonymous in relation to each other. Thus "ox" is to "apostle" as "eye" (organ of sight) is to "eye" (leaf-bud of a potato); there is some inherent connection in both cases. If there were another separate word for "eye" meaning "leaf-bud of a potato" (say, "optispud"), it would be a synonym to "eye" meaning leaf-bud of a potato, as Paul regards "apostle" to be a synonym of "ox" in this case. The occurrence of "optispud" in the context would bring out the polysemous, metaphorical, peripheral meaning of "eye" as leaf-bud of a potato.

In both pairs of senses – the two polysemous meanings of "eye" and "ox" in its core sense and its figurative sense of "apostle" –

there is a bridge of likeness between the two meanings in the pair, as well as some difference. The likeness is some similarity of appearance, as in the case of Tullius the man himself and Tullius a replica of the man (ambiguous-equivocals-in-use, related to the same source). The metaphor implicit in eye as leaf-bud of a potato has become established in the language. Paul's reading of the passage in Deuteronomy strikes us as more of a unique signification (there cannot be many contexts in which "ox" takes on the meaning of "apostle"). But when authoritative readers such as St Paul offer interpretations of authoritative texts such as the Bible, such interpretations can become established convention and so become part of the contexts by which the text is read. As a result, the metaphorical sense becomes more expected, more believable; it elicits not so much surprise at the figure's rhetorical ingenuity as a sense that the resources of the word's literal meanings have been developed.

Just as the grammarians saw in the authoritative texts of the classical poets the profundities of philosophy, cosmology, and mythography, so too Augustine finds in Scripture, following the lead of Paul, an excess of meaning in its figuratively polysemous words. Such habits of reading lead to an expectation of discovering depth and infiguration in the text, a hope that may even influence how the things in the world designated by these ambiguous words come to be regarded. The exchange of meaning between words and things becomes reciprocal. Real oxen can come to look different for the reader of Scripture as a result, just as sowers, tillers, and plowmen can come to be regarded as preachers and teachers of the Word; we can come to realize that, indeed, the sea is laughing, as Levin says.

In *De doctrina christiana*, Augustine, in treating of how to approach scriptural signs that prove to be ambiguous in a homonymous way (the third category), examines some of the varieties of ambiguity set out in *De dialectica* (3.2.2–3.4.8, trans. 79–83). He draws some of his examples from the perspective of construing phrases or clauses rather than from the viewpoint of individual words. Here he repeats his point about the first category, unknown literal signs, about incorporating additional meanings, if they can be accommodated to the context: if more than one understanding of an ambiguous verbal grouping is in keeping with both the overall teaching of scripture and the immediate context, "there is nothing to prevent our punctuating the passage in any of the various possible ways" (3.2.5, trans. 80).

Taking a more lexical perspective brings Augustine to consider homonyms. He gives the example of Latin *os*, which can mean either "bone" or "mouth" (3.3.7, trans. 82). At Ps. 139:15, he thinks it must mean "bone" – but, carrying over the principle enunciated above for several possible options for punctuating a passage, he asks whether something can be gained from taking both meanings of the word as possible here. As he says later, "For what could God have more generously and abundantly provided in the divine writings than that the same words might be understood in various ways" (3.27.38, trans. 102). Such an assumption sees ambiguity conjunctively as a resource of language and reads Scripture expecting to find wordplay. Because Scripture constitutes a finite field of language, the repetition of the word in another sense elsewhere in Scripture may add to the meaning of the word in any one occurrence; the various homonymous or polysemous occurrences of the word "oscillate" with each other.

The fourth category of scriptural words consists of the intersection of categories 2 and 3: multiplicity both vertically and horizontally, as it were, creates ambiguity that is figurative, but also homonymous in its figurative significations. "Ox" has its semantic elements, its focal point of meaning, that relate it to "apostle," but it has other potential complexes of metaphorical meaning as well that other contexts might release. These focal points of signification at the periphery of the semantic field of the word can be so far from each other, so much like homonyms, that they seem to be opposites. This is the case of Augustine's favourite example for this category (the figurative equivalent of "os"): the lion is to be metaphorically understood in one scriptural passage as Christ; in another, as the devil (3.25.36, trans. 100). The synonyms for these two metaphorical senses of lion (Christ, the devil) differ so much that they fit the grammarians' terms *in bono, in malo* used by Servius. It is hardly likely that, in any one scriptural passage, "lion" would be conjunctively ambiguous in both figurative senses, yet opposites can give richly complex semantic reverberation to each other.

Educated in these arts doctrines, readers of Scripture would generate multiple homonymous or polysemous meanings out of the several occurrences of the same ambiguous word and would

generate multiple synonymous meanings out of the several occurrences of the same meaning in different words. Lexical ambiguity
has about it a nearly sacred power, as Quilligan remarks with
respect to Langland in particular (79). This being so, a sacred text
particularly should manifest abundant proliferations of meanings
(Irvine, *Making*, 270). As Augustine wrote in *Confessions*, "And ...
we believe you, Lord, to have said about both representation and
interpretation, 'Increase and multiply' (Gen. 1:22). By this blessing
you allowed us the means and ability to express in many ways that
which we have in our understanding as one [i.e., by synonymy]
and to understand in many ways that which we read obscurely put
in one particular way [i.e., by homonymy]" (264, my own trans.).
This scheme of the networks of sameness and difference in the
ambiguities of Scripture seems to be salutary for the devout reader:
Christ the Word, in his incarnation and his manifestations in Scripture, has a healing influence by virtue of differences and similarities, just as medicine works by similarities and differences (*De
doctrina christiana*, Prol. 1.14.13, trans. 14–15).

It was this reconstruction of the classical arts of discourse in *De
doctrina christiana*, focusing on the multiplicity of words, on the
hypersemiosis of lexical ambiguity, that was to be taken up and
reshaped in the twelfth century. For Augustine, exercise in the arts
of the trivium was not what it had been in the long history of
classical culture – not Sophistic education for participation in the
polis and for the cultured practice of the subtlety of words; not
philosophical investigation into the various kinds of confusion that
creep into dialectical exchanges; and not the grammarian's
description and discussion of correct and appropriate usage in the
canonical texts that constituted the erudite study and veneration
of the ancient poets. For Augustine, attention to the language of
Scripture, its multiple intricacies of sign and signified, consituted
discovery and exploration of the wealth of biblical meaning and
the full, true understanding of it. For the reader of the Bible,
following these arts-of-discourse procedures made possible a meditative renewal of truths already known, an imbuing of the familiar
with the unfamiliar, the same with the different, as discovery
merges with recognition. For the preacher, reading in this way
serves as a procedure of invention for homiletic address that
involves the whole Christian community in this meditative activity;
together, speaker and congregation share the experience of the

indwelling of God's Word as they come to recognize the coherence and richness of the multiple meanings of Scripture.

For Augustine, as for Langland, the intricate networks of language seem to be a resource for the discovery and exploration of religious understanding and a basis for the common life of the community. For Augustine what is shared is perhaps a particularly cognitive and contemplative experience rather than a social and practical one. For Augustine, the twelfth-century Paris Masters, and Langland, however, it seems to be language's ambiguity and infiguration, differentiating and multiplying, that help open up the opportunity for the experience and activity of the Word in the Christian community.

MODERN THEORISTS ON AUGUSTINE: STRUCTURALIST AND POSTSTRUCTURALIST VIEWS OF AMBIGUITY

Marrou remarks that Augustine, proceeding as he does according to the classical art of letters (grammar), looks at drawing out the rich significances of Scripture much as the modern critic does the reading of literary texts. Marrou notes especially the similarity between Augustine's delight in Scripture's abundance of multiple meaning and the modern literary "symbolist aesthetic" (*Augustin*, 489), and he suggests that Augustine in effect invites us to read Scripture as if, in some sense, it were the poetry of Mallarmé (649). For both the reader instructed by Augustine and the reader that Mallarmé's work seems to imply, the text sets in motion an intricate interplay of meaning that suffuses the world itself with symbolic significance (649–50). However, Augustine took care to delimit the scope of this expansion of scriptural meaning, something that exegetes in the later Middle Ages did not always do; he mentions the allegorical excesses of the Carolingian commentators in particular (445). Still, throughout the medieval period, figurative exegesis remained in the service of reason, while for the romantic and symbolist poets, it served aesthetic sensibility (490).

Like Marrou, several recent theorists – notably, Eco and Todorov – have sought to compare the Augustinian/medieval notion of figurative ambiguity with the notion of the symbolic in romantic poetics. Eco, in *Semiotics and the Philosophy of Language*, would make a distinction, however, between Augustine's exegesis and the sorts of reading implied by nineteenth-century poetry. He regards Augustine's procedures for interpreting biblical words as "panmetaphorical" or allegorical (103–4, 151–2), while the romantic–symbolist view of poetic language is "symbolic." The metaphor and symbol signify differently. The metaphor signifies by a transference of names that brings about an imagined exchange of properties (91, 93–4). It is the set of semantic properties that ox and apostle share that makes for the bridge by which the two become synonyms and over which the properties are exchanged. The symbol, in contrast, signifies by suggestion in a way that leaves the signification incomplete, indefinite – conveying only "nebulous content" (130, 132, 144). Interpretation of both metaphor and symbol involves contextual inference, as does all comprehension of signs (8, 35, 136–7).

For Eco, Augustine's schema in *De doctrina christiana* "for correct textual disambiguation" (*Limits*, 13) reined in the symbolic indefinition possible in an unrestrained reading of Scripture and brought it within a still open, but not unlimited, network of "panmetaphoricism." The "inferential walks" (*Role*, 32) of the exegete take place within the world context or "encyclopedia" as established and elaborated by the patristic synthesis of classical and Christian learning (*Semiotics*, 104, 149, 151–2; *Role*, 51–2; *Limits*, 11–14). In this system, while there remain ambiguity and multiplicity of signification (and so the richness of scriptural language that Augustine celebrates), equivalent meanings accumulate as a consequence of the exegete's recourse in interpretation to the rule of faith – i.e., the overall, summative content of biblical teaching. In this way Scripture presents itself not as spilling out into a nebulous and boundless array of symbols, but rather as constrained in its meaning by a system of distinct, if ambiguous, significations.

And yet, just as Marrou remarks on the excesses of the Carolingian exegetes, so Eco speaks of a certain tension in medieval exegesis between the need to constrain and to systematize scriptural meaning and the conviction that the Bible's profundity is inexhaustible, that the reaches of its meaning have no limit (*Semiotics*, 149, 152). This potential of the symbol for indefinite expansion even to the extremes of inconsistency or idiosyncrasy is given full range in the Neoplatonic and Kabalistic exegesis of the Renaissance (*Semiotics*, 153–4; *Limits*, 10, 18) and also in romantic and symbolist poetry (*Semiotics*, 156–7; *Limits*, 20).

In a recent book, Eco complains that his statements about the openness of the text have been misunderstood as granting unlimited rights to the interpreter (*Limits*, 6). He may very well have had Roland Barthes particularly in mind, for Barthes writes of medieval exegesis as "breaking up" the system of the scriptural text, breaking it out of the restraints on its meaning, destablizing it to the extreme (Barthes, "From Work to Text," 161). In the same essay, Barthes speaks of the text's irreducible plurality, which makes possible an explosion of potential meaning that bursts open signification and carries it beyond mere ambiguity (159). In *Criticism and Truth* (70) as well, Barthes speaks of "the freedom of the symbol" to which the Middle Ages gave full scope in its theory of scriptural interpretation (68). It is here that Barthes cites with approval Eco's book on the openness of the text (67). But Barthes may be supposing Eco to be too much the poststructuralist like himself, rather than the structuralist semiotician that he is.

Eco would reply that Barthes has not given sufficient consideration to how Augustine's schema for interpreting biblical language constrains scriptural infiguration – making the Bible's network of surplus meaning multiple and open, but not indefinite or inconsistent. Eco's distinction between metaphoric and symbolic signification clarifies the restraining function of Augustine's analysis of ambiguity in the Bible; he regards Augustine's procedures for interpreting polysemous metaphoric meanings as adequate for structuring and containing scriptural significance. But Eco's view carries with it certain assumptions that were not Augustine's: namely, that the patristic and medieval "panmetaphoric" way of looking at the world was culturally rather then ontologically based (*Role*, 222; *Semiotics*, 104) and that language comprehension is fundamentally top-down – inferential in relation to a cultural code, rather than compositional, i.e., primarily built up from the consecutive processing of incremental lexical units. Irvine's perspective on the semiotics of interpretation, from which he surveys the development of the art of grammar, is that of Eco in this regard: both the classical commentators on the pagan poets (*Making*, 133, 148) and Augustine in *De doctrina christiana* (180, 246) resort (whatever they may claim otherwise) to inferences from a particular cultural code to find texts meaningful.

Eco's differentiation of Augustine's "panmetaphoricism" from romantic symbolism corresponds to Su's differentiation between ambiguity and vagueness: "The senses of an ambiguous word are multiple but distinct; vagueness does not enjoy such distinctness in its meaning, which is more appropriately described as a semantic nebula" (Su, 116). This lack of clear definition of meaning characteristic of both symbolism and vagueness is present also in indeterminacy of interpretation which Su analyses as involving a lacuna in the text's network of meaning which readers are left to fill in as best they may. Su refers here to Bahti, who suggests that even with respect to indeterminacy some theorists stress that the text still tends towards its completion in a coherent understanding while other theorists insist that the indeterminate material remains "uncommunicative or incomprehensible," open to unrestrained flights of interpretive imagination (Bahti, 217). Even in the case of textual indeterminacy, then, there are structuralist and poststructuralist positions, just as there are also structuralist and poststructuralist views of what sort of openness is allowed by Augustine's schema for understanding scriptural words, whether seen as ambiguous (Eco, structuralist) or as symbolic (Barthes, poststructuralist).

Todorov is another theorist who, like Eco, pays attention to how Augustine analyses the multiplicity of lexical meaning in Scripture and compares it to the theories of nineteenth-century poetics. Like Eco, he sees how "the affirmation of the unity of meaning of the Bible" in *De doctrina christiana* holds in check the multivocity of scriptural language (*Symbolism*, 109; see also 107–9, 130). His discussion of romantic theories of the symbol, in contrast, suggests possibilities for bridging the disagreement between Eco and Barthes, so that ambiguity and symbol become not so much mutually exclusive as overlapping. Augustine's procedures for reading Scripture could then be taken as releasing forms of meaning that are at least partially symbolic. This stance has particular relevance for *Piers Plowman*, since Langland's wordplay takes place perhaps where the ambiguous and the symbolic overlap.

Todorov shows how Augustine's schema for reading Scripture as set out in *De doctrina christiana* has certain affinities with romantic poetic theory. Both Augustine and the romantics seek to give an account of what they as readers particularly value in texts – "superabundance of meaning," "a plurality of meaning" (Todorov, *Theories*, 191, 194) that reaches for the inexpressible. This hypersemeosis is "symbolic" for Todorov if it is achieved by "indirection" as opposed to resulting from a direct, simple means of multiplying equivalents. This pair of terms, indirect/direct, Todorov takes from Goethe, but he also mentions Mallarmé (*Theories*, 273; *Symbolism*, 88). Goethe associates indirect signification with the symbol, contrasting it with allegory, which limits metaphoric representation to a single point of contact (*Theories*, 199, 201–3). In indirect signification, the sign retains a certain "opacity" (*Theories*, 201), a certain persistent resonance of the nature of the thing that is appropriated as a figurative representation.

Todorov takes up Augustine's (Pauline) example of "ox" from *De doctrina christiana*; it is an instance of symbolic, indirect expression because various features of what oxen actually are like may carry over to suggest certain things rather indistinctly about apostles. Su's semantic analysis might explain this phenomenon in this way. The ambiguities of "ox" include not just that metaphorical complex of semantic properties that makes it possible for "ox" to be synonymous with apostle (i.e., both have a role to play in the harvest), but other connotative senses as well – such as strength and endurance. Other associations and polysemous meanings for "ox" besides the one that makes for the strongest connection to apostle can thus be set to reverberating in an almost symbolic way. Thus some figurative significations in some contexts may be not so much distinct and therefore ambiguous as indistinct, vague, indeterminate, nebulous, "weakly evoked" (Todorov, *Symbolism*, 82), and therefore nearly symbolic. The positions of Eco and Barthes therefore seem bridged by a sort of continuum of possibilities. The purposes and dispositions of readers must surely affect the resonance of ambiguities, even though texts call out to be read in certain ways.

But the indirect reverberation of surplus connotations given off by metaphors is not the only way in which ambiguity can approach the symbolic. Even homonymous wordplay can "create symbolic effects," says Todorov, as meanings beyond the obvious come into consciousness (*Symbolism*, 55). When ambiguity is compounded, as in Augustine's ambiguous figurative expressions (his example of "lion"), something like the indefinite signification characteristic of symbols can occur, especially if the reader's knowledge of Scripture is extensive enough to bring to mind other occurrences of the expression. Ambiguity can be compounded also when the reader amasses richly ambiguous expressions into complex clusters that overwhelm him or her with the growing accumulation of interrelated significance. This experience is familiar to readers of *Piers Plowman*; for instance, such "combinatorial explosion" can occur in a reading of the Samaritan's sermon in Passus xvii, as I show below.

Augustine recognizes the plenitude and multiplicity of the language of the scriptural text as a resource for gaining insight and understanding regarding the Creator and the created world. It is a multiplicity based on ambiguous signification and metaphorical meaning that is stable and distinct enough to be systematized by the art of grammar. The reading of the Bible according to arts-of-discourse procedures and in keeping with the analogy of faith involves both a common experience of the religious community in worship and in hearing God's Word and the individual experience of meditative renewal. Barthes and Todorov see in the method of patristic exegesis a potential symbolization that opens up an indefinite boundlessness of meaning, an excess that can pull readers away from common norms of understanding. But the assumption of the unity of scriptural meaning, the rule of faith, and the systematic procedures of reading that open up scriptural language to yield forth its wealth of signs all limit the potential for symbolic extravagance (by the limits of reason, as Marrou would say; by metaphoric codification in relation to a certain encyclopaedic world-view, as Eco would say; or by limiting the power that indirect signification has for symbolic evocation, as Todorov would say). In such ways the Christian community strives to preserve itself intact by preserving some measure of commonality in the reading of the text that holds it together.

But as the Christian community comes to define itself differently, as it did fundamentally in the twelfth century, and new intellectual and practical concerns common to all Christian society come to challenge primarily devotional and contemplative ones, making sense of the multiplicity of scriptural signification comes to entail a new way of using the arts of discourse in the public preaching of the Word. It is this homiletic adaptation of the discourse arts, oriented by new social concerns, that also influenced Langland.

CHAPTER THREE

The Twelfth Century
and Arts of Discourse

TWELFTH-CENTURY ARTS
AND AMBIGUITY:
PETER THE CHANTER

The years around 1200 saw a revolution in preaching (d'Avray, 25; Murphy, 310; Longère, 78). Peter the Chanter was at the centre of this revolution; his popular work on applied theology and practical ethics, *Verbum abbreviatum* – which Langland almost certainly, as we saw above, at least consulted, if not read – is itself of a homiletic nature in the preaching mode (Baldwin, 14). In a famous passage, the Chanter states that Scripture is dealt with in three different ways: *lectio* (commenting on the text), *disputatio* (raising and responding to particular problems, or *quaestiones*), and *praedicatio* (preaching). *Lectio* serves as the foundation of all three; *disputatio* puts up the overall structure; *praedicatio*, which subsumes the previous two, covers over the building with a roof that protects the faithful (*Verbum*, 25AB).

Other works by Peter the Chanter circulated that originated in the school-classroom pursuits of commenting and disputing. He took up the gloss tradition in his own biblical commentaries – for example, following for the Psalms the *magna glosatura* of Peter Lombard (Baldwin, 92, 95; Hunt, *Schools*, 100); and his *Summa de sacramentis* is a collection of questions dealing particularly with pastoral theology (Baldwin, 14, Evans, *Language: Earlier*, 147–8). Peter also wrote two works that in different ways apply arts-of-discourse principles to the material dealt with in glossing and disputing: *De tropis loquendi*, a rather technical treatise on clearing up possible misunderstandings caused by the wording of Scripture, and *Summa "Abel"*, a dictionary-entry guide to the ambiguous words of Scripture – a *distinctiones* collection of the sort that has attracted the interest of readers of *Piers Plowman*. Both exemplify well the twelfth-century preoccupation with ambiguity and the multiplicity of meaning in the arts tradition.

The efforts expended by twelfth-century writers in accumulating and sifting through authoritative but divergent opinions, especially in the form of the *quaestio* literature, constitute the larger context for the emphasis that Peter the Chanter places on ambiguity. Peter Abelard's *Sic et non* and John of Salisbury's *Policraticus* are illustrative instances here. In the Prologue to his work, Abelard observes that biblical and patristic writings sometimes appear to us not only as differing (*diversa*), but even as contradictory (*adversa*) (89, ll. 1–2). Not at all disconcerted, he adds that such "dissonantia" (discrepancies) (103, l. 331) should spur the reader to a greater eagerness in seeking after truth. Often, of course, the same words can mean different things in different passages (96, ll. 185–7). In sorting out such differences, Abelard is making use of distinctions drawn in the logical tradition for cases of disjunctive ambiguity. He had available to him doctrines on logical fallacies from Aristotle's *De interpretatione* with the commentaries by Boethius, as well as from the recently recovered *On Sophistical Refutations*. These texts, as we saw above, deal with equivocation, homonymy, and polysemy (De Rijk, I, 24–48; 82–112; 165).

Book II of *Policraticus* explores the reliability of various kinds of signs, such as omens, portents in the heavens, and prophetic dreams. John of Salisbury seems interested more in the range of possible interpretations and the difficulty involved in confidently assigning any one meaning to signs than he is in providing a logical procedure for deciding definitively among possible significations – just as in the work overall he seems to vacillate on key issues. John's interest in ambiguity shows perhaps less of a logical than a grammatical orientation. In several places he draws a parallel between signs in nature or in dreams and signs in written language – both can pose difficulties of interpretation because of their ambiguity (*Policraticus*, ii.26, 144, ll. 26–7, trans. 124; ii.16, 99, ll. 37, trans. 81). Words are ambiguous because of the variety and range of meanings that they convey; distinctions need to be made among these multiple meanings (ii.17, 102, ll. 16–22, trans. 84; ii.24, 138, ll. 17–20, trans. 118). In this context, John uses the very rare word *polixenus*, meaning "polysemous" (ii.16, 99, l. 8, trans. 81), which he probably encountered in a text from the grammatical tradition (Servius, *In Vergiliu*, i.1, commenting on "cano").

Peter the Chanter's *De tropis loquendi* applies to the Bible these twelfth-century grammatical and logical interests in ambiguity (Evans, "Ponendo," 4, "The Place," 235). In the Prologue, Peter explains that he seeks to demonstrate the unity of Scripture, to show that its seeming multiplicity, diversity, or disparity comes down to one consistent meaning – i.e., that the truth of Christ "brings together a superficial contradiction of words into a unity of meaning and clear understanding, so that in this way Scripture is brought to agree with itself through and through" (109). One preserves the Bible's unity by demonstrating that what appears contradictory is only apparently so, that things disconcertingly similar are in fact different on closer consideration, and that certain similar things are indeed alike in ways that reinforce the unity of the Scriptures as a whole (105–6).

The Chanter evidently completed only the first part of this three-part program, viz., providing the procedures for reconciling apparent contradictions (Evans, "The Place," 238). Because demonstrating the unity of Scripture limits the overall effort to clear up sources of confusion and misunderstanding, the treatise takes a rather disjunctive, Aristotelian or dialectical approach to biblical language. Accordingly, it presents polysemy and ambiguity as stumbling blocks, rather than as resources. The twelfth century's subtlety in logical analysis is apparent in the very close consideration given to the range of meanings manifested by syncategoremata, or function words, such as *secundum* (94–5). Even so, an essential category in the analysis is *improprietas*, i.e., transferred signification (Evans, "Work," 52–3; "The Place," 234–5), a term that derives almost certainly from Augustine's *De doctrina* and the grammatical tradition. The version of Peter the Chanter's *De tropis* that appears in the Rawlinson Ms. in the Bodleian contains the remark that arts-of-discourse doctrines are to be studied as the keys to theology and to improve preaching (*De tropis*, 96); *De tropis* seems to have been meant (perhaps among other things) as an aid to preachers, though quite an advanced and technical one (Evans, "Ponendo," 3, "The Place," 241).

The Chanter's dictionary-entry guide to the figurative significations of Scripture, the *Summa "Abel,"* was also an aid to preachers, but it instead displays the richness and multiplicity of the resources of scriptural meaning. The antecedents for the *Summa*, itself apparently the first of the *distinctiones* compilations, are three-fold: the *differentiae* glossaries of late antiquity, based on the cultivation in classical literary culture of distinguishing subtleties of vocabulary; Augustine's systematization of the kinds of multivalent biblical signification in *De doctrina christiana*, and collections such as those of Eucherius and his Carolingian successors who followed Augustine's principles by drawing up glossaries of metaphorical meanings in Scripture (Evans, *Alan of Lille*, 27–8).

The twelfth century was a great age of compilations of all sorts: dictionaries, summas, anthologies. Peter the Chanter's *distinctiones* collection is representative of this activity in the schools. As well, the elaboration of the various occurrences of ambiguous expressions in Scripture as a characteristic means of homiletic development came into vogue at about the same time (i.e., c. 1190–1200: Rouse and Rouse, "Statim," 213, 215). Peter of Cornwall heard a sermon delivered in the *dictinctiones* manner and tells of being greatly taken by its force and by its display of Scripture's richness of expression. He comments with admiration especially on the sermon's abundance, copiousness, and multiplicity of signification (passage given by Hunt, "English Learning," 41). A *distinctiones* collection would be put to good use in the composition of such sermons.

The alphabetically arranged entries of *Summa "Abel"* are organized like a fan that spreads a single sign into the multiplicity of its various manifestations in Scripture. This principle is evident in the layout of the page in Corpus Christi College, Cambridge (cccc), ms. 47 as lines from the entry words along the left extend out like spokes to the multiple significations, which can thus quite easily be picked out. The entries facilitate easy searches by preachers (Rouse and Rouse, "Statim," 213, 216). This fanning out of meaning assumes two principles: multivocity by homonymy and by synonymy, in keeping with Augustine's scheme of analysis in *De doctrina christiana*. In metaphorical homonymy, the Chanter shows that a single word has several figurative meanings; thus "lion" can mean either the devil or God in Scripture, and he cites passages in the Bible where the one or the other meaning occurs (f. 89^r). This was Augustine's very example in Book 3 of *De doctrina christiana.* In synonymy, he shows that a single meaning has several figurative expressions; thus, the devil is signified by either a lion or a hunter in Scripture (ff. 46^{r-v}), and again he cites appropriate biblical passages. *Summa "Abel"* has no prologue, but one manuscript does have this note at the top of the first page: "He who does not know the differences among similar things [i.e., different meanings expressed by a single word, or homonymy] cannot properly be said to see the Lord, nor can that be said of him who does not know the similarities among different things [i.e., the same meaning expressed by different words, or synonymy]" (cited by Wilmart, "Un répertoire," 336–7 n., quoting from Ms. Mazarine 774). Thus the assumptions of the arts-of-discourse doctrines that Augustine incorporates into his interpretive scheme for reading the ambiguous signs of Scripture here reach their logical conclusion in the form of a massive glossarial compilation.

But the entries do more than present the rich multiple signification of biblical language; they also explain why things are represented by the signs they are, in their contexts within the closed set of the biblical text as a whole. Thus they offer not only the multiplicity of scriptural meaning but also often the rationale for the multiplicity. It is perhaps here that dialectic and attention to theological *quaestiones* have made their contributions. The formulas of wording in the entries imply why there should be just these figurative manifestations of an idea within Scripture and why there should be just such a range of ideas that a particular metaphor represents. Each appearance of a concorded instance of a word seems to contribute to the complete development of Christian teaching.

In the title entry, the sign "Abel" is an unknown figurative expression in Augustine's terminology; it is not also figuratively homonymous, because it signifies figuratively only *one* thing in all of Scripture: the founder of the church (f. 1^{r}). But what is said of Abel in the Bible (Gen. 4; Matt. 23 – with some exploration of the contextual situation beyond the words themselves) shows that he is made to signify the founder of the church for three reasons: his innocence, his martyrdom, and his virginity, for he was a shepherd and so did not sow seed (should this be called a figure within a figure?). It is as if these three reasons are the necessary and sufficient attributes of the church's founder. Sometimes the Chanter groups the reasons, if they are numerous, and the scriptural passages that give rise to them into two classes, *in malo* and *in bono.* This formula seems much more general in its application than when Servius used it in commenting on Virgil to distinguish "poison" from "medicine," or even when Augustine used it in *De doctrina christiana*, but the principle, one of opposition, is the same.

Occasionally Peter the Chanter offers several sets of meanings or expressions, several "fans" under one entry, each set supplying multiple significations with their occurrences in Scripture and perhaps with accompanying explanation as well, to give different but overlapping arrays of meaning for the same word. "*Anima,*" for example, has six sets of meanings, each with its marginal heading, from which lines fan out to the several senses with (usually) their occurrences in Scripture. The fourth set of the six on "*anima*" presents seven different synonyms for the several senses of the word as differentiated by function: *anima* can mean the same as *animus* when it wills, *mens* when it thinks, *memoria* when it recollects, and so on (f. 9r). No instances from Scripture appear. These polysemous senses go back to Isidore of Seville; they occur in his *De differentiis*, where he differentiates, in the manner of the grammarians, between the similar words *animus* and *anima* (col. 84BC). In the Corpus Christi copy of the *Summa "Abel,"* the marginal heading that is most appropriate to this Isidorian set (set four) is displaced and given as the heading for the first set. It reads, "the various names for *anima* are differentiated according to its various functions" (*Anima pro diversis actibus diversa sortitur nomina*). This is almost identical to Langland's introduction to his listing of all the names for Anima, taken from Isidore, near the beginning of Passus xv (B.xv.39a.): *Anima pro diversis accionibus diversa nomina sortitur.*

The fifth set (f. 9v – *Anima ponitur*) is typical of the method of the early *distinctiones* collections. Its content overlaps with several other entries, with their attention to the capacities of the soul in its various states – during life on earth or during the afterlife. This fifth set has four meanings for *anima*, with a scriptural instance for each: *anima* is put sometimes for the capacity of the senses for pleasure, as at Ps. 78:18 (Vulgate 77:18) – "and they tempted God in their hearts by asking meat for their desires (*animabus suis*)"; sometimes for life on earth, as at John 12:25 – "he that hates his life (*animam suam*) in this world keeps it for eternity"; sometimes for reason, as at Gen. 2:7 – "the Lord God breathed into his face the breath of life and the man became a living soul (*animam viventem*)"; and sometimes for that superior part of the soul that is capable of knowing God, as at Ps. 103:1 (Vulgate 102:1) – "Bless the Lord, O my soul (*anima mea*)." Such an entry would clarify seemingly incompatible polysemous senses of the same word in different passages yet reveal for homiletic discourse the range and richness of the word's hypersemiotic signification of use. That there should be (as in the case of *anima*) several sets of meaning for one word reflects the various sources from which the compiler drew, as well as the belief, shared by Augustine and by others with respect to etymologies, that the more meanings the better, as long as all are instructive.

Thus already the *Summa "Abel,"* first of the *distinctiones* collections, while clearly showing all that it owes to arts doctrines on ambiguity and to Augustine's *De doctrina christiana* in particular, reveals the potential developed during the thirteenth century at the hands of the friars. Progressively, the *distinctiones* compilations become less a collection of the multiple significations of words and figures in Scripture and more a catalogue of divided and subdivided topics in pastoral theology (such as the seven deadly sins), to which they linked scriptural passages as markers, or illustrations, or confirming proof-texts. (Rouse and Rouse, "Distinctions," *Preachers*; Giusberti, 88–92; d'Avray, 236; von Nolcken; Wilmart; Longère, 189–90). The resulting "school sermon" had moved away from exegetical commentary with its focus on words (Rouse and Rouse, *Preachers*, 66–83). The affinity of *Piers Plowman* with the *distinctiones* compilation is mostly with the form early in its development.

De tropis loquendi and *Summa "Abel"* represent well the tension in medieval symbolization on which Eco, Barthes, and Todorov have remarked. *De tropis* is disjunctive, on the side of constraining meaning, in setting out to demonstrate Scripture's consistency and unity of meaning, in solving problems of ambiguous wording. *Summa "Abel"* is conjunctive, on the side of releasing, expanding meaning, in setting out to show the rich multiplicity of the signification of biblical language. In this way, too, these two works of the Chanter's are successors to Augustine's *De doctrina christiana*.

Verbum abbreviatum seems to have been intended for a readership beyond the schools (Baldwin, 16). It incorporates both *lectio* and *disputatio* into the homiletic practice of the arts of discourse in the service of broad pastoral purposes. There are clearly identifiable stretches of continuous gloss as well as *quaestiones* embedded in the exposition – problems raised and solutions offered (Baldwin, 13).

But at least in the short version, which is the version printed in
PL 205 (see Baldwin, 14–15, on the versions; also his Appendix II,
246ff.), there seems to be little or nothing of the technical grammatical and dialectical analysis of *De tropis loquendi*. As prolix as
Verbum abbreviatum is, Peter would presumably insist that it does not
constitute a superfluous excess of words because it encompasses a
consistent and integral scriptural teaching ("abbreviated" in that
sense), directly relevant to the practical affairs of life. Several times
he insists that his purpose is to convey a knowledge of things (*scientia
rerum*) that would inform right action in practice and that would
sustain and deepen the faithfulness of a Christian's life in society
(24A–B; 30D–31A; 36D). This suggests a new emphasis in the assimilation of the arts of discourse to rhetorical purposes of teaching,
motivation to moral action, and solicitude for spiritual welfare,
addressed to a wide and inclusive audience. The Chanter seems
concerned with specific applications of learning, particularly scriptural study, to social and institutional situations and with the function of popular preaching as a discourse now perhaps for the first
time directed to all of the Christian public. These interests appear
to indicate an approach to learning and its uses that is fundamentally both scriptural and moral, reminiscent also of Langland's.

Occasionally *Verbum abbreviatum* incorporates an entry from
Summa "Abel" into exposition. The *Summa* has a number of entries
under "preaching" (*praedicatio*), including the rather surprising
item "*praedicatio suspenditur*" (133ᵛ). Very personal circumstances
might have suggested to the Chanter the usefulness of an entry on
discerning when preaching could become too much of a good
thing! The Chanter offers four reasons for curtailing preaching:
because the listeners are unworthy of the effort, because they have
not the capacity to understand the discourse; lest indifferent listeners become severe critics, and so risk sinning; and lest too much
persistence in making sermons alienate even the well disposed.
This is a *distinctio* by overlapping causes: equivalent elaborations
are set out for "curtailing of preaching," with scriptural passages
given for each instance. These four reasons occur also in *Verbum
abbreviatum*, somewhat differently presented, incorporated into a
chapter entitled *De bona taciturnitate* (194B–C). This borrowing
shows how in preaching materials the same patterns and subject
matter are able to be reformatted and repeated in different configurations in different contexts – in works close to the arts tradition

such as *Summa "Abel,"* in works of practical theology such as *Verbum abbreviatum* – as if by successive turns of a kaleidoscope (d'Avray, 246–7, for this metaphor).

The achievements that resulted from the practice of the arts in the twelfth-century schools tumbled into new configurations when turned to the purposes of popular preaching in the evangelical renewal and were available to take on a yet somewhat different design in Langland's poetry.

LINKING THE TWELFTH-CENTURY ARTS OF DISCOURSE AND LANGLAND

Langland's relationship to his intellectual background is, Murtaugh remarks, "always indirect and idiosyncratic" (56). Still, as I mentioned above, several readers of *Piers Plowman* have argued that Langland was probably familiar with the work of Peter the Chanter (see p. 22 above). There are other channels through which the arts doctrines of the twelfth-century schools could have become available to Langland; these doctrines, and Augustine's in *De doctrina christiana*, appeared in the sermons collected in anthologies of preaching.

John Baldwin, in *Masters, Princes, and Merchants: The Social Views of Peter the Chanter and His Circle*, has shown the wide range of the Chanter's concern with practical issues and the extent of the learning on which he drew to address those issues from a scriptural perspective with a notable evangelical commitment. His teachings were influential; several prominent English churchmen either were his students or had an education and interests that parallelled his. Especially important among these were William de Montibus and Thomas of Chobham.

William de Montibus was probably not a student of Peter the Chanter's, as some have thought (see Goering, 12 n. 33), but he was active in the Paris schools at the same time as Peter, and their pursuits in the arts of discourse took very similar paths (11). William returned to England in the 1180s to become chancellor of Lincoln, one among the churchmen of remarkable abilities assembled there by Bishop Hugh of Avalon. As chancellor, William both taught theology and preached.

Joseph Goering has argued that Peter the Chanter and William de Montibus both fit in the "biblical–moral" school of theology, given their attention to Scripture, their concern more with moral than with speculative questions, and their commitment to teaching and preaching on practical matters relevant to the care of souls (36–40). Within this broad concurrence of interests, both men also wrote about how the arts doctrines on ambiguity apply to the theological study of Scripture. Thus both prepared a *distinctiones* collection (William's is referred to by Judson Allen, in his article on the idea of *detractor* in *Piers Plowman*, 353–4). And both wrote a work on ways in which grammatical and logical analysis can serve to sort out difficulties posed by apparent inconsistencies in Scripture and the theological perplexities to which they can lead. We have looked above at Peter the Chanter's work on this subject: *De tropis loquendi*; William's comparable treatise is *Tropi* (Goering, 50–1, 349–88). Both works are found together in Worcester Ms. F.61, where Langland could have come across them in the fourteenth century.

William de Montibus's own implementation of arts-of-discourse strategies in theological pursuits is apparent both in his *lectio* on the Psalms and in his sermons. Very much in the manner of some of the Paris Masters, William uses the differentation of word meanings to sort out for his students various interpretations of the Psalter text and to follow pertinent theological and pastoral issues suggested by them (Goering, 47, 497–503). The ambiguity of words here not only is a source of potential stumbling blocks to be cleared up but also allows the reader to explore the surplus meanings of words in all their abundance. His sermons, too, had their uses for instruction in the application of the arts to theology (56–7, 516). Like Peter the Chanter, William would have regarded preaching as one of the most valuable outcomes of theological learning. Although he wrote for the classroom, one of his students, Richard of Wetheringsett, produced an epitome of his master's teachings, including characteristic strategies derived from the arts, cast as a *summa* of preaching. This, the "*Qui bene presunt*", was meant to be accessible to readers beyond the schools and became a popular and influential resource for clerical education in the later Middle Ages (Goering, *William*, 86–95, "The Summa '*Qui* ...'"). In that era, three copies of Richard's work were at Worcester Cathedral (Bloomfield et al., *Incipits*, #4583), where Langland might have consulted it.

Thomas of Chobham, while subdeacon of Salisbury, wrote an *ars praedicandi* treatise – *Summa de arte praedicandi* – clearly indebted to Peter the Chanter and remarkable for the breadth of its perspective (Morenzoni, Intro. to *Summa*, xl and lxiii; Murphy, 317–25). Thomas's discussion of the arts-of-discourse principles that undergird exegetical preaching contains much that is derived, as might be expected, from Augustine's *De doctrina christiana*. The Prologue offers the widest possible view of signification, restating Augustine's distinction between things and signs, which prepares the reader for the analysis of things *as* signs (5, 8). Again, like Augustine and like Peter the Chanter in *Summa "Abel"* and *De tropis*, Thomas pays particular attention to transferred or metaphorical ambiguity (6). Thomas seeks to account for the multiplicity of scriptural meaning, particularly the figurative senses generated from numbers, proper names, and the properties of things (8–10). His attention to how shared properties enable metaphorical signification (how bridges between focal points of meaning allow for semantic transferences) characterizes his approach to the homonymy and synonymy of figurative language. Thomas shows how the reading of similitudes can get out of hand. Figurative meanings must be inspired by God or be in keeping with scriptural teaching. The connotations and polysemous senses of words bridged in metaphor cannot be so distant from each other as to be completely without connection: there would be nothing edifying about understanding "lion" in a scriptural passage as meaning horse (8). And even if something edifying could be gained from regarding a wolf as a metaphor for God, such a comparison would have unacceptable overtones (280–1). The constraints on scriptural meaning that Augustine mentions (and which Eco emphasizes in Augustine) are explicit here.

The overall perspective of Thomas's treatise seems to be that of a preacher appealing to a group of listeners – not so much sharing the contemplative experience of reading the sacred text together as presenting to the public of a Christian society the knowledge of things – *scientia rerum*, in Peter the Chanter's phrase. Here, the arts-of-discourse procedures involved are less from grammar and dialectic than from grammar and rhetoric. While Augustine studied the multiplicity of scriptural language to reveal the richness of the Bible's meaning, for Thomas its point is that it lends itself to addressing a diverse audience drawn from various sectors of society (276). Taking the ambiguities of biblical language figuratively not only preserves the consistency of scriptural teaching and releases the richness of scriptural meaning but also makes for lively and accessible homiletic discourse that holds the attention of the listeners (279). Similitudes, Thomas explains, teach more effectively than does the naked truth (282). Such a remark anticipates Langland's poetic appropriation of principles of invention from the arts tradition and preaching.

Besides dealing with figurative signification in terms of similitudes based on shared properties, Thomas considers the differentiating of ambiguous expressions in *distinctio* fashion as one of several means by which divisions can be made anywhere in the sermon. The several means of division that Thomas uses come from Boethius's *De divisione*, which notes that the division of a homonymous expression or syntactical ambiguity into several significations has a basis only in convention, not in nature (*De divisione*, 878D–9A). While Thomas, like Augustine in *De doctrina christiana*, devotes more space to explaining this sort of multiplication of meaning than to any other and urges on the preacher the importance of understanding how it functions (285), Richard of Thetford, in an *ars praedicandi* written a decade or two after Thomas's, disallows this means of division for the preacher: "not every way of dividing should be used in preaching. What does it matter to the layman to know the multiple senses of some word?" (Richard of Thetford, "Octo modi," 17ᵇ.36 – for attribution to Richard, see Charland, 77; Longère, 199). Dialectical means of differentiating seem to be preferred here to grammatical – i.e., lexical ones – as the school sermon, during the thirteenth century, comes to have less about it of the gloss and more about it instead of the formalized exposition of reasons, causes, and authorities. Langland's own literary practice – his attention to words and their range of meanings – seems closer to Thomas and his twelfth-century antecedents than to those of the thirteenth century.

Manuscript copies of theological works on the arts and resources for preaching would have been available to Langland in Worcester, at the friaries there or at the cathedral, and certainly at any number of places in London, where he must also have resided for part of his life. The procedures of the arts of discourse were not the exclusive domain of a few circles of learned clerics. Vernacular preaching to the laity in the later Middle Ages does draw on resources from the schools of the earlier period. Collections of popular English sermons compiled around the time Langland was writing *Piers Plowman* show definite affinities in their forms of development with the theological uses to which the arts were put in the late twelfth and early thirteenth centuries, before the professionalization of Latin preaching in the *ars praedicandi*. Leith Spencer remarks on the prevalence in late-fourteenth-century English sermons of development by the elaboration of similitudes, word associations, *distinctiones*, and wordplay, "a manner of thought and expression which originated in twelfth-century developments in spirituality and learning" (86 – see also 151, 268, 271). She shows as an illustration the extent to which later preachers in English drew on the Latin sermons of Odo of Cheriton, who taught in the Paris schools in the early thriteenth century and whose sermons on the gospels drew on the writings of Peter the Chanter and his circle (Friend, 646–7; Baldwin, ii.29 n. 261).

The Fourth Lateran Council of 1215 directed that more effort be made to preach the faith to all of Christian society – and encouraged another development that tended to reduce the distinction between clerical and lay: the founding of town grammar schools (Rouses, *Preachers,* 56, 58). Grammar schools offered a rather more elementary version of the arts of discourse than did the cathedrals, the emerging universities, and the mendicant study centres, but it was none the less an arts education that contained the essential elements of more advanced pursuits. Two small works something like *distinctiones* collections had great currency as textbooks there. *Synonyma* and *Aequivoca* of John of Garland were specialized glossaries in verse of words that the student of Latin vocabulary might tend to confuse because of their closeness of meaning (synonymy) or of form (homonymy) (Orme, 90–1; Miner, 144). Making such differentiations had been standard practice in literary education since the time of the Sophists, as we saw above.

Langland's interest in the ambiguity of words is thus quite in keeping with the grammar-school curriculum that he would have known as a student or perhaps was familiar with as a school master. His attention to the various polysemous senses of the soul in B.xv, for instance, could have been prompted by John of Garland's *Synonyma*, where, however, the treatment of the various meanings of the word "*anima*" is versified and considerably more elaborate than what could have been found in Isidore (*Synonima cum expositione magistri Galfridi anglici*). In speaking to the Dreamer about the several names that have been attributed to himself, Anima mentions not only Isidore but also Augustine: "Austyn and Ysodorus, either of hem bothe / Nempnede me thus to name – now thow myght chese / How thow coveitest to calle me, now thow knowest alle my names." (B.xv.37–9). The differentiation of various senses of a word is a grammatical procedure appropriately associated with the methods of both Augustine and Isidore. Isidore's treatment of *anima* (*De differentiis*, 84BC, or *Etymologiarum sive originum Libri XX* ['Origines'] xi.i,13), found its way into the twelfth-century *distinctiones* collections such as *Summa "Abel"*, as we saw above. Langland might have come across it in such reference works.

The various meanings for the word that serves for Anima's name may not have any important narrative function in the course of Passus xv (although they may have contributed to the cast of mental faculties that peoples the third vision – B passus viii–xii). But the polysemous significations of other characters' names certainly do come to play a major part in the story elsewhere in the poem. Thus Clergie, "that kan manye thynges" (B.x.169), is in one sense Learning, husband to Scripture in B.x, but as one of the guests present at the banquet with Conscience in B.xiii and later, in Passus xx, as one whom Conscience calls on for help during the siege of Unity Barn, he is rather the order of clerics. The Middle English word had both meanings, and Langland is clearly interested in the interrelation between them. Also Wit, in his conversation with the Dreamer in B.ix, explains the range of meanings and roles that Kind takes on, both as word and as character; its several significations are further explored in what seems to be a systematic way by the Samaritan in his sermon in Passus xvii, as we see below. But the most striking instance of narrative significance given to the ambiguity of a word used as a proper name is the case of Lady Mede (Passus ii, iii, iv). Conscience seems to be speaking out of the arts-of-discourse tradition itself when he disjunctively differentiates the two meanings of "*mede*" at B.iii.230–1, a speech that is the pivot of the entire episode: "'Nay,' quod Conscience to the kyng and kneled to the erthe, / 'Ther are two manere of medes, my lord, by youre leve.'" Lady Mede has it in her to act both parts – to dispense corrupting bribes, to bestow just rewards. Clearing up this lexical misunderstanding has particular *social* importance. From these several instances it is evident that ambiguity is a valuable resource in the macrostructures of the poem's narrative; it is crucial also in the microstructures of the text's surface networks.

A patterning something like the multiple array of polysemous meanings so explicitly set out for *anima* in Passus xv is more intricately woven into the textual surface of Langland's poem in numerous extended passages: the writer searches out the range of distinctions of a word's meaning, homonymy and synonymy provide avenues for the extension and display of signification, the text explores the resources of scriptural words and figurative uses for what they can teach and how they can move us to reflection and understanding. Exegetical preaching, in the manner of Augustine's *De doctrina*, and the arts doctrines on ambiguity that underlie it, particularly as made available by the twelfth-century masters, is the means of this preparing and multiplying of scriptural meaning taken up in the poem.

CHAPTER FOUR

Piers Plowman:
The Resources of Ambiguity
in the Samaritan's Sermon

In Passus xix of the B text, Pentecost, understood as the occasion when the disciples received light and a knowledge of languages, is the founding event for Christian society, and it is then that Grace appoints Piers as his plowman (B.xix.262). The oxen of his team are the Gospels; they are the *team* that is also the *theme* of Piers's tilling/telling (This is the context for Huppé's example of Langland's wordplay on the ambiguity of *tille* and *teeme*). Once the entire field is plowed by Gospel teaching, it is harrowed by a team of the Fathers; thus patristic commentary, with its arts-of-discourse procedures of exposition, helps to enrich and make finer an understanding of the scriptural text, and the soul (soil? – perhaps there is a play here on the Middle English near-homonyms "soul," "soil") is the better prepared by this cultivation to grow a crop of virtues (264–77). The interweaving of the multiplication and differentiation of the significations of certain key words into the text of Langland's poem has the similar purpose of cultivating the collective understanding in order to help the Christian community grow and change. The elaborate play on the words and similitudes that come into the Samaritan's preaching on the Trinity at the end of B.xvii illustrates the ways in which Langland proceeds in his poem by exploring the complexities of ambiguous expressions according to arts-of-discourse doctrines; it is a passage representative of this major aspect of Langland's poetry.

The Samaritan's teaching about the Trinity in *Piers Plowman* B.xvii consists of an intricate interweaving of distinctions differentiating the three Persons of the Triune God and the sins associated with each. In addition, homiletic similitudes of the fist and the candle; a distinction among polysemous senses of a vernacular word, the Middle English word "*kinde*" (the range of meanings stretches to the homonymous); and the figurative meanings of a conflation of texts from Proverbs all fit together into kaleidoscopic patterning like Augustine's way of reading Scripture in *De doctrina christiana* and the twelfth-century arts-of-discourse procedures used in developing sermons. The Samaritan sums up the entire complex with a concluding exposition – of a saying drawn from three texts in Proverbs – anticipated, even aimed for, in his own speech that precedes it. In *Piers Plowman* a passage often leads up to a key word, figure, or scriptural passage as if the poet were working backwards from that point in his composition of the poem. (See also the passage leading up to the quotation from Chrysostom at B.xv.118.) Accordingly I proceed backwards in my discussion of Passus xvii from the elaboration of this saying derived from Proverbs (the three-vexations saying) back to the similitudes that lead up to it (the candle and, before that, the fist).

THE THREE-VEXATIONS SAYING

The Samaritan concludes his sermon at the end of Passus xvii with a saying derived from Proverbs about the three vexations that drive a man from his house: a nagging wife, a leaking roof, and a smoking fire. This saying conflates and recontextualizes several different verses in the Book of Proverbs (from Prov. 10:26, 19:13, and 27:15): "Thre thynges ther ben that doon a man by strengthe / For to fleen his owene hous, as Holy Writ sheweth. / That oon is a wikkede wif that wol noght be chasted: / Hir feere fleeth hire for feere of hir tonge. / And if his hous be unhiled, and reyne on his bedde, / He seketh and seketh til he slepe drye. / And whan smoke and smolder smyt his sighte, / It dooth hym worse than his wif or wete to slepe" (B.xvii.317–24).

The saying itself had wide currency in the Middle Ages (it appears in William de Montibus's *Numerale*, 243, in Goering), but Langland seems to have taken the figurative interpretations for the three vexations (as Skeat suggests in his edition [EETS, 1869], Notes, 393) from a passage in Peter the Chanter's *Verbum abbreviatum*. Langland's interpretation coincides exactly with the Chanter's for one of the alienating vexations: the "wikkede wif" is taken to

be a cause of sin, "oure wikked flessh" (l. 330), the Chanter's
"carnis tentatio" (331C). For Peter the Chanter, this vexation and
its interpreted meaning legitimate the incorporation of the verses
from Proverbs into chapter 135 of *Verbum*, on gluttony, drunken-
ness, and lechery. But the Chanter's interpretation of another of
the vexations as a cause of sin – that of the smouldering fire as
blinding ignorance – suggests another set of associations: ignorance is countered by the Son, the Person of wisdom and understanding, and the three vexations are then easily taken up into the
Samaritan's sermon on the Trinity. But for Langland, it is not the
smouldering fire but the leaking roof corresponds to ignorance –
ignorance now specifically of the benefits of suffering. This lack of
understanding lines up with Christ as both the Crucified One and
Judge: "The reyn that reyneth ther we reste sholde / Ben siknesses
and othere sorwes that we suffren oughte, / As Poul the Apostle
to the peple taughte: / *Virtus in infirmitate perficitur.* / And though
that men make muche doel in hir angre, / And ben inpacient in
hir penaunce, pure reson knoweth / That thei han cause to contrarie, by kinde of hir sikness; / Hath mercy on swiche men, that
so yvele may suffre" (B.xvii.335–42).

   The third vexation – smouldering – now corresponds to malevolence towards others as a cause of sin, the sin against the Holy
Spirit. Langland repeats here the word 'quench,' which is key to
the Samaritan's previous development of his sermon, as we see
below. Somewhere at the root of this image lies a verse from First
Thessalonians (as Schmidt notes): "Do not quench the Spirit"
(1 Thess. 5:19): "Ac the smoke and the smolder that smyt in oure
eighen, / That is coveitise and unkindenesse, that quencheth
Goddes mercy" (B.xvii.343–4). Ill-will smothers that very human
quality, the spark of loving-kindness, divine in its source, a manifestation of God's love for us. It is this sin against the Holy Spirit
that is most central to what the Samaritan preaches. Something
very like Peter the Chanter's arraying of ideas and images from the
three-vexations saying seems to be in the poet's mind here; it is a
set of figurative significations that fan out as three synonymous but
connotatively different causes of sin, each aligned by opposition
with one of the Persons of the Trinity, each with its scriptural verse,
in the manner of entries in the early *distinctiones* collections.

   In the twelfth century, Peter Lombard drew together the opinions of the Fathers on the topic of the Sin against the Holy Spirit

in a section of his great compilation of theological doctrine, *Sententiae* (Sentences) (Liber II. Dist. 43); it includes distributing three causes of sin among the three Persons – against the Father, sins caused by weakness (*infirmitas*); against the Son, sins caused by ignorance (*ignorantia*). The Lombard sorts out as the sin that is opposed by the activity of the Holy Spirit (who among the Trinity most represents love and good will) the malicious and obstinate rejection of God's proffered benevolence. Thus Langland may very well have adjusted the Chanter's triads as he did, putting ignorance with the leaking roof rather than with the smouldering fire, by taking from the Lombard this aligning of the sin of malice, the sin that quenches love, in opposition to the Holy Spirit.

Peter the Chanter also considers this sin, the Sin against the Holy Spirit, in one of his several sets of entries under "*Peccatum*" in the *Summa "Abel."* With the three Persons are arrayed three causes of sin in terms very like those found in *Sentences*, but with this difference: the sin against the Holy Ghost is not exclusively a matter of the relationship between the individual and God, but is understood as a sin against one's fellow Christians. Because the Holy Ghost is associated with *benignitas* and *dilectio* (love), the matching cause of sin is *malignitas* and *induritia* (hardness of heart; 47 f. 123ᵛ), which seems, however, to read "*industria*"). It is this understanding of the Sin against the Holy Spirit that Langland takes up, applies to the Christian's attitudes, words, and actions towards others, and matches with the third vexation caused by the smouldering hearth-fire, now understood to represent the resentment harboured by the angry master of the house against the negligence of the servant who has failed to tend the fire: "And whan smoke and smolder smyt in his sighte, / It dooth hym worse than his wif or wete to slepe. / For smoke and smolder smerteth hise eighen / Til he be bler eighed or blynde and [the borre] in the throte, / Cogheth and curseth that Crist gyve hym sorwe / That sholde brynge in bettre wode, or blowe it til it brende!" (B.xvii.323–8). It is very characteristic of Langland to emphasize the dimension of social morality, particularly love of neighbour.

The Samaritan's explication of the three-vexations saying focuses on the third vexation, then – the smoldering hearth-fire – which corresponds to the sin of malice or hard-heartedness towards others, as shown by the resentful master of the house towards his servant – the Sin against the Holy Spirit. It is with this part of the saying that the immediately preceding teaching by the Samaritan, the similitude of the triune candle, links up. That link between the similitude and the three-vexations saying consists of several mutually reinforcing strands – metaphors and multivocities twisted together, very much in ways that the twelfth-century masters incorporated the arts of discourse into preaching. First, there is the figurative contrasting pair, "quenched, smouldering fire" / "blazing fire" (of the hearth, of the candle) understood as meaning that the Holy Spirit's benevolence (the fire of love) can be thwarted by people's malice towards one other. This is twisted together with the polysemy of the Middle English word "*kind*" and the play on its near-homonym "*kindle*," which seems to be called up by the repetition of its opposite, "*quench*."

"QUENCH" AND "KINDLE"

In the exposition of the three-vexations saying, already considered above, Langland seems careful to have the Samaritan repeat the word "*kinde*" or one of its derivatives in the interpretation of each of the three vexations. Thus *the weakness of the flesh* (kind) that the nagging wife, the first vexation, represents is said to be an inevitable feature of our human nature: "The wif is oure wikked flessh, wol noght be chasted, / For kynde clyveth on hym evere to contrarie the soule" (B.xvii.330–1). ("*Kynde*" means here "natural bodily instincts"; see MED, s.v. "*kinde*," noun, 5a.)

And similarly, despair and resentment, consequences of ignorance of the benefits of suffering, represented by the leaky roof, the second vexation, are said to be not unexpected outcomes of circumstances, *a typical result* (kind): "The reyn that reyneth ther we reste sholde / Ben siknesses and othere sorwes that we suffren oughte, / As Poul the Apostle to the peple taughte: / *Virtus in infirmitate perficitur.* / And though that men make muche doel in hir angre, / And ben impacient in hir penaunce, pure reson knoweth / That thei han cause to contrarie by kynde of hir siknesse" (B.xvii.335–40). ("*Kynde*" here means "natural action"; see MED 6a.) "*Kinde*" in these two of its several polysemous senses is thus distributed to two of the verses from Proverbs that make up the vexations saying, in the manner of the *distinctiones* collections.

In the case of both of these operations of natural forces, the sins that result are forgivable because they follow from Nature, "*Kinde*."

But the unnatural sin of malice towards innocent people, inexcusable by any circumstance, is unforgivable – and is the sin against the Holy Spirit that the smouldering, partly quenched, unkindled fire represents, the sin that most occupies the poet: "Ac the smoke and the smolder that smyt in oure eighen, / That is conveitise and un*kynde*nesse, that quencheth Goddes mercy. / For un*kynde*nesse is the contrarie of alle kynnes reson; / For ther nys sik ne sory, ne noon so muche wrecche / That he ne may lovye, and hym like, and lene of his herte / Good wille, good word – bothe wisshen and wilnen / Alle manere men mercy and foryifnesse, / And lovye hem lik hymself, and his lif amende" (B.xvii.343–50). (*"Kynde"* here means "innate moral feelings"; MED 5b.) The careful repetitions of *"Kinde"* or its derivatives (or "paronyms," Cruse, 130) for each vexation oscillate among each other and so help explain what is exceptional about the one unforgivable sin – it is unnatural, "un-*kynde*liche."

This careful distribution of three different senses of the polysemous word *"kinde"* in the expositions of the three Scriptural metaphors in the vexations saying is very much in the manner of the twelfth-century compilers. Langland's elaborate linking up of these three metaphors (a nagging wife, a leaking roof, and a smoking hearth-fire) with three causes of sin (the flesh, ignorance of the benefits of suffering, malice towards others), matched in turn with the Persons of the Trinity, probably (as we saw alone) owes something to Peter the Chanter. The ambiguity of *"kinde"* thus fans out into meanings used to make theological distinctions that have their substantiation in metaphors from Scripture in an astonishingly intricate array that seems embedded in the resources of language itself. Langland has focused especially on the third metaphor, the hearth-fire – quenched by malice towards others, but kindled by the breath of the Holy Spirit – this metaphor and its meaning he has carried over into his elaboration of the vexations saying from his exposition of the candle as a similitude for the Trinity.

Already in this previous exposition (B.xvii.204–316) (I continue to move from back to front in my analysis of the passus), the Samaritan in his sermon has played on the various meanings of the word *"kinde."* Here the repetition of it and the fanning out of its several polysemous senses is an essential part of the Samaritan's homiletic development of the burning candle as a similitude for the Trinity. Again, as if in anticipation of what will be said about the meaning of the smouldering fire in the interpretation of the three-vexations saying, the focus in the candle similitude is on the sin against the Holy Spirit. The Father is the wax of the candle, the Son is the wick, and the flame itself, which can burn down to a mere glow or flare up to give heat and light, is the Holy Spirit (B.xvii.204–17).

In his note to this passage in the C text of *Piers Plowman* (C.xix.167, 313), Pearsall draws attention to the interest that medieval writers showed in the physical phenomenon and symbolic potential of the burning candle. William de Montibus in his great compilation of mnemonic verses, the *Versarius*, includes the following line under the heading *Deus Trinitas*: "The one Triune God – the mind, the sun, a fountain, a candle, a hand" (Goering, 412, no. 261). This verse clearly sets out a series of similitudes for the Trinity that theological teaching has to offer to the preacher, like those commended by Thomas of Chobham. The Samaritan's sermon develops the last two – the hand and the candle.

In developing the Trinitarian significance of the candle, the Samaritan interweaves in a complexity all his own two similitudes of three-in-one: fire, wax, wick; fire, heat, light: "For to a torche or to a tapur the Trinite is likned – / As wex and a weke were twyned togideres, / And thanne a fir flawmynge forth out of bothe. / And as wex and weke and warm fir togideres / Fostren forth a flawmbe and a fair leye / So dooth the Sire and the Sone and also *Spiritus Sanctus* / Fostren forth amonges folk love and bileve, / That alle kynne Cristene clenseth of synnes" (B.xvii.204–211). William de Montibus mentions both of these Trinitiarian similitudes in his works (*Similitudinarium*, 316, in Goering, s.v. *candela*; *Numerale*, 12.1 "De articulis fidei," 259 in Goering), and the second (fire, heat, light) is also elaborated by Richard of Wetheringsett in his popular "*Qui bene presunt*" (10–11 in Goering's typescript of the text).

The Samaritan's development of the candle similitude involves a complex reticulation of the various senses of the word pair "*kinde*"/"*unkinde*," this time rather less systematic than in the development of the senses of "*kinde*" in the passage on the three-vexations saying. The pair ("*kinde*"/"*unkinde*") or its derivatives (such as "*unkindenesse*") sometimes appear in a rather loose sense very much like that most common for the word "kind" in modern English, describing the benevolent attitude that stems from innate moral feeling (MED 5b). Twice the word in this sense occurs in the phrase "unkynde to thyn evenecristene" (251, 262), and once in the example from the Bible of the stingy and ungenerous Dives: "Dives deyde dampned for his unkyndenesse" (B.xvii.265).

Contrasting with this rather general sense of "kinde" as benevolent, the concreteness of the candle image is elicited by putting "unkindenesse" with the verb "quench": "Thus is unkyndenesse the contrarie that quencheth, as it were, / The grace of the Holy Goost" (B.xvii.271–2). And a few lines before this appear these lines: "The Holy Goost hereth thee noght, ne helpe may thee by reson; / For unkyndenesse quencheth hym, that he kan noght shyne, / Ne brenne ne blase clere, for blowynge of unkyndenesse" (B.xvii.255–7).

These lines, by their juxtaposition of "unkyndenesse" with "quench," call up in the reader's mind the opposite of "quench" and the near-homonym of "kinde" – "kindle." This recalls immediately preceding lines in which the very materiality of the concrete image of the candle makes possible a sense of "kinde" proper to natural history and in keeping with "kindle": the candle is composed of certain elements with their natural qualities (MED "kinde," sense 4e) – including the quality of flammability, with its affinity for taking the element of fire, a "kinde" or natural propensity to "kindle." Unkindness quenches the benevolence of the Holy Spirit, but people have a natural propensity to catch the fire of love for others: "Ac hewe fir at a flynt foure hundred wynter – / But thow have tache to take it with, tonder or broches, / Al thi labour is lost and al thi long travaille; / For may no fir flaumbe make, faille it his kynde. / So is the Holy Goost God and grace withouten mercy / To alle unkynde creatures … " (B.xvii.245–50).

Although "kindle" is not in Langland's text, Goodridge uses it in his translation of these lines (251), and Schmidt also mentions it in his note to line 248 (300). "Kindle" seems to hover above these passages. Such ambiguity, in which the near-homonymity ("kinde," "kindle") is brought out by opposition ("quench"), is described by Su as "punning by antonym" (128–9). More precisely, Cruse terms this sort of opposition not an antonym but a "restitutive," since it is a pair "one of whose members necessarily denotes the restitution of a former state" (228). In this case, the rekindling naturally reasserts itself; it is our natural condition to burn with the flame of love of neighbour.

According to the theologians, the Person of the Holy Spirit, like the candle in its flammability, has about it a defining nature that is the contrary of *unkindenesse* – that is, divine benevolence or benignity, conjunctively God's nature (*kinde*) and God's goodness (*kindenesse*) both: "The grace of the Holy Goost, Goddes owene *kynde*" (B.xvii.223). One way God's generous nature is manifested is in the Creation itself, (*"kinde"* can mean both the natural Creation and the Creator – MED 8a, 8c), particularly in the fashioning of the human person according to the Maker's image, a likeness developed in terms of *kinde* in Passus ix (B.ix.25–66). Thus all those who live according to their created being, showing kindness to others, in some way is similar to the candle that represents the Triune God: "For every maner good man may be likned to a torche, / Or ellis to a tapur, to reverence the Trinite; / And whoso morthereth a good man, me thynketh, by myn inwit, / He fordooth the levest light that Oure Lord lovyeth." (B.xvii.278–81).

What *Kinde,* the Creator, brings into existence human malice can destroy: "For that kynde dooth, un*kynde* fordooth" (B.xvii.273) or "[un*kynde*] forshapeth," as the Samaritan adds (290) – that is, malevolence can uncreate, unmake us. This undoing of God's graciousness in Creation by an unnatural malevolence is the unforgivable Sin against the Holy Spirit; the collocation "un*kinde* creatures" (B.xvii.216, 250) comes to seem almost a paradox: the handiwork of the Creator should be naturally kind. The likes of Dives, in being "un*kinde* to hise" (i.e. God's) (B.xvii.269), destroy those who have a particular closeness to God as His *kinde* – that is, as His *kind*red (MED 10). God's kindred are the needy and the innocent who are unjustly persecuted (B.xvii.266, 288–94).

To pick out here in this way the numerous polysemous senses of *kinde* and its derivatives (paronyms) or near-homonyms in their various parts of speech (the word *"kinde"* meaning: benevolent, innate quality, to inflame, the Creator, kin group; as well as the words meaning their opposites: malevolent, unnatural flaw, to quench, the destroyer of Creation, enemies of God) suggests that each repeated instance of the word has its own disjunctive, univocal meaning. In fact, the manifold network and array of the ambiguous meanings receive a certain interactive resonance from the poem: each instance of *kinde* registers secondarily with other proximate meanings – similar, opposite, or somehow associated: as, for example, *"kinde"* (benevolent feeling) resonates with *"Kinde"* (Creator). The meaning in each occurrence dynamically oscillates with (see Tynianov, 67–70) or is interinanimated by (Richards, 70) or semantically interacts with (Lawton in Alford, *Piers Plowman*, 240) its other significations. Alliteration serves to reinforce such resonances. Each instance of the word seems to extend and elucidate the other, in a manner reminiscent of Augustine's assumptions about reading Scripture according to the doctrines of the art of grammar. The semantic constructions become even more complex and more dynamic if the corresponding passages of the C Text are laid over the B text – as if, Augustine might say, the later version were another translation or perhaps another turn of the kaleidoscope, giving new patterns to the same or closely related materials, the two configurations lending further potentials of meaning to each other. There results a complexity of conjunctive polysemous and homonymous ambiguity, a "combinatorial explosion," that Todorov would say approaches the symbolic in its effect. The interconnections among the two networks that extend out from "*kinde*" and "*unkinde*," among themselves and as set over against each other, become so intricate that the reverberations fade away to the indistinct, the indirect, the nebulous. Language thereby shows the mystery of its own power to reveal by hypersemiosis. It is as if language has ideas of its own (Culler, 15) that the poet has sought out and disclosed.

THE FIST

Before the similitude of the candle, the Samaritan had already offered the hand as a metaphor for the three Persons of the Trinity: the fist is the Father; the fingers, the Son; the palm, the Holy Spirit (B.xvii.139–203). This similitude anticipates that of the candle by showing already the role of the Holy Spirit and the unique gravity of the sin against it (Biggs, 23). The Holy Spirit is the palm that enables the hand to reach forth and extend itself in order to minister to and lay hold on those whom God chooses to help: "The pawme is pureliche the hand, hath power by hymselve / Otherwise than the writhen fust, or werkmanshipe of fyngres; / For the pawme hath power to pulte out the joyntes / And to unfolde the fust, for hym it bilongeth, / And receyve that the fyngres recheth and refuse bothe / Whan he feleth the fust and the fyngres wille" (B.xvii.174–9; see also 142–5). The Holy Spirit works in unison with the other Persons but exercises a key role in extending God's mercies.

Those who reject that benevolence proffered by the Spirit commit the unpardonable sin because they quench the Spirit's gift of grace: "So whoso synneth ayeyns the Seint Spirit, it semeth that he greveth / God that he grypeth with, and wolde his grace quenche" (B.xvii.202–3). This key occurrence of "*quenche*" here at the end of the Samaritan's development of the Trinitarian similitude of the fist seems to set in motion the elaborate play on metaphors and word ambiguities in the rest of the sermon. This word is repeated several times in the Samaritan's subsequent development of his sermon (B.xvii.256, 271, 344) and so ties together the various parts and emphasizes their accumulated complexity. The focus continues to be on the sin against the Holy Spirit, but "*quenche*" is taken up first in the similitude of the candle flame and in the polysemous multiplication of the ambiguous word "*kinde*," near-homonym to the absent but peculiarly present word "kindle," a restitutive opposite to "*quenche*." In the development of the three-vexations saying, too, the scriptural texts from Proverbs about the smouldering fire tie into and further extend the play on *quenche*/kindle. The matching arrays (the Persons of the Trinity, the three causes of sin, the three vexations) seem to owe something to Peter the Chanter, as we saw above, and are similar to the fan-like patterns to be found in the twelfth-century *distinctiones* collections. This intricate reticulation of filiations, likenesses, differences, and multiplications of meaning relies on procedures of development based in arts-of-discourse doctrines regarding ambiguity.

The Samaritan's sermon reflects back on the conversation early in the Passus between the Dreamer and Moses (Hope) and Abraham (Faith). There the Dreamer had put the rather clumsy question (B.xvii.25–6) of which virtue, Faith or Hope, most deserves allegiance – (or perhaps rather, as the Dreamer apparently thinks of it, allegiance to which virtue would offer the easier way out). The Samaritan's sermon that follows repeatedly associates the Holy Spirit with grace and benevolence, tending to identify the Holy Spirit and Love, despite the clear identification of Love with the Samaritan who is Christ, the Second Person. The Samaritan's development of the similitude of the candle in particular (wax, wick, flame are inseparable) suggests that the other theological virtues, Faith and Hope, can be realized only if they stem from Love, for these three virtues inhere in each other in something of the way in which the three Persons of the Trinity do. This serves as an answer to the Dreamer's question – he must try to embrace all three virtues; no one of them can be picked out by itself. Thus the Samaritan's sermon does function, in a way, as a response to the Dreamer's question.

Thus all of Passus xvii coheres in the metaphor of the flame, which comes into the similitudes of the candle and the vexatious smouldering fire. The entire passus seems to be aimed in particular at the figurative exegesis of the verse from Proverbs about the smouldering hearth-fire. In leading up to that figure, the Samaritan has developed two metaphors, the fist and the candle, similitudes for the Trinity that are listed together in William de Montibus's *Versarius* and very much of a sort commended by Thomas of Chobham. Particularly remarkable in the Samaritan's teaching, when compared to the theologians' compilations and preachers' aids, is the emphasis on Christ's humanity and on Christians' showing compassion and generosity to others. The key word "*quench*" is associated in various complex ways to the Sin against the Holy Spirit, which is shown to be malevolence and lack of generosity. The Good Samaritan (Christ) himself represents just the opposite traits – love and good will towards others. It is thus qualities of Christ's humanity in particular that the poet elaborates by drawing on the richness of language's resources (for Langland's concern with the humanity of Christ, see Aers, 121).

Like Augustine reading Scripture according to the procedures of the *De doctrina christiana*, Langland has traced out in the sermon of the Samaritan an elaborate network of the multiple meanings of words and figurative association, in wordplay that suggests a shared cognitive experience of devotional reflection between poet and readers. But important to the passage's exposition is an exploration of the senses of a *vernacular* word, "*kinde*" – and the sense of a struggle to live a life of apostolic faithfulness in the everyday circumstances of fourteenth-century Christian society. This attention to both the vernacular and the currently lived situation gives Langland's reformulations of fundamentally twelfth-century ideas and procedures new and deeper resonances. His poem is in the idiom of the public discourse of preaching meant for all England, in the attempt to teach and move all members of Christian society to renew their lives in responsibility for themselves and regard for others. Attention to language as a resource, in all its multiplicity and richness, is Langland's means for making such an appeal.

In this passus, in a manner quite representative of much of the rest of the poem, Langland has, by drawing out wonderfully rich and intricate reticulations, elaborated and interconnected polysemous, conjunctive ambiguities of the word "*kinde*," played on oppositions among word meanings (*"quench"*/"kindle"), tied two similitudes of the Trinity (fist, candle) into a figurative understanding of a scriptural metaphor (the smouldering hearth-fire from Proverbs), and displayed these complexities of words and figures in matchings with sets of theological distinctions – the three Persons, three causes of sin. The resources of language, as made available by the arts of discourse, in ways reminiscent of Augustine and the twelfth-century Paris Masters, seem in this way to be the creative source of the poem. If the narrative of Will's journey intersects these networks and sometimes gets lost among them, it is because the concatenations between words and things generate the poetry as much as the story line itself does. Here language, particularly the *vernacular*, in the rich excesses of its signification and filiations, brings the transcendent into the everyday.

Transition

This brief epilogue to part I is meant to serve as a transition to part II. I draw out some of the key ideas from part I that can serve this purpose, particularly the idea of the unity of literal, ambiguous meaning, and situate my view of this in relation to some opinions of others. I then connect this topic with the other kind of ambiguity, the ambiguity of words as words, which I deal with in part II, and I attempt to show how this can be both literal and ambiguous, though in somewhat different, transposed, respects.

In part 1, I argued that the potential for surplus meaning is contained in language, that repetition of various sorts brings out this ambiguity in such a way that the same is gone over again, but also something different emerges. The resources of signification inherent in words can be explored by the commentator, the preacher, and the poet in a way that leads to greater understanding, deeper insight. Words have about them a power and mystery in their richness of meaning; they seem to have ideas of their own, if their full range of signification is explored. A major aspect of Langland's poetry seems to me to follow from these assumptions about language, which derive from a long tradition regarding ambiguity in the arts of discourse.

Among those who have regarded the doctrines of ambiguity as central to medieval vernacular literature in general, and to Langland in particular, some have judged that the predominant view of ambiguity held by medieval writers, Augustine and Langland included, is one in which language in its richness of signification is not so much a resource for knowledge as an unreliable version of reality, tainted by materiality, which is to be distrusted and finally left behind in the pursuit of higher truth. This view is essentially dualistic, it seems to me, while the understanding that I have tried to explain seems unified and incarnational – i.e., the signifying word, comprising its several focal points of related meanings and even distant significations as well, is a source for disclosing the nature of the world. Gillian Rudd, like Mary Carruthers before her, sees Langland's view of ambiguity in language as dualistic; Irvine sees Augustine's view likewise as dualistic, if in a somewhat different way.

In *The Search for St. Truth* (1973), Mary Carruthers had taken the central concern of *Piers Plowman* to be "the analysis of words as ambiguous tools of thought" (4). That analysis proves only to reveal language's inherent "inexactness, ambiguity, and obscurity" (36), its unreliability in any search to understand the truth of things. The figure of Piers does offer some inkling of the possibility of a redeemed language, but it would be one that was figural and spiritual, one that transcended the literal (78, 170–1). Ambiguity is here regarded as a fatal flaw that can be overcome only by replacing human language with a medium of understanding that derives from another, higher realm of experience.

In much the same way, Rudd, in *Managing Language in Piers Plowman* (1994), remarks that "a concern with the ambiguous nature of language is fundamental to the poem" (xi), but she takes this concern to be anxiety about language's untrustworthiness rather than an interest in exploring its richness of signification. Rudd suggests that Langland is occupied with distinguishing and determining the nature of two kinds of discourse, deductive (*scientia*) and affective (*sapientia*), both subject to their own sort of ambiguity – we might associate the rational discourse of deduction with disjunctive ambiguity and the affective discourse of contemplation with conjunctive ambiguity. In any case, the poem's conclusion is that both uses of language are disappointingly unreliable; reliance on them must be somehow superseded (204). Ambiguity becomes compounded with ambiguity when it emerges that Langland is ambivalent about these two discourses – and seems finally to embrace a (somewhat-postmodern) ungrounded plurality of representations (229).

Irvine argues that for Augustine, as for the commentators on Virgil, "Interpretation supplies another or substitute text – the commentary, 'other words' – which represents itself as a disclosure of what the text would say if stripped of its surface rhetorical vehicle, the text as if freed from the fixed textuality of concrete expression" (*Making*, 245–6). This other version, the "de-allegorized" one, assumes "semiotic supplementarity," whereby a separate, additional signification replaces the literal original ("Interpretation," 34, 39–40, 66). Such a dualistic view of interpretation is necessary particularly for authoritative religious texts, understood to have been written "according to a rhetoric of concealment" (*Making*, 182); once the esoteric spiritual insights are unlocked from the text, the vehicles of language, tied as they are to the material world of the senses, are merely empty husks, of no further account (183). The hidden meaning, revealed in the gloss or commentary, leaves behind the merely instrumental literal signification.

This dualistic mode of interpretation holds that hidden meaning and verbal container have really nothing to do with each other. Suzanne Reynolds, in *Medieval Reading* (1996), has challenged this view and has proposed a way of understanding how medieval readers schooled in grammatical culture took up the richness of language in literary texts that is similar to my own. Instead of regarding the glosses to Horace that she studied as supplementary and extrinsic to the meaning of the text, she finds them "instruments of a literal reading." Text and commentary are not fundamentally separate but inhere in each other: the gloss but brings out some intended points of meaning, contained in the literal words, that might have been missed (148–9). Accordingly, Reynolds questions the common opinion that allegorical interpretation should be the dominant model for medieval reading. Rather, medieval readers of most texts tended to assume, she suggests, that words taken literally include the figural or metaphorical in their potential for various possibilities of interpretation (133–5). Meanings are not divided off into literal and allegorical but encompassed within one interconnected configuration of focal points of significance. This unified or incarnational view of language, based on ambiguity rather than allegory, brings out what is common in the range of a word's meanings, the same in the different. Seen in this way, just as no strict line divides polysemy and homonymny, so no strict line can separate the literal and the allegorical.

A bit of slippage in the meaning of the word "literal" can accomplish the transition from consideration of lexical ambiguity, the subject of part 1, to the consideration of the ambiguity of words as words in part II. "Literal" can refer to the most common or central meaning of a word ("eye" as "organ of sight"), but it can also refer to a meaning embodied in the word itself, the letters or sounds that make it up, or in its concrete relation to other words in the system of language. For example, the Hungarian word for scissors, "*ollo*," graphically, "literally," conveys a sense of the shape of the thing designated, though this might be missed if an expert in language did not point it out. In this way, the "literal" meaning, the meaning incarnated in the material medium of the language itself, becomes one among other possible meanings of an ambiguous word that it could well take a grammarian to explain.

Among the subdivisions of ambiguity that Augustine distinguishes in *De dialectica* is the category "ambiguous equivocals in art" (as we saw above). By this he means what the Stoic Chrysippus seems to have had in mind in saying that all words are ambiguous: that is, words can be regarded for their signification, but also metalinguistically as words. Augustine's term, "ambiguous equivocals in art," refers to the art of grammar, which deals with words in themselves, apart from what they mean. Another sort of repetition, another take on the word, in some contexts can release a hypersemiotic potential of language beyond polysemic or homonymic ambiguity. It is not other focal points of signification, but properties of the word itself and their implications as discerned by the art of grammar, that allow for this multivocity. The very material, "literal," make-up of the word; or its derivation, how the word or its components connect into a network of related words; or the morphological patterns and syntactic categories that it displays in its range of uses – any of these aspects of words as words might serve to expand the meaning if the context allows for it. In these ways, there can arise an isomorphism between some feature of the literal word itself and its signification that extends meaning beyond what would otherwise be discerned.

To use this means of exploring the resources of language involves indicating the appropriateness of the word's make-up or patterning for its meanings in a particular context; this would be to demonstrate the sign's motivation, to use Saussure's terminology. The indicated appropriateness is much more than simply that the word and its signification must be bound together in such a way as not to imperil the integrity of the language system as a whole; rather, there is significant content that can be obtained from the word's being what it is. Onomatopoeia is probably the most representative instance of such motivation; there is certainly something to be learned from the fact that the English word that identifies the bird of the species *cuculidae* is "cuckoo." We "literally" hear its song in the word for it. This is not the only possible name for this bird that could inform us about it in some way, but it is one. The material itself out of which the word is made is a manifestation of the thing in the world that is signified. The sign is partially motivated to be what it is by being an expression of one feature of the referent's nature. Sound symbolism, of which onomatopoeia is only one type, is coming to be seen by linguists as playing a larger role in language than has previously been thought (see Hinton, Nichols, and Ohala, 1–12).

The ambiguity of words as words raises, even more acutely than lexical ambiguity, philosophical, particularly epistemological, questions regarding the relationship between language and the world. If words at least sometimes embody something of their meaning, then words and things bear a certain appropriateness to each other; reality matches up with, corresponds to, its representation in language, and that representation is largely adequate to making the world intelligible. "Grammatical Platonism" accounts for this correspondence by positing the reality of ideas that both lend essentiality to the identities of things and also articulate the formalities of words and the language system. This incarnational view of language allows for the word to touch its meaning and the things in the world to which it refers, instead of being isolated within its own separate system. Investigation into the word as word, into its concrete particularity, can be a source of learning about the world; the grammarian's study of names can lead to knowledge of things. The meaning that a word shows by being just what it materially is makes it ambiguous, an ambiguity of word as word.

That the Hungarian word for scissors, "ollo," graphically configures what it means may strike us as only a chance oddity. But Cruse in *Lexical Semantics* gives an example of how investigation of the make-up of words can reveal the physical laws of the universe in a rather surprising way. Cruse discusses what he calls "reversive pairs," opposites in which one word denotes some action and the other, its "undoing" – pairs such as "dress"/"undress," "pack"/ "unpack." The "normal" action denoted in each pair is the one that requires human effort to overcome the entropy of the physical universe – thus "coming undressed" or "coming unpacked" is more likely to happen of itself in the course of events than their opposites, so that the action most focused on in human experience ("normal") is the one that involves exerting energy to oppose those tendencies: "to dress," "to pack." The normal actions, expressing exertion, are designated by words that are not compounded with a negative prefix (*un-* in this case). Thus looking into patterns of how words are made up from their components gives evidence for the second law of thermodynamics. Reality in this way contributes to the word's being what it is. For the ancient and medieval grammarians in the arts of discourse and for Langland this principle of the motivation of the sign is a given fact in language phenomena.

It is those features of the word itself described by the art of grammar that have particular potential for word-as-word ambiguity in Langland – for example, the components of the word; etymologies, that is, derivative links to a network of associated words; and the categories to which words belong. If there are some striking instances of the very rightness of a word, expressing by its very form and relationships to other words something of what the thing is that is thereby named, then all who use language (but especially the poet and the preacher) have an obligation not to go against language in their speaking and their actions. This is an important concept for Langland, as we see below. As Schmidt remarks, "Langland sees clerks and makers as bearing a special responsibility towards language" (*Maker*, 10). The nature of language being what it is calls on us to act in accordance with the order that obtains in this network of "lele wordes," trustworthy words (10 n. 18); this is but part of acting appropriately as creatures in the larger world of created nature.

PART TWO

The Ambiguity of Words-as-Words in the Arts of Discourse and in Piers Plowman

CHAPTER FIVE

Words-as-Words: Context, Ground, and Overview

GRAMMAR, "GRAMMATICAL PLATONISM," AND *PIERS PLOWMAN*

As we saw above, understanding how the arts of discourse inform medieval exegetical preaching can help readers of *Piers Plowman* when they confront the poem's complex inventiveness with words. Both preaching and poetics in the Middle Ages were grounded in the textual culture of the art of grammar, as David Lawton has written, remarking on the relevance of this fact for Langland's work (237). Grammar figured significantly in part I, but it comes into play even more in the poet's development of lexical hypersemiosis via his exploration of the ambiguity of words-as-words, as he brings the doctrines and methods of the art of grammar to bear on the make-up and classes of words in order to disclose what language itself can reveal about reality – the world, the Creator, the self as God's creature. Investigating this metalinguistic sort of ambiguity clearly entails philosophical assumptions about the relationship between words and things – "motivation of the sign." Twelfth-century reconceptualizations of the art of grammar shape this aspect of Langland's work, recastings of grammatical doctrines and ideas about the ontology of language that derive ultimately from the pursuit of the discourse arts in classical antiquity and from the writings of Augustine.

Previous readers have noticed Langland's interest in some of the fine points of the *ars grammatica* and have explained some of the poem's key constructive elements in terms of grammatical doctrines and practices. Paula Carlson has claimed that grammar orders the narrative development of a major section of *Piers Plowman* – what some have called the *Vita* – by providing it with its progressive structure according to the adverbial degrees of comparison (Carlson, 118). John Alford has remarked that nearly half of the poem's substance is translation or commentary on quoted text, so that the mode of discourse is fundamentally the grammarian's practice of exposition on a text, the *enarratio* (*Guide*, 2, 6). From this point of view, grammar is pervasive in the poem and a key to its structure.

Further evidence for the role of the art of grammar consists of Langland's apparent familiarity with common grammatical formulas and his use of several rather obscure metaphors taken from the art. The importance of such grammatical metaphors in the poetry of the 1190s, especially in Alanus de Insulis's *De planctu naturae*, suggests some affinity with Langland (Curtius, 414; Ziolkowski; Alford, "Grammatical Metaphor," 751–4; Amassian and Sadowsky, 457; Carlson, 96–115). Cynthia Bland has shown that the phrase "*ex vi transicionis*," occurring in Patience's notoriously obscure riddle (B.xiii.151), is a commonplace of the grammar-school classroom (Bland, 126); and Derek Pearsall has noted that Langland's phrase "*hic et haec*" is a formula for indicating gender in Latin grammar books, where some such expedient is necessary because Latin lacks the article (Pearsall's note to C.iii.404; see, for example, Donatus, *Ars Minor* KGL, vol. 4, 356, l. 25; Reynolds, 68–72). Some of the earliest examples for English words denoting technical grammatical concepts occur in Langland (Thomson, xiv; and see MED articles, such as that for "*substantif*"). Langland seems to have been breaking new ground in vernacular English poetry by using technical terms and metaphors from the art of grammar in a manner reminiscent of the twelfth-century poets writing in Latin.

Jill Mann has pointed out another twelfth-century poetic practice that implicates the art of grammar into poetry, especially pertinent to the attention that Langland pays to the ambiguity of words-as-words: the punning in "goliardic" satire that implies a substantive relation between words and things. The impetus for pursuing this connection comes from the following lines in the Prologue (a procession of kings, knights, and clergy suddenly appears in the Field Full of Folk; these prominent figures are greeted by several cryptic addresses, one from an angel, to whom a "goliardeis" replies): "Thanne greved hym a goliardeis, a gloton of wordes, /

And to the aungel an heigh answeres after: / *Dum "rex" a "regere"*
dicatur nomen habere, / *Nomen habet sine re nisi studet iura tenere'"*
(B. prol. 139–43).

In the Latin couplet, the Goliard offers an etymology that seems
meant to have some force of argument. *"Rex"* (king) is from *"regere"*
(to rule); but a leader has only the name (*nomen*) of king without
the thing of kingship itself (*res*), if he does not govern justly
according to the laws. The assumption is that the etymological
relationship *should* be borne out by the state of things. A certain
grammatical self-consciousness comes into making the point with
the explicit adducing of an etymology and with the use of the terms
"nomen" and *"res."* Mann suggests that such an argument assumes
some sort of philosophical realism and entails as well the position
that language is wholly adequate to representing, even participating in, the world. She mentions in this regard the "grammatical
platonism" that Jolivet has described as an element in the philosophy of Thierry of Chartres and other twelfth-century masters (68).
Such philosophical positions can lead to the view that language
has about it a certain moral authority that grammar is able to draw
out. As Mann writes, "the judgement on the satiric object is made,
as it were, by the language itself" (69).

The particular etymology offered by Langland's Goliard has a
significant lineage. Skeat noted the close likeness to satiric verses
printed by Wright in *Political Poems* (Skeat, ed., *Piers Plowman*, EETS,
Part IV, Sect. 1 [Notes], 21). The etymology is mentioned by the
twelfth-century writer John of Salisbury in a passage distinguishing
king from tyrant in his *Policraticus* (ed. Webb, Bk. VIII, ch. 17,
vol. 2, 346). Ultimately the *rex*-from-*regere* derivation comes from
Isidore's *Origines*, Book I, a grammatical treatise in itself, where it
is given as a prime example of etymology (OCT, I.xxix, 3). Thus
important precedents for the Goliard's reply to the angel appear
in twelfth-century writers and in late classical or early medieval
summaries of arts doctrines that go back to antiquity.

Schmidt also pays some attention to the Goliard's verses and,
with a reference to Mann's article, takes it as important that the
lines emphasize the close bond between word and thing (*Clerkly,*
81). Later in his book Schmidt suggests that Langland's dealings
with language imply a sort of sacramentalism that shows on the
poet's part "a powerful sense of the relation between outward sign
and inward reality" (90–1), so that "words operate sacramentally,

enacting that which they signify" (109). Even before the appearance of Mann's article, Anne Middleton had recognized the relevance to Langland of a "realist metaphysics," whereby relationships in grammar match those of real entities (185), or, as Alford has put it, a metaphysics whereby language and nature are identified ("Metaphor," 754–5). Sister Mary Davlin has also remarked on the significance of these ideas for Langland's poetics (*Game*, 20 and n. 25, 114–15).

Davlin discusses an example of the development of word-as-word ambiguity that entails the "grammatical platonism" or "sacramentalism" that readers have seen as inherent in Langland's poetics. Holy Church is paraphrasing a verse from the Epistle of James ("Faith without works is dead," 2:26), saying "That feith withouten feet is [feblere] than nought" (B.i.186). The statement says that religious belief that lacks the means to go abroad in the world to act in accordance with the conviction it affirms is a faith so weak as to be as nothing; but the very make-up of the words themselves says the same thing but differently: i.e., if we take the word "feet" out of the word "*feith*" (i.e., *feeth*), then there is nothing left but a weak breath (h), a mere inarticulate aspiration, which is an element of, but less than, the word "*nought*." As Davlin says, "'feith', 'feet', and 'nought' are read also as words which denote words" (41). The two ways of taking the statement match up with each other, bearing each other out, so that a certain state of things in the world is confirmed to be true by the analysis of language. In this example the grammatical analysis is only implied, not indicated by some technical term or procedure clearly taken from the arts, as was the case in the example of the Latin verses by the Goliard.

There has been considerable recent critical interest in medieval theories about the nature of language and the relevance of these ideas to medieval and renaissance literature in general. Readers have differed over how best to identify the various theories about language, which theories predominated during the Middle Ages, and the relevance of these ideas to poetics. Eugene Vance and Jesse Gellrich both stress the mutually exclusive opposition between the theory that language is based on arbitrary convention and the theory that it is based instead on the realities of nature, but Vance sees conventionalism as predominating in the medieval arts of the trivium, while Gellrich sees realism or naturalism as predominant to the point of having the status of myth (Vance, xi, 258; Gellrich,

35 n. 13, 101). Correspondingly, for Vance, it is the conventionalist view of language that is subverted by poetry, while for Gellrich it is the naturalist view that is subverted by both poetry and biblical exegesis (Vance, 272; Gellrich, 134–5, 138, 249, 253). Like Gellrich, Richard Waswo sees a revolution in semantics, from a naturalist referentialism to a conventionalist relationalism, as leading to poetic creativity ("linguistic energies [become] manifested in literature," 288–9). However, for Waswo, this revolution occurred not in the fourteenth century, but in the sixteenth.

R. Howard Bloch and John Alford, in contrast, believe that the differences between the nominalist and realist positions could yet coexist in an "easy co-presence" (Bloch, 44; Alford, "Grammatical Metaphor," 736). For Bloch, the two views are "inadequately synthesized"; medieval theorists had not yet sufficiently worked out the full extent of their mutually exclusive consequences (46). Bloch speaks as if the medieval soul were torn between the *knowledge* that language was only a set of conventional rules and attributions of meaning and the *belief* that reality and language were bound together by real relations (44). Isidore of Seville's "ontology of words" (56) was not dislodged even by the triumph of Aristotelian logic in the later twelfth century; rather, Isidore remained "monumentally important" for the later Middle Ages (57). It was as though medieval theorists about language lacked the nerve to give up their naturalistic beliefs.

Such analyses, whether the two positions are seen as kept distinct or as mingled together in some confusion, tend to assume that the history of the philosophy of language is a series of progressive developments on the way to the empiricist positivisms of Saussure or Bloomfield. Historians of linguistics have sometimes given such an account; Robins's *Ancient and Medieval Grammatical Theory in Europe* (1951) is an example. But Chomsky's universalistic innate conceptualism and other more recent developments in grammatical theory, such as the Husserlian realism or objective idealism of J.J. Katz in his *Language and Other Abstract Objects* (1981), have challenged that version of the narrative; positivist linguistics can no longer be seen unproblematically as the inevitable goal of progress in the history of linguistics. Readers of medieval literature, perhaps especially of *Piers Plowman*, with its poetic exploration of meanings inherent in lexical ambiguity, might consider alternative theories that somehow accommodate medieval ideas about the relation between language and reality without either disposing of it or aestheticizing it.

ESTABLISHING THE
THEORETICAL GROUND:
ONTIC *LOGOS*

To discover meaning in the very make-up of words and in the system of word classes, as Langland does, involves a certain realist view of the relation between words and things. In order to better understand and appreciate this conceptual grounding of Langland's poetics, I trace these ideas back to traditions of particular relevance to Langland, to the twelfth-century masters, to Augustine, and to the classical philosophies of language on which Augustine draws. To prepare for these historical pursuits, I offer in this section a theoretical framework for the classical and medieval ideas about the nature of language. First, I show the consequences of adopting a triadic as opposed to a dyadic semiotic and then go on to present concepts from Charles Taylor that will be carried over into later sections.

Any position that holds that language is grounded in reality and that words and things can be shown to be linked according to such means of analysis as motivation, sound symbolism, and isomorphism of word classes must be committed to a triadic semiotic. Speculations on the nature of language have always been either triadic or dyadic. The former view dominated classical antiquity and the Middle Ages; the latter predominates at the present time – Saussure's synchronic linguistics is a notable instance of the dyadic model (see Noth, article on the "sign," especially 83–91). Boethius, in his important and influential commentary *On Aristotle's "De interpretatione"*, written at the end of classical antiquity, sets out the three-point schema in terms of "*vox*" (word vehicle), "*mens*" (conceptual meaning), and "*res*" (thing referred to) (col. 297B). A twentieth-century formulation of the same position is that of Ogden and Richards in *The Meaning of Meaning* (10–11).

Ogden and Richards represent the triadic semiotic by an equilateral triangle with "symbol" (word vehicle) at one side, "thought" at the top, and "referent" at the other side. The line along the bottom is not solid like the other two sides of the triangle, but dotted: "Between the symbol and the referent there is no relevant relation other than the indirect one, which consists in its being used by someone to stand for a referent" (11). But the connection between word vehicle and referent is the very line that the "grammatical platonist" regards as susceptible to becoming solid if carefully investigated. Word and thing invite the mediating subject to notice how they, vehicle and referent, mutually inform each other. There is much to be learned about both from considering the ways in which they are alike.

Ann Bertoff has argued that adherence to a triadic semiotic avoids many of the pitfalls that contemporary literary theory, with its Saussurean assumptions, has dug for itself. The dyadic model postulates an arbitrary matching up of signifier and signified that leaves an unbridgeable gap between the two orders of words and things; the triadic model allows for the mediation of interpretive thought between language and the world, allows even for a two-way dialectic, whereby words reflect reality but also are instrumental in understanding it (9–10). Saussurean dyadic entails as well a referential agnosticism. The language-user must remain sceptical about the capability of the language system to provide an adequate reading of the world. Bertoff remarks, "The dyadic insistence that the map [signifier] is not the territory [referent] becomes the claim that without the map there is no territory" (18). The dyadicist tends to end up committed to an extreme form of the Sapir–Whorf hypothesis.

Boethius, and most ancient and medieval language theory, saw the grounding of signification as flowing triadically from reality through the comprehending subject and unproblematically into language; this object-to-language direction I call "objective," after the objective order of things that is taken to ground signification. Modern theories of language usually see signification to derive and flow, often dyadically, in the opposite direction, i.e., from language into the concepts that language distinguishes and so into "reality," whatever that might now mean (is there territory beyond the map of it?); because according to this view understanding of the world is linked fundamentally to the system of language itself, the language-to-object direction I call "linguistical." Structuralism takes this direction as fundamental to its position. Charles Taylor and K.O. Apel describe the ancients as (for the most part) assuming a triadic and "objective" view, i.e., taking it for granted that the world is rational, that it makes sense in a way that the inquiring subject can comprehend and give an adequate account of in discourse. Apel speaks of "the intersubjective identity of possible meanings as correlated to the ontological structure of things" (36–7); similarly, Charles Taylor speaks of a "powerful line-up of an ontic *logos* [in reality] ... which was followed by a *logos* in the thinking subject" ("Language," 222). This *logos* is manifested as a medium for communication in natural languages.

Taylor argues that language itself can be thought of as relating to things as triadically mediated by the subject in either of two ways: in a *designative* or in an *expressive* way. These are not mutually exclusive; each catches a meaningful aspect or dimension of reality (218). (Cruse also makes this distinction – his terms are "propositional" and "expressive" – and he explains that it is the expressive trait that differentiates synonyms, in that they are words with identical meanings, but with a different feeling about them; 171–4). The designative and the expressive are Taylor's mutually complementary alternatives to the exclusionary conventionalist and naturalist ways of thinking about language of which other critics such as Vance and Gellrich have made use. Representation by *designation* serves to specify or identify things, selecting them out for attention; it involves a certain demonstrative, neutral stance, and implies a lack of connection between the object designated (referent) and the means of signifying it. Representation by *expression* serves to offer a direct, immediately available manifestation of things; it involves a certain closeness and oriented disposition in its stance and implies some sort of incorporation of the object into the means of signifying it (Taylor, 218–19).

The expressive aspect works to make solid that dotted line between "symbol" and "referent" in Ogden and Richard's semiotic triangle. In the "objective" direction, along this line from "referent" to "symbol," words take on the cast of what they signify, as in the case of the name of the cuckoo; this is motivation. But, as Pierre Guiraud has suggested, if this expressive impulse is taken in the other direction, the "linguistic" one, from the "symbol" to "reality," things come to take on the cast of the words used to refer to them; language transforms reality so that it is in keeping with words. This is "retro-motivation"; it accounts for the earwig's being regarded as having traits that derive from its name (Guiraud, 407). Guiraud sees this expressive dynamic in both directions as fundamental to our everyday verbal activity and as an important source of literary invention (409; see also Culler, 11, 13). In this regard, he mentions several medieval poets and Valéry in particular and discusses this phenomenon of motivation and retro-motivation with respect to medieval etymologizing, one sort of developing "words-as-words ambiguity," as we see below.

Charles Taylor goes on to suggest that there is something expressive about the object-to-language, "objective" way of seeing signification's grounding. This is especially so in Christian thought, in which the Creator brings into existence a world that manifests the divine ontological plenitude and intelligibility. As Taylor puts it, "what we have in Augustine and his successors is an expressive theory of meaning embedded in their ontology. The originator of meaning, God, is an expressionist. This sets the framework for the theories of the Middle Ages and the early Renaissance, what one would call the semiological ontologies, which pictured the world as a meaningful order, or a text" ("Language," 223). The creature made in God's image, the human person, is particularly enabled to understand this text, for we find within us a special affinity between ourselves and Creation. (As we see below, this is a crucial idea for Augustine, Hugh of St Victor, and Langland). Furthermore, Christians, because they accept a "semiologizing ontology" that regards reality as endowed with an immanent significance or *logos*, would presumably regard as especially expressive the words of a sacred text that reveals the historical meaning of that expressively created world. In this way, Augustine and those who follow him in how he reads Scripture take the words of the Bible as invaluable resources for understanding Creation.

If expressive representation and designative representation are not incompatible but are both needed for an adequate theory of language, then perhaps these two directions of the founding of signification, the "objective" and the "linguistical," can somehow be taken up into a more encompassing understanding of meaning, whereby language not only represents the world, but also enters into the realities that it describes. Meaning flows between language and the world in both directions, then, a triadically mediated dialectic. Perhaps reading Langland from the vantage point of medieval notions of a "semiologizing ontology" that encompasses both designative and expressive sides can contribute to a full appreciation of the experience of language.

This theoretical groundwork can help to draw out the philosophical implications of Langland's development of the ambiguity of "words-as-words." The example given by Sister Mary Davlin and discussed above assumes that there is much to be learned from investigating closely the imprint that reality makes on language. Holy Church restates the truth taught in the letter of James that works are the essence of faith: "For James the gentile jugged in hise bokes / That feith withouten feet is [feblere] than nought … " (B.i.185–6). The meaning of the statement is confirmed and extended by the implied analysis of the word "*feith*," analysed into its components. There is a repetition involved here, the word over again, same, but different: as a whole, "*feith*"; as made up of its components, "feet-h." The grammatical analysis serves to trace meaning back along the line, understood to be solid, that constitutes the base of the triadic model, "referent" to "symbol." The very word in its make-up expresses some essential feature of what faith is; what faith is motivates the word that signifies it. That these correspondences hold seems to contribute to the force of the interpretation's moral authority. The world and language are mutually informative. The very nature of reality is suited to being manifested in the make-up of discourse; ontology thus shows itself to be semiological.

PRELIMINARY OVERVIEW OF TWELFTH-CENTURY ARTS TRADITION

Twelfth-century thinkers profoundly reconsidered the three-point interrelationship between Creation, philosophical knowledge, and language. At that time, in the urban schools of France, masters and their students took up authoritative texts with a renewed commitment to exploring the phenomena and meaning of the natural world, the full range of what the intellect could pursue, and how language interrelates and expresses these natural and conceptual orders. Besides new texts to assimilate, they had new methods and new purposes to bring to a fresh examination of old texts. What is manifested by Nature in Creation and what resources the arts tradition offered to Reason for its understanding especially occupied the masters. They brought a remarkable energy and thoroughness to their explorations and an optimistic assumption that a way could be found to pursue Reason and scriptural revelation together in the achievement of a greater understanding of the world. This understanding was to be put to the purposes of enabling ordinary members of Christian society to live more faithful lives, especially in the context of the towns (LeGoff, xvii, xix).

To turn intellectual endeavour into channels for reforming the life of Christian society through preaching and pastoral ministry was an impulse that originated in the desire to follow the apostolic life that also characterized the century. These concerns that occupied the masters of Chartres, Paris, and St Victor have a particular sympathetic resonance with the issues that seem also to hold Langland's attention. Compendia of sermons and reference books in the arts are the most likely means of transmission of these twelfth-century concerns and practices to the fourteenth-century poet.

Readers of *Piers Plowman* have sometimes mentioned Hugh of St Victor, particularly as the author of *Didascalicon*, for his role in the reformulation of the arts for the Christian culture of the high Middle Ages, which had consequences relevant to the reading of Langland (James Simpson, 59; Murtaugh, 63–95; Carlson, 36–40). The Victorines, Hugh and Richard the most prominent among them, were in a unique position to mediate the encounter of the new intellectualism with patristic tradition. The Abbey of St Victor was a community of canons organized according to the rule of St Augustine, but committed by its founder, William of Champeaux, to the enterprise of learning within the environs of the Paris schools. The community served as a bridge between the earlier monastic tradition, which looked back to the Fathers but was reinvigorated by the reform movement, and the emerging academic activities in the cathedral schools (Chenu, "Imaginatio," 260; Smalley, *Study*, 196; Chatillon, "La culture," 149; Evans, *Language: Earlier*, 28).

Hugh in particular was seen even in his own time as an interpreter of St Augustine and the bishop of Hippo's successor in redefining a program of the arts in the service of the church. Hugh's *Didascalicon* sets out an approach for reading Scripture that owes a great deal to *De doctrina christiana* in its attention to figurative meaning and in its grounding in arts-of-discourse doctrines (Zinn, 50; Sweeney, 61–2; Margaret T. Gibson, 42). In both Augustine and Hugh, grammar plays a pivotal role at the beginning of the inner ascent from the arts to theology. If anything, the arts are even more important in Hugh's program than in Augustine's, for he wrote at a time of intense activity in the trivium arts and sought to take into account those developments (Sweeney, 63–4).

In the autobiographical sections of his *Metalogicon,* John of Salisbury offers a glimpse of the teaching of the arts masters at Paris. The art of grammar figured prominently in their pursuits. Twelfth-century grammarians drew on the long tradition of commentaries on Donatus and Priscian and like them focused on the parts of speech. As Fredborg has remarked, with reference to two of the leading grammar masters of that time, theirs was a "purely semantical grammar," but the ontological issues raised by this attention to the properties of words and word classes were central to their considerations (Fredborg, 44). This is the context of the "grammatical platonism" of Bernard of Chartres that has interested Jill Mann as a reader of Langland. The twelfth-century masters pursued lines of thought that led them from the analysis of words to a philosophy of language.

Augustine, as we saw above, was concerned with aspects of the art of grammar in his works and thought deeply about our experience of language and how it facilitates our knowledge of things both corporeal and incorporeal. His dialogue on the philosophy of language, *De magistro,* takes the form of a grammar lesson, with himself as master, his son as student. The way in which Augustine appropriated and recast the classical arts for use in the "middle age" of a Christian culture was to be authoritative for centuries to come. His fascination with language and the resources that it held for Christian purposes, the mystery of its origin, and the inwardness of language experience all received the attention also of medieval thinkers who read his work or were influenced by it. Langland knew at least something of Augustine's reputation in this respect, for in B.xv Anima mentions Augustine as an authority on the inner experience of the soul and on the identification of its various roles by names (B.xv.37); Anima goes on in the passus to instruct the Dreamer about names in a sort of grammar lesson.

Augustine pondered the relation between words and things, language, the arbitrariness of language conventions on the one hand and the relation of words to what they signify on the other, as that issue was part of his inheritance from classical philosophy and language teaching. Classical philosophers and practitioners of the arts, from the sophists to the Neoplatonists, bequeathed a rich legacy of speculation about the nature of language, the motivation of the sign, and what could be gained from investigating the ambiguity of words-as-words.

CHAPTER SIX

Augustine on Words-as-Words

SOURCES OF THE AUGUSTINIAN SYNTHESIS: CLASSICAL ARTS DOCTRINES ON THE AMBIGUITY OF WORDS-AS-WORDS

In addition to studying the multiple meanings of words, the Sophists examined the relations of words to the reality they were meant to signify. It was they who posed the problematics of language addressed by later philosophers from Plato on. Only after several centuries did grammar emerge as a separate study in its own right.

The central issue as formulated by the Sophists was the question of what constituted the "correctness of names," i.e., what determined that words were rightly put, appropriate, apt with respect to their referents and to each other. Plato mentions that Protagoras wrote on this subject (*Cratylus*, 391ᶜ; *Phaedrus*, 267ᶜ). The question is related to the larger Presocratic concern with how adequately discourse can give an account of reality; not all, by any means, accepted the doctrine of "ontic *logos*," in Taylor's term. Those who did not gave various reasons for not doing so. For Heraclitus, reality was always changing, it did not persist long enough to be seized by discourse; for Protagoras, each person's experience was radically his or her own, not intersubjectively shared and exchangeable; for Gorgias, there is a total incompatibility between experience and expression in discourse that makes impossible the use of language to convey truth.

What grounds language, how it can be capable of getting across the truth about things, is just what is at issue in Plato's dialogue *Cratylus*, where Plato refers explicitly to the opinions of Heraclitus and Protagoras (402ᵃ, 386ᵃ). The Presocratic and Platonic ideas about how names relate to reality and how they can provide knowledge about the world contributed to later Stoic and Neoplatonic notions about language that were incorporated into Hellenistic and Roman arts-of-discourse doctrines, especially grammar (Amsler, 24; Pinborg, 77–8; Wagner, 62). The Stoics especially addressed the ontological dimension of the study of language and worked out what could be learned from investigating metalinguistic ambiguity – i.e., the surplus meaning to be ascertained from the make-up of words, their derivations, and the category distinctions of word classes.

The breadth of discussion in *Cratylus* makes it a useful point of departure for consideration also of Stoic and Neoplatonic views of language (views that seem to have had particular importance for Augustine), in so far as we can reconstruct them from obscure and fragmentary texts. Socrates in *Cratylus* associates the issue of the correctness of names with the Sophists (384ᵇ, 391ᵇ⁻ᶜ). For him, the rightness or truth of the lexical elements of discourse (385ᵇ⁻ᶜ) consists in their capability of reliably indicating the natures of things. He provisionally sums up the progress of the discussion at one point: "the correct name indicates the nature of the thing" (428ᵉ). Elsewhere Socrates remarks that language would need to be capable of such correctness in order to fulfil both of its functions of teaching and of distinguishing natures (388ᶜ).

But how do things come by their names? Socrates touches indirectly on the possibility that names (proper names in this case, which are not seen as exceptional instances of language signification) develop along with their referents in the regular course of nature, just as people take on their own names in keeping with their stations and destinies (394ᵃ–395ᵃ). (*Piers Plowman* B.v, Repentance's portrayal of Gluttony's stopover at Beton the Brewster's place, affords many examples of proper names that indicate something of how those named have lived, what they are like, as "Tymme the Tynkere," "Pernele of Flaundres," and so on – 307ff.) However, throughout most of the argument the participants in the dialogue talk as though things come by their names through their originary imposition according to the judgment of a lexical artisan or semantic legislator (e.g., 389^d, 431^e) – maybe even a more-than-human power (397^c, 438^c). But Socrates raises the possibility that givers of names could be mistaken, resulting in a mismatch between word and thing (436^b), and one of the other speakers offers as a counter-example the wilful master who frequently changes the names of his slaves, exercising his caprice by so doing (384^d). (W.S. Allen provides an anecdote that reinforces the counter-example in the dialogue: a similarly capricious ancient philosopher called his slaves by the names of various Greek particles – words that by themselves lack any meaningful content; W.S. Allen, 42.) And the arguments that Socrates appears to borrow from the Sophists seem shaky at best. They proceed, as Socrates says, either by breaking the single word up into a phrase or by associating it (or a part of it) with other similar words (421^{d-e}), in both cases explaining words in terms of other words and so always repeating the process, around in a circle in an endless chain, never breaking out to establish meaning on firm ground (see Genette, 26).

But at this point Socrates proposes a new method (422^b), which analyses names into their constituent letters as transcribed representations of certain sound elements. (The analysis of "feeth"/ "*feith*" that Holy Church suggests in B.i has about it something of both this approach and the previous one: identification of a component as another word ("feet"), identification of a sound element associated with a certain meaning ("h") – a mere aspiration, almost nothing at all.) Determination of the several gesture-like actions of sound production (422^e–423^b) and their signifying content can show that complexes of sound imitate complexes of ideas. In this way certain "primary names" (422^c) can be shown to imitate vocally the essence or nature of what they name, and the rest of the lexicon can be derived from these primary names by appropriate modification of them (427^c). This theory shows more promise than the previous Sophistical ones, but even it seems unable to support the position that names should reveal the essential natures of what they name, although they may be sufficient to convey the general character of the thing (432^e), some of its traits, or to make it in some way more intelligible (434^e).

Plato seems to be assuming that the view of language as underwriting words' ability to account for the self-manifestation of the world would require combining the denominative and the expressive sides of language, bringing into complete accord designation and signification, to use Genette's terms in *Mimologiques* (Genette, 23). But natural languages seem not to attain this ideal, to Socrates' apparent disappointment (435ᶜ). The Stoics and Neoplatonists persisted, however, in this quest, holding to an understanding of ideal correctness similar to that on which Plato seems to give up.

For the Stoics, language and its meanings are isomorphic; there are correspondences that hold between them, shapes that match. This congruity is grounded in a theory of the vocal imitation of semantic content that resembles Socrates' "new method" – i.e., there are certain primary names whose elements portray in sound the defining features of the thing named (Holtz, 60). A wise man or philosopher-king originally imposed these true denominations; the Stoics seem to have thought of this event in rather more historical terms than had Plato. Since that event, derivative names have descended from those primary ones, some paralleling in their vocal material the semantic development from the original meaning, some deviating anomalously. By tracing these changes back in time, the grammarian is able to recover truth about things. The Stoics thus put considerable store in etymology, differing from Plato also in this (Pinborg, 95–7; Frede in Rist, ed., 68–70; Holtz, 8; Amsler, 22–3; Irvine, "Interpretation," 37).

At the end of *Cratylus*, Socrates speaks of a dream he has that all things "do not leak like a pot" (440ᶜ), that while a particular instantiation of what can be identified by a name is always changing, yet that by virtue of which it is so named does persist, can be reliably grasped by knowledge, and so can be correctly named (439ᵈ–440ᵇ, 397ᵇ). Socrates here again rejects the Heraclitean view, as he had also Protagoras's that there can be no intersubjective identification and nomination of things by language (386ᵈ⁻ᶜ). It was the Neoplatonists who dreamed most elaborately Socrates' dream of an ontic *logos* that does not dribble away, that is discernible in common. If Proclus's late commentary on *Cratylus* is any indication, the Neoplatonists read the dialogue as an attempt to establish a theory of language that ties discourse securely to Being.

In his conversation with Cratylus late in the dialogue, Socrates denies that investigation into names offers reliable knowledge about the world (436ᵃ⁻ᵇ); he speaks of an alternative way of knowing things, a true and natural way, "through their affinities ... and through themselves" (438ᵉ, 439ᵇ). But as Georgios Anagnostopoulos has argued, the course of conversation in some of the other dialogues suggests how difficult it is to arrive at the definition of something, such as virtue, solely on the basis of the evidence offered by things themselves and things related to them – and yet the inquirer apparently has some notion of what is sought, identified as it is just by the naming of it (Anagnostopoulos, 335).

In *Meno*, Socrates proposes an explanation for how we seem to know already what it is we are seeking: the fact that a slave can seem already to have known the truth of a geometrical theorem, about which he can accurately answer questions but about which he has not been taught, suggests that knowledge about things is present before our experience of them; and "if the truth about reality is always in our soul, the soul must be immortal" (*Meno*, 86^b), i.e., "we *implicitly* know, through some prior direct acquaintance, the nature of what the term means" (Anagnostopoulos, 337). This explanation, unlike the alternative theories whereby we find things out by investigation into names or into things themselves, gives an account of our knowledge as having sprung up with our being. This idea of the recollection by the soul of knowledge from a previous existence was taken up by the Neoplatonists and associated with their theology of emanation and return, which linked the cosmogony of *Timaeus* with a theory about how language is grounded in reality.

Proclus, in his commentary on *Cratylus*, seems to maintain that a name is something more than an imposed indication of the nature it denominates, but is instead somehow co-substantial with it, a possibility that Socrates raises only indirectly when considering family names and titles (394^a–395^a) (Bastid, 48, Note: for Proclus's commentary I am wholly dependent on chapter 2 in Bastid's book). Bastid several times remarks on the obscurity of Proclus's text.) If name and nature are innately bound up with one another, it is because they both flow from the same source, the source also of the soul, which has gained its intuition of the things indicated by words from this originary connection. The soul participates in the Mind that joins word and thing in a particularly closely linked triadic relationship. In fact, the soul's power of recognizing what things are and of discerning the identifying propriety of names shows the soul's origin and affinity with the Demi-urge, Fashioner of the cosmos. There is a relation between the eternal patterns of essences by which the Fashioner formed and sustains the world and the array of words that emerges with it, and the soul is able to recover this relation. The descent of transcendent Spirit into materiality and the activity of intermediary beings have tangled up language somewhat, but the devout philosophical-grammarian can reascend to a clear apprehension of essential and lexical realities (Bastid, 49). This doctrine constitutes what could be called a Neoplatonic mythic semiologizing ontology.

The Stoic etymologist also traces words back through their gradual deterioration to a form that fully realizes language's manifestation of reality, but this is historical work rather than esoteric. The study of language, by recovering the primary forms of words, may not reveal the essential natures of things, but for both Stoics and Neoplatonists, for the grammarians who draw on their philosophical traditions, and for Augustine, it can reinforce the teachings of the wise or help foster the soul's reminiscence of what it already knows from its noumenal origins. While Plato seems not to have put much store in the Sophists' arts of discourse and the application of them in the reading of the poets, the Stoics and Neoplatonists saw the pursuit of language studies as having considerable potential for revealing truth about the world and for elucidating the profundities to be found in poetical texts. Stoic methods of etymological research were a great resource for the grammarian's explications (*enarratio*). The poets came to play something of the role of Plato's Giver of Names, so that it could be assumed that the analysis of usage in poetic texts would reveal a word's essential meaning, and vice versa, i.e., that the meaning of a word that was arrived at by etymological reasoning would be just the signification expected to be found in the poets. And when the arts treatises themselves came under the commentator's scrutiny, the grammarians came to be cast in the role of the Legislator of language.

The Stoic doctrine of the isomorphism of language and reality led to the alignment of grammatical with ontological categories: words constituting a class by their being identical in form are names of entities also constituting a class by their being actually identical in some respect. The Stoics, on this basis, were the first to distinguish between common and proper nouns: common nouns, having a certain set of endings, are the names of classes of things that have natures in common with others in their class, like "people" and "horses"; proper nouns, having a different set of endings, are the names of particular individuals, like "Socrates." This principle of isomorphism becomes important for the definitions of the parts of speech in the long tradition of the art of grammar and is present already in the treatise *On Voice* by the Stoic Diogenes the Babylonian, abridged by Diogenes Laertius (*Lives*, VII.55–9). This work seems also to anticipate the overall format of many of the later treatises on the art of grammar, including Donatus's *Ars grammatica* (Frede in Rist, ed., 42; Holtz, 9; Irvine, *Making*, 34).

Both Stoic and Neoplatonic traditions offered not only theories about language and methods for pursuing the art of grammar, but also a mythology of cosmogenesis of which commentators found traces in the texts of the poets. Christianity came to the classical arts tradition with a different narrative of the coming into existence and destiny of the world and of its redemption, but pagan theories and methods of language could be accommodated into Christian culture all the same (Irvine, *Making*, 88–9). After all, Christianity, too, had its authoritative texts for the exegetes' attention, and their story told of a God who brought about Creation by speaking things forth, who oversaw the naming of creatures, the imposition of names, by the first man and who created and redeemed the world by the agency of the Word. The Alexandrian Christian writers and Jerome in particular showed how the grammarians' procedures for exegesis of the pagan poets (*enarratio*) could be combined with the traditions of Jewish scholarship in the interpretation of the Christian Bible (Holtz, 46; Fontaine, 31–2; Amsler, 87, 118; Irvine, *Making*, 163).

There was no reason that Christian readers of Scripture should not avail themselves of the classical arts tradition's assumptions about the relation of language to reality and about the procedures of grammatical exegesis that those assumptions allow for. Christian commentators would accept the idea that the world, which is comprehensible in a way that language is able to account for adequately, is itself a manifestation of the Creator's Being – i.e., theirs would be a particularly expressivist "semiologizing ontology." They would also believe that the human person, made in the image of that Creator and made capable of language, would have an originary affinity with the logos that brought forth all things according to their natures. The natural languages can thus be regarded as having a source in the transcendent, which enters into their triadic relationship to reality.

AUGUSTINE ON THE ARTS
AND ON THE ONTOLOGY
OF LANGUAGE

We saw above how arts doctrines on ambiguity underlie the exegetical procedures for homiletic invention in Augustine's *De doctrina christiana*. In other early writings, Augustine reflects on the more philosophical aspects of grammatical theory, on the grounding of words in reality, and on what can be learned from investigating the make-up of words and the distinctions of word classes. Words-as-words have the potential at least to convey surplus meaning beyond their mere designations. In his thoroughgoing rethinking of the nature of language and how it is possible at all, Augustine is oriented partly by Stoic and Neoplatonic doctrines, but he seems ultimately to be in line with Plato's more indeterminate inquiries, but pursued to essentially Christian conclusions. The very act of reading and the language that is processed in comprehending text become objects of meditative self-reflection that leads inward to discern how the Christian God is present in our interior experience of meaning. Grammar takes on the particular role that it has in Anima's remark in B.xv: – Grammar is "the ground of al" (l. 371).

Augustine recognized both the expressive and the designative sides of language; as for Plato, so also for him, both aspects had their mysteries about them. Augustine does offer some striking examples of isomorphic reasoning in the Stoic manner, which demonstrate the expressiveness of language structures, lexical patterns configuring the reality that they denote. In one example, Augustine finds significance in the forms of the verb *morior,* "to die" (*De civitate Dei,* 13.11). Just as dying defies human analysis (it seems not to be an event that actually occurs, but to be only a passing from life to death), so the forms of the word *morior* do not follow the usual conjugation patterns for their word class (Marrou, *Augustin,* 649–51; Alford, "Metaphor," 737; Amsler, 48–50). While this anomaly itself has meaning (indeed, "it has turned out this way not unsuitably nor inappropriately, and not by any human action, but as God would have it"), elsewhere, in a similar instance, Augustine finds that the form of language does not at all express what things are. He observes that the system of regular verb classes as he taught it to his pupils represents the present tense as having a concrete reality that it does not in reality have; for the present, despite the table of verb forms in that tense, happens only as the future becomes the past and so does not really exist (*Confessions*, XI.17). Like Plato in *Cratylus*, Augustine is aware of contradictory evidence on the matter of whether language conforms to reality.

Brian Stock has recently argued that Augustine's spiritual biography can be narrated almost entirely in terms of situations of reading and writing (*Augustine the Reader*). The context and usual procedures of the grammar-teacher's classroom is not infrequently at the back of Augustine's mind in his works. One instance is his recourse to the etymologizing of grammatical terms, a practice that grew out of the classroom treatment of grammar treatises as themselves texts deserving comment. The usual derivation for the name of the art, from the Greek word for "letter," γράμμα, is given in *De ordine* (II.12.37). In the course of *De magistro* – a dialogue that takes the form of a grammar lesson – the word for noun, *nomen*, is said to come from *noscere*, "to know," since names make things known (V.12) by marking them out with a sort of identification tag ("*notamen*"; for a similar etymology, see *De genesi ad litteram, imperfectus liber* – [sec. III, part 2], 477). In the same passage of *De magistro*, *verbum*, "word," is said to be composed of *aurem* and *verberare*, "to strike the ear" (see also at VII.20). Collart has observed that this etymology recalls Stoic theories of language that stress the materiality of sound, such as that presented in Diogenes of Babylon (Collart, 291; Diogenes Laertius, *Lives*, VII.55).

Despite this apparent acceptance of the commonplaces of the grammatical tradition, this etymology for *verbum* seems to be held up by Augustine for scorn in the chapter of *De dialectica* on the origin of words (92[9], l. 8). Here his reservations seem to be the same as those of Plato in *Cratylus*: such etymological explanations go on indefinitely because they but explain words in terms of other words; and, besides, it seems possible to come up with a more or less reasonable explanation for any number of different derivations (92[9], ll. 3–7). Like Plato too, Augustine goes on in *De dialectica* to set out the principles for a "new method" (but here attributed to the Stoics – 93[9], l. 18; 94[10], l. 10) that traces lexical origins back to certain primary words whose sounds somehow resemble the things they indicate (94[10], ll. 2, 10). However, a counter-example even to this principle troubles Augustine in *De magistro*: *caenum* ("filth") and *caelum* ("heaven") are almost alike in sound but so different in sense! (ix.25). Thus, while Augustine sometimes accepts assumptions of the Stoic grammarians, especially regarding word-class isomorphism and the validity of etymological derivations, elsewhere his philosophical probings undercut them.

Although Augustine did not regard the details of lexical composition and morphological patterning to be as informative as the Stoics and Neoplatonists had, like the Neoplatonists he found in the arts of discourse the basis for thinking his way self-reflexively within and back to an understanding of the source of human existence. His formulation and rationale in *De ordine* for the seven liberal arts (the three arts of discourse and the four mathematical disciplines) seem to constitute the first conceptualization of the liberal arts as a coherent program (Hadot, 101). In this context, Augustine's discussion of the art of grammar emphasizes the designative side of language, but the self-reflective study of the arts leads one to see that the indirect connection between word and referent through the intermediary of the intellect has ontological implications of its own, for one comes to realize that the inherent apprehensibility of things is matched by the mind's capability of discerning the identities of things designated by words. The best explanation for this matching is some predisposition of the soul to know already how realities are articulated in the world, a theory, again, of "ontic *logos*" like that suggested by Plato in *Meno*. There may be in addition certain instances in the configuration of the world, history, language, and Scripture itself in which God reveals some special significance in the expressive conformity of thing, event, word form, or biblical passage to its meaning; the word forms of *morior* are such an instance. But such special instances, short cuts, as it were, along the base of the triadic diagram, referent to word, are not to be expected as a rule in language.

Towards the end of Passus x of the B text of *Piers Plowman*, the usually reticent Dreamer bursts out in exasperation at the many indications that he has been given of learning's uselessness; in reply, at the beginning of xi, Scripture admonishes him with the stern rebuke, "*multi multa sciunt et seipsos nescient.*" This statement apparently comes from a work attributed in the Middle Ages to St Bernard, but the idea and its implication that true knowledge leads back to the self are in keeping with how Augustine sees the purposes that the liberal arts should serve: the program of the arts, as is explained in *De ordine*, constitutes a journey in intellectual pursuits that brings the inquirer back to self-understanding. That journey begins with thinking about language, with grammar in particular, first of the arts of discourse. Langland, too, has an interest in this aspect of the liberal arts program.

De ordine is one of the Cassiacum dialogues, written between Augustine's conversion and his baptism. In it, he and his interlocutors try to understand the place of evil in the world, brought into existence as it has been, in some sense, by a benevolent God. At one point in the dialogue, Augustine suggests that their conversation itself, their way of pursuing the question, is disordered, and he remarks that they need to reflect on the order of their discussion lest they make a mistake like that of a grammar master who would teach about syllables before introducing the letters that constitute them (II.vii.24). Augustine later returns to this apparently off-hand example, taking it as the starting point of a course of intellectual pursuits that can lead reliably to a philosophical understanding of divine things. The art of grammar discerns in language a reasonableness in its very structuration that is the consequence of the originary founding of language by human agency exercising its rationality (*De ordine*, II.xii.35, II.xi.31). Human reason, responding to the need of people to communicate the common intelligence that they all possess, was able to order the indefinite profusion of things and of sounds by its apprehension of number; language receives its efficacy from being arranged by number into meaningful patterns of classes and sequences (II.xii.35). (In the same way Proclus argues in his commentary on Euclid that mathematics contributes "completeness and orderliness" to all the arts of discourse; Proclus, *Commentary*, Prol.I.24, 21; discussed in Hadot, 117.) This initial act of designative imposition is not unlike the work attributed by Plato to the "semantic legislator"; names and their systems have not grown up as direct expressions of the things with which they go but are the result of a deliberate act of human reason (*De ordine*, II.ii.33).

In sketching out the work that reason accomplished in founding language, Augustine in effect composes a mini-treatise in grammar patterned after the school tradition of the art: an account is given of letters, then syllables, then the parts of speech, then meter (*De ordine*, II.12.35). A lesson according to such a rational principle of order would not make the mistake of getting off course as Augustine's interlocutors in the dialogue had done in their endeavours to understand God. Once reason has reflected on the numbered and ordered rationality of the language system that it has founded, it goes on to discern those principles that made it possible: definition, division, and synthesis (II.13.38, II.11.30). In this way it establishes the art of dialectic and comes to a fuller understanding of the soul's own reasonable nature, its own *logos*.

In his *Retractationes*, thinking back over this argument, Augustine remarks that perhaps he had not sufficiently qualified the Platonism implicit in his view of a separate intelligible reality discovered by the soul in its reflecting on its own powers of reason. But then, after all, he goes on, Plato was not wrong if we understand by "intelligible world" "that eternal and immutable principle of reason (*ratio*) according to which God made the world" (*Retractationes*, I.3.2).

Augustine further examines this connection between the soul's capacity to establish language and the creation of the world according to intelligible forms in his commentary on Genesis. The forms of things (*rationes*) exist first in God and then are brought into created existence through the agency of the Word, second Person of the Trinity, by a divine articulation (*De genesi ad litteram*, II.8.17). As in Neoplatonism, intermediary beings play a certain role here. The soul's power to discern and articulate the world intelligibly in language implies some originary contact with these forms as they exist in the transcendent Creator. Nor would that Creator cease addressing the creatures brought forth in this way, for to do so would be to abandon them to an existence not yet fully realized (I.5.10). Creation is sustained by the Word's continued presence to it, present to humankind most immediately. The soul's discovery of its affinity with reason through its education in the arts makes possible a realignment of the individual human person with the Creator and thereby a further completion of the purposes for which the world was given being. The journey inward into the self leads to a deeper understanding of the world's beginning and of the human creature's affinities with the intelligibility that brought Creation about and that continues to sustain it.

In *De magistro*, written a few years after *De ordine*, Augustine again reflects on the mystery that language is possible at all, considering this time not the founding of language according to intelligible order, but rather the immediate experience of being able to comprehend and convey significance with words. The mind's progress is again inward, and again there to be discovered within is the Creator of the world and of its meanings as well as the immediately apprehensible Word. Both are present in the recesses of the memory.

Much of *De magistro* investigates the similarities and differences among the four terms identified in chapter 5 of *De dialectica* as the factors involved in the signification of language: *verbum, dictio, dicibile,* and *res.* The exact meaning of these terms is not certain (see chap. 5, n. 7 and 9, 126–7), but the argument of *De magistro* seems to dwell on the difficulty of matching up the *dictio,* the word as signifier, with its *dicibile,* what is being picked out of reality by the *dictio.* Augustine argues that language cannot explain the meaning of a word (*dictio*) if we have not already had in the past and kept in our memory some experience of an encounter with the thing which that word signifies (*De magistro,* 10.33–5); nor can we know what in our immediate experience is being identified (*dicibile*) as what it is that the word picks out – Is it "walking," or the "pace," or the "distance" walked that is being signified by the *dictio,* "walking"? (3.6, 10.29). As with Plato in *Meno,* the only explanation for language's functioning successfully in our dealings with the world seems to be an originary articulation achieved at the Creation and present to the memory (11.36). As for *in*corporeal things, we can have knowledge of them only through the immediate presence of the Inward Teacher, the Word (11.38–12.40).

Thus we come to language with the distinctions according to which reality is differentiated already present in our minds, "inscribed" there not by being mapped on from an arbitrary language system, but by being shared with the Creator. The three factors of the triadic semiotic – thing, idea, word – are, as it were, already predisposed to line up with each other – another consequence of the "ontic *logos*" being immanent in things, in our minds, in language. Given all that the memory provides to make language possible, Augustine in his *Confessions* reflects with wonder on the richness of its resources: "The wide plains of my memory and its innumerable caverns and hollows are full beyond compute of countless things of all kinds. Material things are there by means of their images; knowledge is there of itself; emotions are there in the form of ideas or impressions of some kind. ... This is the power of memory" (X.17.26).

In searching the faculties of the mind for analogues to the Trinity, Augustine again discovers, within, the articulated content of language present from the beginning: "in that realm of eternal truth from which all things temporal were made, we behold with our mind's eye the pattern upon which our being is ordered, and which rules all to which we give effect with truth and reason" (*De Trinitate*, IX.7.12). This content is called the "locutions of the heart" (XV.10.18: *locutiones cordis*) and is likened to the Word, which brought forth Creation. This inner apprehension consists of coherent "imprints" or "marks" (*"vestigia memoriae"* [*De catechizandis rudibus*, 2.3.4]) ("impressed ideas" is Rist's term, 31), which are intersubjectively present in common among people but must be incarnated in the sounds of a particular language in order to be communicated. *De catechizandis* explains that these mental imprints are the direct manifestations of the realities that they make intelligible and, in that way, are like the expression of a person's face (2.3.5–6). But the translation of that mental imprint into language was not also a direct expression, as the Neoplatonists and Stoics would have it; at least this should not be the expectation. And yet the study of language in the arts of discourse does lead the inquirer to discover the resources within, the transcendent resources on which language depends, and so it brings the soul back to its Creator. The pursuit of the art of grammar itself takes on a surplus meaning when it explores the theological dimensions of the mystery of language.

Charles Taylor has remarked that "it was Augustine who introduced the inwardness of radical reflexivity and bequeathed it to the Western tradition of thought" (*Sources of the Self*, 131). Rist, too, has stressed how influential has been Augustine's emphasis on the power of introspection (86–7). That journey within and back was for Augustine less mythological than it had been for the Neoplatonists, more personal instead, an ascent of the creature in loving pursuit of the Creator. The liberal arts in this way became assimilable to Christian culture, relevant to the individual believer's own progress in sanctification – and central to Will's search for Piers Plowman. Scripture's rebuke to the Dreamer – to come to know himself better – could be an admonition to pursue the metalinguistic and theological implications of the arts of discourse before presuming to argue on the basis of Scripture. While Augustine's inward reflections on language are driven by love for God, Langland, as we see below, gives particular significance to love of neighbour as the impetus for the pursuit of all learning, including the study of language. "Word" and "work" belong together, the study of language and compassionate action for the sake of others.

CHAPTER SEVEN

The Twelfth Century
and Words-as-Words

THE ART OF GRAMMAR
FROM AUGUSTINE TO
THE TWELFTH CENTURY:
NAMES AND ETYMOLOGIES

Augustine's deliberations about language were one major source of ideas for the twelfth century about the relation between language and reality; another was the pedagogical tradition in the arts of discourse, especially in grammar, but also in rhetoric and dialectic. The pedagogical tradition in grammar survived through late antiquity and into the Middle Ages in the form of commentaries, whose material was from time to time shaped into authoritative compendia, such as Priscian's *Institutiones* and Isidore's *Origines*, which were subsequently mined for more commentaries. This tradition gave prominence to the parts of speech, especially the noun, and to etymological derivation, doctrines that ground the investigation of words-as-words.

The school tradition in grammar concentrated on the study of the pagan poets. However, already at the time of the barbarian kingdoms Cassiodorus and Isidore, following Augustine, had reconfigured the trivium in such a way, giving precedence to grammar, that the arts were readily incorporated into monastic education for meditative reading (Amsler, 133, 166, 171; Leclerq, *Love of Learning*; Irvine, *Making*, 195–225). Some scholars have postulated a "Christianized Donatus," written about 600, which added biblical citations to supplement or replace the illustrative examples that Donatus had taken from Virgil and other pagan poets (Irvine,

Making, 212, 226). The process of incorporating the classical art of grammar into Christian culture was taken further by Carolingian commentators on Donatus, such as Smaragdus of St Michel and Remigius of Auxurre, both Benedictine monks (Smaragdus, *Expositio*; Remigius, *In artem Donati*).

Two fourth-century practitioners of the arts of discourse, themselves perhaps colleagues (Holtz, 16–17), directly influenced two of the greatest Church Fathers: the rhetorician and Neoplatonist Marius Victorinus inspired Augustine by his conversion to Christianity (*Confessions*, VIII.2); the grammarian Donatus was the teacher of Jerome. Both contributed significant speculations about the nature of language to the pedagogical tradition.

In his Commentary on Cicero's *De inventione*, Marius Victorinus (155–6 in Halm) offers a reason for studying the arts that is Neoplatonic in inspiration and close to Augustine's in *De ordine*: pursuit of the arts enables the soul to regain something of the incorporeal and the immortal that it has from God. For Victorinus, grammar has a speculative side that asks profoundly significant questions about how language can lead to knowledge of reality. "*Nomen*," in its broadest sense, refers to the names that all things have, whether tangible objects, actions, or whatever. These names seem to signify that to which they are applied. To account for this, many say that some very wise and excellent person (Adam? Plato's semantic legislator? the Stoics' wise ruler?) has imposed names on everything (214). Elsewhere in his commentary Victorinus suggests that it is the forms which make it possible for everything to be named. Whether some person did this or that may be controverted, but things are what they distinctively are by virtue of their forms and accordingly have a name given to them that itself cannot be at issue (182). Words and the forms of things are thus somehow interdependent and together prevent the reality of things from leaking like a pot, a possibility that had troubled Plato. The twelfth-century masters delved into these metaphysical questions because Victorinus raised them in his commentary, which was a key arts text in the schools.

Donatus's *Ars grammatica* was the standard grammar text for the rest of classical antiquity and through the Middle Ages. So commonplace did it become in medieval school culture that "donet" came to mean an elementary treatment of any subject; Langland uses the word this way at B.v.205. Donatus's treatise is in the tradition of Stoic and Hellenistic formulations of the art of grammar as transmitted in the instructional context of the schools. The treatise is very succinct in its presentation of the elements of grammar, but philosophical positions carried over from earlier speculations about language are implicit in it.

In the tradition on which Donatus draws, the noun precedes the verb among the parts of speech in conformity with the metaphysical principle that the realm of essences or of concepts precedes the realm of flux and change (Holtz, 64). Donatus uses both formal and semantic criteria to define the noun and to differentiate its sub-classes – that is, formally by inflectional configuration (nouns have case endings) and semantically by what sort of real things nouns designate (for example, both common and proper; II.2, 354); this second criterion follows the Stoic tradition, which makes the classes of words and the classes of the things they signify isomorphic. Noun sub-categories include other semantic classes besides common and proper, such as corporeal and incorporeal, and also etymological classes, such as the primary and derived or the simple and compounded (354). These traces of earlier philosophical views will inspire later developments.

Carolingian commentators on Donatus offer reasons for the primacy of the noun among parts of speech that suggest how bound up with each other are language and our knowledge of the world. In the chapter on the noun in his *Expositio super Donatum,* Smaragdus states that it was nouns that were first imposed on all the things that came to be at Creation in heaven, earth, and water; the other parts of speech were formed in order that people could speak about the entities named by nouns (4, 8). Nouns are thus key to human beings' ability to situate themselves in nature. Remigius of Auxerre comments that without nouns to name things we could not obtain any understanding of the world ([13], 8) (he takes this statement from Isidore, *Etymologiarum,* I.7.1). Words match up with the identities that comprise reality and make possible their articulation.

Two great compilers, Priscian and Isidore, gave their own authoritative shape to grammatical doctrine in works that extended the domain of the art and its relevance to all learning; their influence continued into the twelfth century. Both drew on the rich tradition of commentaries that had grown up around Donatus's *Ars grammatica*, particularly that of Pompeius (Pompeius in Keil, 4; for Priscian: Amsler, 60, 72; for Isidore: Fontaine, 191–2). Donatus is the basis for Priscian's much more detailed exposition of grammar (Priscian, *Institutiones*, 2 and 3), but Priscian, unlike his predecessor, insists that the criteria for definitions of the parts of speech be exclusively semantic (55). It is Priscian who introduces the term "substance" into the definition of the noun: the noun signifies entities of substance (*substantia*) whether corporeal or not and identifies further the sort of thing these entities are (their *qualitas*), namely, whether common or proper (55, 56–7). An etymology for "*nomen*" supports this understanding, an etymology that Augustine had also offered: "*nomen*" is said to come from "*notamen*," identification mark (57); thus designation and knowledge are again closely connected. In considering sentences that offer definitions, Priscian seems to allude in his Book XVII to Neoplatonic ideas about the grounding of language: distinct entities are identifiable as what they are from their forms, which were present in the mind of God before they were brought forth into materiality (3.135 no. 44; Gersh, 777).

Isidore's encyclopaedic *Etymologiarum sive originum libri XX* ("*Origines*") begins with a theoretical treatment of the art of grammar, in the first book, that again owes much to Donatus (*Origines*; Fontaine, 188; Irvine, *Making*, 212); but, more important, grammatical procedures, etymology especially, pervade the entire work as universally reliable methods for apprehending the essential natures of things (Fontaine, 29, 37, 50, 202–3; Amsler, 145; Irvine, *Making*, 222–3). Isidore again relates *nomen* to *notamen* (identification tag), for the name, "by its application to things, renders things known to us" (I.7.1). Etymology reveals the knowledge of the thing to be found in its name, for "to understand a word's origins is to grasp readily its force of meaning; every investigation into something is advanced by pursuing the derivation of its name" (I.29.2) (see Fontaine, 42–4; Amsler, 137–41; Irvine, *Making*, 221–2). Zumthor has emphasized that this relationship between origin and derivative was regarded not as historical but as ideal; the connection reveals the intelligible identity of the concept denoted by the derivative (147, 155). Book X of *Origines* is the application of this principle in an alphabeticized general lexicon of words, a reference book that anticipates the great etymological encyclopaedic dictionaries of Hugutio of Pisa and Johannes Balbus in the twelfth century and later.

Isidore's *Origines* continued to be read in the later Middle Ages and remained "monumentally important" (Bloch, 52). Etymologizing became a habit of mind for medieval writers. Jonathan Culler has noted that an etymology is a sort of historicized pun (2): that is, the derived word and the elements from which it has developed are connected not only by a supposed historical descent but also by a relation of meaning that is taken to be informative about the thing designated by the etymologized word. Thus, "*rex*" (king) is said to derive from *regere recte*, i.e., to rule righteously. Something is learned from the study of the word "rex" as a word regarding kings and how they should act. Words, particularly nouns, are identification tags; off them one can read what things are as they subsist in reality. Words have both a designative and an expressive side. Referent and word are connected by the knowing mind of any user of language, but particularly by that of the grammarian, who is able to draw on expertise in the arts to pursue what can be learned from investigating the interrelationships between words and things.

TWELFTH-CENTURY ARTS AND THE ONTOLOGY OF LANGUAGE: HUGH OF ST VICTOR AND OTHERS

Jean Jolivet's article, to which Jill Mann has drawn the attention of readers of Langland, discusses several cases of "grammatical platonism" in the twelfth century and precedents for it in the writings of Isidore and several Carolingian authors. Jolivet regards it as having been developed independently of philosophy, out of the Neoplatonic elements embedded in doctrines of the art of grammar ("Quelques cas," 98). He characterizes "grammatical platonism" as "an ontology of language" (96), according to which "the universes of words and of things are homologous" (94); "words and things are forever bound together" by virtue of the forms that subsist in the divine mind according to which the world was created. Clearly this is one version of the "ontic logos" that Charles Taylor has described, whereby language and the world it both designates and expresses are adequate to each other and come together triadically in the human soul, which somehow is by its origins capable of contact with the mind of the Creator. This position suggests that there is much to be learned from an investigation of words-as-words and of the language system.

Jolivet singles out Thierry of Chartres among the twelfth-century masters as holding this view, and he attributes its development more to renewed interest in the arts tradition than to a reworking of Augustinian theology. But some of these ideas regarding the relations between words and reality had been explored by Augustine, as we saw above. In the twelfth century it was Hugh of St Victor who carried forward the Augustinian tradition of the role of the arts in the interior journey to God; for him, as for Augustine, that journey begins with grammar and ascends through reflection on the experience of language to realization of the human mind's affinities with the divine intelligence. As Hugh argues, the rational soul takes stock of its power to understand all the things of Nature and is drawn on in its pursuit of Wisdom by its sympathy with the intelligibility immanent in Creation. This could be possible only if the soul in itself somehow partook of the realm of forms. As Hugh quite strikingly puts it, "the rational soul could by no means comprehend all things unless it were also composed of all of them" (*Didascalicon* I.10, 18, and of Taylor, "Introduction," 57). This connection of intelligibility between the human creature and the Creator Hugh identifies in *Didascalicon* (I.8) with the image of God in the human person, marred by Adam's sin, partially restored by the pursuit of Wisdom. Murtaugh has argued that "the image of God constitutes a chief poetic recourse in medieval thought and ... Langland recognized it as such" (3).

Contemporaries called Hugh "another Augustine" – "*alter Augustinus*" (Taylor, "Introduction," 162 n. 22). His *Didascalicon*, like Augustine's *De doctrina christiana*, sets out doctrines of the discourse arts as preliminary to the exposition of Scripture; but, although both writers attributed great importance to self-reflective reading, particularly of Scripture, as the beginning of divine knowledge, the arts had a greater role to play for Hugh than they did for Augustine (Sweeney, 63, 65; Taylor, "Introduction," 32), as was appropriate in the context of the renewal of learning in the Paris schools. *Didascalicon* and the dialogue, *Epitome*, are the principal works in which Hugh sets out his program and rationale for the arts as preparatory to higher studies in philosophy and theology, although his great work on the sacraments offers some relevant passages as well.

The way to Wisdom begins for Hugh with the realization that the human creature is capable, through language, of apprehending the intelligibility that is manifest in the world. The Creator allowed Adam to name the animals so that he would recognize in himself his reason's capability of discerning the natures of the creatures (*De sacramentis*, I.6.13; the Latin text that Deferrari translated is apparently unavailable; see note by Deferrari, vii, and Chatillon, "Les Ecoles," 832 n. 104). It was reason's understanding of the distinctiveness of things, accountable to their forms, that made it possible for Adam to sort out the impressions that his imagination receives from his senses. The faculty of imagination (*imaginatio*) functions at the intersection of sense and spirit; it configures the data of sense experience, makes it susceptible to comprehension. (Chenu, "Imaginatio," 594; Baron, *Science*, 58; Taylor's note 37 to *Didascalicon*, I.5, note on 201, with references to Hugh's *De unione corporis et spiritus*). It is reason that is able to define and name what *imaginatio* presents to it (*Didascalicon*, I.3, Taylor, 49–50, Buttimer, 9, quoting from Boethius on Porphyry). The rational soul is able further to appropriate sensible experience to higher understanding, if it does not allow itself to become preoccupied with material things (*Didascalicon*, II.5, Taylor, 66, Buttimer, 29). Each faculty in turn thus processes at a higher level what the perceptions register, the understanding recognizing the intelligibility of what words designate. Thus self-reflection on the mind's ability to articulate reality in language is the starting point for the inquirer's search for Wisdom in learning and the beginning of the work both of the self's liberation from some of the limitations of sin and of the restoration of Creation (*Epitome*, 194, trans. in Taylor, "Introduction," 12; *De sacramentis*, "Prologue" to Bk. I.2, 3; and see note 166 to Taylor, "Introduction," 172–3).

In this way the study of language serves to renew the image of God in us: "This, then, is what the arts are concerned with, this is what they intend, namely, to restore within us the divine likeness, a likeness which to us is a form but to God is his nature" (*Didascalicon*, II.1, Buttimer, 23, Taylor, 61). Grammar initiates the progress through the subjects of instruction that runs from the arts of discourse (*trivium*) to the mathematical disciplines (*quadrivium*) to *philosophia* to *divinitas* (*Epitome*, 206, and Baron, 246–7 n. 50).

While the sequence of mental faculties *sensus–imaginatio–ratio* is engaged at the lower end of the progression through the subjects, *intellectus* (understanding) is reached at the higher end (Chenu, "Imaginatio," 595–6, quoting from Hugh's *De unione corporis et spiritus*). The trivium prepares the way for those readying themselves to advance in philosophy, not only by providing the initial basis for self-reflection, but also by providing them with the skill in language needed to discern the truth in discourse (*Epitome*, 198, and Baron, 236–7, n. 32). Hugh accordingly offers this etymology for *trivium*: it is as if the three arts were *tres viae* – i.e., that which furnishes the *routes* or approaches to philosophical pursuits (*Epitome*, 205; also *De grammatica*, 122). This is a role that Augustine also attributed to the arts, at least in the Cassiacum dialogues, which are early. And like Augustine in *De ordine*, Hugh insists on the coherence of all seven arts: they "so depend on one another in their ideas that if only one of the arts be lacking, all the rest cannot make a person into a philosopher" (*Didascalicon*, III.4, trans. Taylor, 89, Buttimer, 55; Baron, *Science*, 89).

Hugh's *Epitome* is followed in the best manuscripts (Baron, "Introduction," 175, 177) by Hugh's treatise on the first of the arts, *De grammatica*. Like *Epitome* also, *De grammatica* is a dialogue, and the interlocutors in the two works are the same. It is as if this methodical treatment of the fundamentals of grammar were offered as a paradigm of what an art is, just as Augustine in *De ordine* regards the grammar lesson as the defining case for Reason's ordering of knowledge. As Hugh remarks in *Didascalicon*, quoting Isidore's *Origines*, "knowledge can be called an art when it comprises the rules and precepts of an art, as it does in the study of how to write" (II.i, Taylor, 61, Buttimer, 23). Similarly, grammar is defined at the outset of *De grammatica* as a subject ordered according to the principles of the arts and serving as a model and starting point for the others (ed. Baron, 76).

Hugh regards grammar along with the other arts of the *trivium* as part of *logica*, perhaps following Boethius in this (*Didascalicon*, I.11, Taylor, 59, Buttimer, 21; *Epitome*, 192), but there is precedent for such a classification also in Augustine's *De dialectica*, which evidently was read in the twelfth-century schools (Jackson, "Introduction" to *De dialectica*, 18–19). Hugh sometimes contradicts this larger context for grammar, with its Stoic antecedents, by defining the art narrowly, limiting it to facility and correctness in language use (*Didascalicon*, II.29, Taylor, 80, Buttimer, 45–50; *Epitome*, 195, 205). This difference reflects the sources – on the one hand, Donatus's rather reductive treatment of the elements of the school tradition, and on the other, Isidore's *Origines*, Bk. I.

One of the interlocutors in the dialogue needs to hear how it is that grammar should include some of the Isidorean practices that lead to such richly productive interpretive strategies as glossing and etymology: it is because grammar is a distillation of and training in all that there is to know about language in relation to the forms and composition of words (*De grammatica*, 120, 122). Such a definition certainly opens the way for a broad understanding of what the art of grammar is good for. In telling something of the story of his own elementary education, Hugh sounds like a little Isidore: "I worked hard to know the names of all things that my eyes fell upon or that came into my use, frankly concluding that a person cannot come to know the natures of things if he is still ignorant of their names" (*Didascalicon*, VI.3, Taylor, 136, Buttimer, 114). The names of things reveal their natures, and reflection on how this could be so is the beginning of the mind's ascent through the faculties and through the course of the arts to a higher understanding. Hugh of St Victor's view of the arts of discourse stresses more than had Augustine, but in a similar way, what can be learned from the study of language regarding the divine intelligibility immanent in the world.

John of Salisbury and the masters who taught him at Paris and Chartres in the mid-twelfth-century focused rather more exclusively on the classical practices of the arts, although their understanding of the way language is grounded in reality is much the same: the writings of John and some of the Paris Masters contain notable instances of the "grammatical platonism" noted by Jolivet. John's teachers addressed themselves directly to the texts of Cicero, Boethius, and Priscian, among others, and so their view of the trivium is oriented less by Augustine and the other Fathers than Hugh's had been.

In *Metalogicon*, John of Salisbury presents himself as defending the arts of discourse against their detractors, who argued that they were useless and should be dispensed with; in the course of his defence he mentions his own teachers and some of their methods and doctrines. Among them was William of Conches (*Metalogicon*, I.24 and II.10: McGarry, 71, 97, and cccm, 54, 71), a student of

Bernard of Chartres, a grammar teacher who particularly excites John's admiration – "the foremost Platonist of our time," who propounds the Platonic doctrine of Ideas (II.17, IV.35: McGarry, 113, 259, and CCCM, 82, 173). John tells of one of Bernard's teachings about the interrelations of words that involves a co-substantial participation of language in reality reminiscent of Proclus's commentary on *Cratylus*: the word "whiteness" (*albedo*) passes into its derivatives, "to be white" (*albere*) and "white," as a modifier (*albus*), in a way that takes part in how the thing itself, whiteness, processes into derived modifications of being: from subsisting to implying a subject (*albere*) to inhering in a material object (*albus*). While the poets use grammatical doctrine as metaphor in their poetic narratives, Bernard employs a poetic metaphor to illustrate this grammatical doctrine of derivation or descent of substance into the concepts of verb and modifier: the thing in itself (*albedo*) is like a virgin, pure and integral; passed into a state that implies a subject (*albere*), the thing is like a virgin admitted to a bridal chamber, presented for conjunction with the groom, corporeal reality; passed into a state that involves inherence in a material object (*albus*), the thing is like the bride whose union with her husband has been consummated, once and for all joined to a body (III.2: McGarry, 151–2, and CCCM, 106–7). That the grammatical tradition gave precedence to the noun among the parts of speech is obvious here.

Jolivet has said that this teaching of Bernard's amounts to a "paronymy of being and language," i.e., words and reality derive together into their other manifestations (Jolivet, "Éléments," 137–9; see also Chenu, "Un cas," 667–8, *La théologie*, 95–6). Chenu also attributes to Bernard a theological opinion mentioned by Abelard: the words spoken at the consecration of the Host have an objective efficacy that implies that language, especially nouns, partakes of essential reality (Chenu, "Un cas," 666–7). The precedence given to substance in such thinking underlies the listing of the noun first among the parts of speech according to the ancient grammatical tradition: grammatical categories and relationships follow the order of reality in an identical succession.

John of Salisbury was familiar with the teachings of Bernard's brother, Thierry of Chartres, at first hand (*Metalogicon*, II.10: McGarry, 97–8, and CCCM, 72). Thierry was renowned as a teacher of the liberal arts and brought together in one great compendium a number of essential works for the exposition of both the trivium and the quadrivium; this compilation, the *Eptateuchon*, included for grammar some selections from Donatus, but Thierry's thoroughness and theoretical interests are apparent from his inclusion in it of all the books of Priscian's *Institutiones* (Clerval, 225). Thierry did comment on Cicero's *De inventione* himself (*Latin Rhetorical Commentaries*), but it is his expositions of a passage in Boethius's treatise *De Trinitate*, which draw on Priscian and on Marius Victorinus's commentary on Cicero, that present most clearly his teaching on the grounding of language in reality.

The theological writings of Boethius, on which Thierry commented, tend to be more Platonic in their philosophical assumptions than do his works on Aristotle's *Organon* (Tweedale in Dronke, ed., 197); they thus provide the opportunity for Thierry's most Platonic speculations about language. A notable instance occurs in Thierry's comments on a passage in *De trinitate* that identifies the subject matter of theology as the incorporeal (II, 8–13); Thierry observes that the things of the created world have their distinctive unity and definability by virtue of the reciprocity between their names and their forms. It is because things are nameable that they are conceivable as particular entities, and vice versa. It is this doctrine that makes possible Thierry's remarkable statement that "names bestow essential being on things" – *Nomina ... essentiant res* (*Commentaries on Boethius*: Commentum super *De Trinitate* Boethii, Abbreviatio Monacensis, item 52, p. 351; Lectiones in Boethii librum *de Trinitate*, item 52, p. 171–2; and Glosa super Boethii librum *de Trinitate*, item 42, pp. 287, 277–8).

This does seem to be exactly the assumption that Plato needs to make in order to answer, in the way that he would wish, the problem raised by the Sophists regarding what can account for the correctness of names. With references to Genesis and Priscian, Thierry explains that the forms subsist in the mind of God, who inspires the initial imposition of names on things by humankind (*Commentaries*: Commentum super *De Trinitate* Boethii, Abbreviatio Monacensis, item 53, 351–2; Lectiones in Boethii librum *de Trinitate*, item 53, 172; and Glosa super Boethii librum *de Trinitate*, items 41 and 42, 277–8; for discussion of these passages from Thierry, see Jolivet, "Quelques cas," 96, 99; Chenu, "Un cas," 667 n. 7; Dronke in Dronke, ed., 372–3). Both Augustine on Genesis and Priscian on definition had written of language's being founded on the forms constituted in the mind of God, and Victorinus in glossing Cicero had written about the interdependence of words and the forms of things. The antecedents for Thierry's explanation lie both in the Fathers and in the classical tradition of the arts of discourse, but more in the latter.

Teaching at Paris in mid-century with Thierry was Peter Helias, another of the great masters of the arts of discourse; John of Salisbury had the benefit of the teaching of them both (*Metalogicon*, II.10: McGarry, 97–8, and CCCM, 72; see also Häring, 319, and Southern, 129–32). Peter composed an exhaustive treatment of the more theoretical aspects of Priscian's *Institutiones*, drawing on earlier commentaries – the *Glosule*, probably by William of Champeaux, founder of St Victor, and the *Glose* by William of Conches, teacher to John of Salisbury and student of Bernard of Chartres (on Peter, *Summa*, see apparatus to Reilly's edition and his Introduction, 16). Peter's *Summa super Priscianum* had widespread distribution in the libraries of medieval Europe, including England; there was at least one copy at the end of the Middle Ages at Worcester Priory Cathedral, where Langland could have consulted it. Peter seems to be at pains to define a grammatical conceptualization of language that was different from a logical one (Hunt, "Studies on Priscian I," 220; de Rijk, *Logica*, II, part 1, 109; Reilly, "Introduction" to Peter, *Summa*, 2). The syncretistic strands in the tradition of the art of grammar continue to be the underlying factor in Peter's treatment of the subject, with the Stoic element predominating (Reilly, "Introduction," 17). That tradition had emphasized the treatment of the noun among the parts of speech. The definitions of "noun" offered by Donatus and Priscian included the terms "quality" and "substance" (Priscian introduced the idea of substance), which invited confusion with similar terms that appear in Aristotle's *Categories*, but which there have a particular ontological significance (Rosier and Stefanini, "Theories," 291, Rosier, "Les acceptions," 299). It was in this context that Peter Helias took up Priscian's definition of the noun as a word that signifies substance and quality.

Peter's formulations can be clarified by (perhaps owe something to) a passage from Thierry of Chartres, which leads us to one of the places where Thierry says that "names bestow essential being on things" (*Commentaries on Boethius: De Trinitate*, 287): "The noun attributes to that which it signifies a sort of form and a sort of underlying matter, because it indicates its meaning as underlying (*substans*) as well as informing (*subsistens*)" (cited and discussed by Rosier, "Les acceptions," 311; mentioned by Reilly, "Introduction," 17). Thierry thereby explains how nouns and the things they signify bear on each other.

Peter makes use of this distinction (*substans, subsistens*) to explain Priscian's definition of the noun. The noun has a material aspect to it as substance (*a substando*) and a formal aspect to it as substance (*a subsistendo*); but both aspects taken together constitute the noun's substance and allow it to have qualities in a certain sense (Rosier, "Les acceptions," 302; *Summa*, 861–3). Helias finds unsatisfactory Donatus's understanding of the quality of the noun as simply either proper or common (*Summa*, 211–12), but he also rejects the logician's understanding of quality as one of the categories (859–60). Rather, substance *a substando* is the aspect of the noun that it has by virtue of something's being able to be said about it as a subject. In this way, anything can be a substance, even a "quality" in the Aristotelian sense, such as white, as long as it has about it sufficient unity to have something predicated of it. This is a very broad sense of substance indeed (Reilly, "Introduction," 37; *Summa*, 189–90, 196, 200).

Then, in its aspect as substance *a subsistendo*, the noun takes on its distinctive meaning as a certain something by virtue of its quality. For example, human beings are qualified as such by their humanity, and Plato, by his Platonity (*homo*, a common noun; *Plato*, a proper noun); it is this quality that differentiates the designated thing from other things, homo from *arbor* (*Summa*, 862). Forms serve to make possible this taking on of identifying qualities (716). Others, Peter notes, have held something like this in saying that the noun in signifying substance indicates "that which is," while in signifying quality it indicates "that whereby it is what it is" (190; see also de Rijk, *Logica*, II.1, 230–4, 521–2). Helias would have found the mention of forms with respect to statements of definition in Priscian, *Institutiones*, Book XVII.

Forms of the verb also facilitate abstract theorizing on the relation between words and reality. The infinitive, according to Priscian (VIII.43, KGL 2, 408–9), like all verb forms, has some indication of tense, though not an exact one. Like the finite verb in that respect, it is like a noun in having a certain nominal force, so that the infinitive "*legere*" has much in common with the noun "*lectio*." The finite forms of the verb add specificity to the infinitive. Describing the uniqueness of the infinitive form in a similar way, in its being part verb, part noun, Peter notes that it shows either an active or a passive side, as other verbs do, but does not specify anyone to whom that acting or being acted on pertains (*Summa*, 496–7). The infinitive conveys the idea of what the action is, in somewhat the same way that a finite verb does, but more indefinitely.

In the *Summa* of Peter Helias it is clear that the art of grammar has its own way of pursuing ontological issues, in keeping with the experience of language. Words are analysed so as to suggest that language manifests aspects of being. The mind's power of apprehension achieves the intelligibility of both words and things in concepts, drawn together triadically. Accordingly, as Reilly remarks, "Human as existing, as intelligible, and as having five letters is all the same" – reference, sense, and words-as-words all come together ("Introduction" 36). It is as though all three points of the semiotic triangle coincided, reinforcing each other.

John of Salisbury, student of these illustrious masters at Paris, was eminent at the cathedral school at Canterbury (Paré, Brunet, and Tremblay, 25). His own *Metalogicon* is a defence and exposition of the arts of discourse, which he groups together under the term *logica*, as do also Hugh of St Victor and Augustine in *De dialectica*, from which John explicitly takes other ideas (I.10: in McGarry, 32, and CCCM, 28; III.5: in McGarry, 175, and CCCM, 121). John's own conceptualization of the arts owes something both to the School of St Victor, with its strong patristic orientation, and to the secular masters, with their focus on classical texts in the liberal arts tradition. Thus he finds in Augustine's *De ordine* the same rationale for the study of the arts of discourse (and of grammar in particular) that Hugh of St Victor had found there – namely, that the study of language is a starting point for reason's recognizing in its own operations indications of divine capabilities that reveal the soul's affinity with the Creator (*Metalogicon* IV.25: in McGarry, 241–2, and CCCM, 163). And in Book IV (chapters 9–19), John traces an ascending progression through the faculties, from sense experience through imagination to reason and wisdom, that recalls Hugh's series, *sensus–imaginatio–ratio–intellectus*.

In common with the Paris Masters, however, John, despite initially denying that languages do any more than designating things
according to the collective decisions of speakers, examines the
rational relations between words and the world. He speaks of how
the initial imposition of names on things was done according to
divine plan and in such a way that language is able adequately
to grasp the essential distinctiveness of each thing as it was made
to be. As well, for John, there is a basis in reality for the classes of
words: the divisions among the parts of speech express divisions
among things (I.14: in McGarry, 39–41, and CCCM, 33–4).

In another aspect of the interpenetration of language and
Nature, words used for things in the world can be applied mean-
ingfully to concepts in language – "properties of things overflow
into words." Thus one can speak appropriately of a "harsh verb"
(I.16: McGarry, 47, and CCCM, 39). This interpenetration, or "reciprocity between things and words" (I.16: McGarry, 50, and CCCM,
41), describes Bernard of Chartres's underlying assumption in his
metaphorical explanation of the derivations of *albedo*. John goes on
to remark that the poet too must respect the affinities between
language and nature (I.17: in McGarry, 51–2, and CCCM, 41–2).
The potential for expressivity in the nature of things, which makes
metaphors meaningful, and the expressivity in language that allows
us to gain knowledge by investigating words-as-words, are related
to each other. Both are resources of surplus meaning available to
the poet of the twelfth century as well as of the fourteenth.

The Paris Masters, in thinking deeply about the grounding of
language in reality and about the rationale for the study of the
liberal arts, grammar in particular, reformulated the trivium by
rereading the Fathers, especially Augustine, and by studying with
new intensity the texts of the classical arts of discourse, with their
roots in the ancient philosophical traditions. Because this reformulation took place where it did, in a context of urban prosperity and
of the church's attempts to keep up with the movements of evangelical fervour among the laity, this renewed practice of the arts
had far-reaching consequences for medieval social, religious, and
cultural life. It was indeed formative – for the church's programs
of public discourse, especially preaching; for the pursuit of studies,
not only at the universities but also at the friars' *studia generalia*
and at other collegiate institutions of learning; and for poetry's
exploring ideas about nature and language, as John of Salisbury

suggests. This twelfth-century reformulation of the arts has particular relevance to *Piers Plowman*.

NINETEENTH- AND
TWENTIETH-CENTURY
THEORISTS ON THE
ONTOLOGY OF LANGUAGE

Certainly there were some among the liberal artists of the twelfth century who deprecated the expressive side of language and denied the grounding of words in reality, as had some of the Sophists and some of the largely descriptive grammarians in the Hellenistic period. Later in the Middle Ages, the nominalists would formulate an alternative to "semiologizing ontology," which modern structuralists and poststructuralists would uphold (Charles Taylor, "Language," 224). But only from the perspective of the modern nominalisms is the narrative of the history of the philosophy of language a story of a progression, with occasional setbacks, towards modern positivist and reductionist theories. Saussure is the epitome of such modern nominalisms, which can be characterized as being dyadic, exclusively designative, and "linguistical" – i.e., flowing in the direction from language to reality, in so far as these theories of "ontologizing semiology" can be said to reach a reality at all.

And yet, as Gérard Genette has shown in *Mimologiques*, in the post-medieval period speculation has continued on the ways in which language recapitulates nature. More recently, there have been those, like Charles Taylor, who have sought to recover the expressive side of language and reconnect it with reality and thereby offset the enormous impact that Saussurean linguistics has had on the human sciences, including the study of literature. Other like-minded theorists, such as Adam Schaff and Herbert Marcuse, have, like Taylor, looked back to romantic philosophers of language, particularly to Herder and von Humboldt, for ideas different from Saussure's.

Saussure disposes of the expressive side of language to assert exclusively its designative side, as Roy Harris remarks, using terms used also by Taylor (122). In giving an account of designation, Saussure, unlike the romantics, allows no role for a referent or for the subject's interaction with the world. His is a dyadic semiotic, in which words are wholly unmotivated – they bear no particular relation to the nature of the things whose concepts they convey. Indeed, Saussure denies the referent to the point that he does not admit even that there are concepts of things for words to designate in the first place, apart from the words themselves (Holdcroft, 11–12). As Saussure says, "instead of pre-existing ideas, then, we find ... *values* emanating from the system [of language]" (trans. Baskin, 117, and C. Bally et al., eds., 162). This system he terms "langue." Once in place, it gives rise to concepts that do possess a separable, definable existence. Those who have thought that language is grounded in anything other than its own structuration have been profoundly deluded: "All our incorrect ways of naming things that pertain to language, stem from the involuntary supposition that the linguistic phenomenon must have substance" (trans. Baskin, 122, and C. Bally et al., eds., 169). The contrast with Priscian and Peter Helias, who use the term "substance" in their definition of the noun, is particularly striking.

Thus for Saussure, "a sign system is adequately defined ... in terms of 'form' rather than 'substance' (which in practical terms means abstracting from the specific channel of communication involved)" (Harris, 31) and so "the choice of actual signs from among the range of possible signs is entirely unconstrained" and arbitrary (68) – i.e., any acoustic or graphic material vehicle would do just as well as any other to signify its concept, although once the language system is constituted the matched elements must stay in place. Saussure says elsewhere, "Language is limited by nothing in the choice of means"; while clothing as a covering is determined in part at least by the natural contours of the body, language "covers" reality without any such constraints – in fact, before language, reality cannot be said to have a shape at all (trans. Baskin, 75–6, and C. Bally et al., eds., 110). It is given shape by its articulation in linguistic forms.

The opposite position, congenial to most in the twelfth century, is expressed in the twentieth century by Edmund Husserl, among others: "the name appears as *belonging* to the named and as *one* with it"; "the perceived object [say, an inkpot] is recognized for an inkpot, known as one, and ... the expression seems to be *applied* to the thing and to clothe it like a garment" (VI,6, 7: trans. Findlay, 690, 688). That both Husserl and Saussure use the same metaphor comparing language to a garment, the first to affirm it, the second to deny it, highlights their contrast in views. Husserl's semiotic is a triadic one, thus allowing for this expressionist mediation (Noth, 90). For Saussure, the natural languages certainly did not grow up with Creation but are equivalent to an artificial signal code that, when put into operation, amounts to a simple, physical energy transmission (Harris, 205–6, 215–16; Schaff, *Introduction*, 77–8).

Herder and von Humboldt, reacting to the Enlightenment precursors of Saussure, such as Locke and Condillac (Harris, 233), offer conceptualizations of language that accommodate both its designative and its expressive sides, as well as placing its development in history and involving it in the human subject's reflectivity, much as had Augustine. Herder reads the Genesis account of Adam's naming the animals in a manner not so different from the way in which Augustine did: "man invented language for himself – from the tones of living nature – as characteristic marks of his ruling reason" ("Essay," 131). The soul, by the capacity of its reason and feelings in response to experience, is able to discern a distinguishing mark for all the things of the world and is able to recognize that thing as what it is on subsequent encounters (Herder, 116–18). The distinguishing mark calls forth a characterizing word (120, 129), and then naming and recognizing the thing become the same (127). This mark resembles closely the idea of identification tag (*notamen*) that some ancient and medieval grammarians include as part of their definition of the noun. The mind, in being reflectively aware of what it is doing in its mediating role of recognizing and naming, enables language to be expressive of the mental resources of thinking and feeling as well as to be designative in its responses to objective reality (Charles Taylor, "Language," 228–9). This is clearly a triadic semiotic.

For Humboldt, "language ... is an involuntary emanation of the spirit, no work of nations, but a gift fallen to them by their inner destiny" (*On Language*, 24). Again, as for Herder, language-making reveals the mediating power of the mind to penetrate "into the nature of a concept, so as to wrest from it at once the most characteristic feature" (26). From the distinguishing mark of the concept, "the sense of articulation discovers the designating sounds" (84). This representing of outer "objects, that speak to all senses at once, and the inner motions of the mind, entirely by [sound] impression on the ear, is an operation largely inexplicable in detail" (72), but the resulting formations of language "emerge from the interaction of outer impression and inner feeling, related to the general linguistic aim of combining subjectivity with objectivity in the creation of an ideal, yet neither wholly internal nor wholly external, world" (105). Herder and Humboldt thus accommodate both the expressive and the designative sides of language in a triadic semiotic. The flow from language to reality and the flow that returns back from the world to the experiencing subject, matching and validating its articulations according to "ontic logos," are both accounted for in a mediated, two-way dialectic. For both men, language is not only constitutive of the reality it is about but also is adequate to its function of meaningful representation (Charles Taylor, "Theories," 273). Names and things rely on each other: names on things for their significance, things on names for their very distinctiveness of being.

Other present-day thinkers besides Charles Taylor have looked back to the romantic philosophers for a theory of language that imparts to words a sure enough connection to reality to give discourse the force of truth so that it can serve to describe and critique the world of experience. A dyadic semiotic that posits an "ontologizing semiology" such that the structures of language "map out" only a self-contained, suspended representation of the world undercuts moral statements. In contrast, a theory of language that binds together thing and word in the concept, so that the actual state of the world can be found to be a counterpart to language, provides the basis for valid descriptions of conditions and value judgments on them. The integrity of the language system in relation to reality suggests to both medieval and romantic thinkers a sort of rightness that has some claim to acknowledgment and moral obligation – a kind of "ecology" of language. As Jill Mann remarks about Goliardic satire, the judgment is made, as it were, "by the language itself."

Herbert Marcuse, in analysing the features of one-dimensional discourse, contrasts its "functionalized, abridged, and unified language" with language as it is conceived by a "classical philosophy of grammar which ... relates linguistic to ontological categories." He then offers an argument, which he goes on to attribute to Humboldt, for the conceptual substantiality of the subject-noun, using terms like those of Peter Helias: "According to this philosophy, the grammatical subject of a sentence is first a 'substance' and remains such in the various states, functions, and qualities which the sentence predicates of the subject. ... If it is not a proper noun, the subject is more than a noun: it names the *concept* of a thing, a universal which the sentence defines as in a particular state or function. The grammatical subject thus carries a meaning in *excess* of that expressed in the sentence" (95–6). There is here something very close to Peter Helias's understanding of Priscian's definition of the noun as composed of substance *a substando*, as subject, and substance *a subsistendo*, as susceptible of conceptual differentiation by virtue of the universal forms.

Adam Schaff also quotes Humboldt on the point of the "dialectic of the objective and subjective factors in the *process* of cognition ... ; a copy [or reflection] of objective reality and a subjective creation of its image in the *process* of cognition do not exclude one another, but complement one another to form a single whole" (*Language*, 18, 139). It is only language conceived as both representation and intervening instrument that can serve as an effective intermediary in the language community's practical activity of dealing with the real world (133).

While there are these contemporary theorists who, like the romantics, hold a view of language compatible with the dominant, generally realist, model of antiquity and the Middle Ages, many recent theorists subscribe instead to a rigorous nominalism. Saussure's concept of the sign provides an appropriate vantage point from which to survey briefly some of these and to relate them to some of the theoretical ideas about the ontology of language raised in previous sections. Saussure is foundational for structuralists, such as the early Barthes, and a point of departure for the poststructuralists, such as Derrida and Baudrillard.

Others have commented on Saussure's pivotal role in the emergence of postmodernism and its immediate predecessors. Harland, for instance, remarks that the "superstructuralist" notion of language is founded on Saussure's concept of "langue," the abstract system of formal linguistic values that lies behind discourse and makes it possible (11). And Christopher Norris has noted how consequential has been Saussure's dyadicism, which excluded "any consideration of language in its referential aspect" (184). Saussure's postmodern successors have continued to lop off corners of

the semiotic triangle: "even when the most recent Superstructural-
ists, the Post-structuralists, propose to dispense with signifieds too
[stable concepts], they are still moving in the same direction: not
back towards the world of referents, but towards a world composed
of nothing but signifiers" (Harland, 19; see also 134). Thus Saussure set the direction in which so many others have since headed
off, following a map that precedes the territory (Baudrillard, 2).
This is what I have called an "ontologizing semiology."

The early Barthes (before 1965) turned Saussure's analysis of the
constituents of the sign to good account by adding a second tier
to his schema: Saussure's sign becomes in a second order of signification a signifier that, taken with its signified, constitutes what
Barthes calls the mythic sign (*Mythologies*, 115, with diagram). This
second generation of signification can occur in either a linguistic
or a pictorial medium. At this second level, in both media, motivation returns again to help make meaning (126).

Barthes's example of a second-order signification in the medium
of written language is a sample sentence, of the sort given in a
grammar textbook, illustrating the agreement of subject and predicate: *quia ego nominor leo* (115–16). The matching of word classes
(singular subject, singular verb; nominative subject, predicate nominative) serves to make the grammatical point that the sentence is
adduced to exemplify in a second, "metalinguistic" order. This doubling of meaning by taking the first-order item as the object of arts-
doctrine scrutiny is exactly the "words-as-words" ambiguity of the
Stoic grammarians and Augustine – "ambiguous equivocals in art."

But Barthes's real interest lies in mythic pictorial signs. Here the
sign is partially motivated at both levels. There is an identifiable
resemblance between the signified (the "analogue") and its representation by an image (or an "icon," in Peirce's term) that bears
it some likeness, such as a photograph. At the second level, too,
there is some recognizable identity of the pictorial sign, now signifier, with what allows it to play into the second order's mythological meaning, as supplied by an obliging interpreter. Barthes uses
this two-tiered schema, derived from Saussure, in his "readings" of
various "cultural texts" – mass-media images and cultural practices,
such as a bunch of roses, a black man in uniform saluting the
French flag, press photos, an ad for Panzani pasta products (*Mythologies*; "The Photographic Message"; "Rhetoric of the Image"). In

all of these, Barthes discovers a richly "polysemous" ("Rhetoric," 38–9) excess of meaning, both denotative and connotative. But when the sign is partially motivated and evokes "a kind of natural being-there of objects," as photographs particularly do ("Rhetoric," 45), aren't we allowing the referent to creep back into the picture as a factor in analysis?

Be that as it may, Barthes places great stress on Saussure's dyadic doctrine of the arbitrariness of the sign. The pictorial image, despite its resemblance to what it depicts, is not a "natural" representation, wholly determined by its referent. It is partially motivated, but it is also partially arbitrary – i.e., the image is coded, stylized in a particular way that enables the representation the more easily to lend itself to mythical or ideological meaning ("Photographic," 18). The mythic image is not as "innocent" as its naturalistic appearance suggests ("Rhetoric," 42, 45).

Barthes thus uses Saussure's rather abbreviated model of language to good advantage in his reading of cultural texts. In adapting Saussure's notion of the sign for these other purposes, he restores something of the full phenomena of language in adding the second tier and giving attention to iconic representation. These extensions reintroduce motivation and something of the expressive side of language.

The first part of Derrida's *Of Grammatology* vigorously attacks Saussure, who at the same time contributes significantly to the orientation of Derrida's thinking, particularly to his key idea of "arche-writing." This repudiation of Saussure marks the turn from structuralism to poststructuralism.

Derrida's ostensible target in part one is "phonocentrism" – giving speech precedence over writing in the investigation of language. But he quickly equates this misconception with a perhaps more insidious error: "logocentrism," the belief that language is adequate to convey reality reliably, that there is, as the ancients would say, a "correctness of names." Just how Derrida makes the equivalence of phonocentrism and logocentrism is not very clear; it is simply the point, as some have remarked (notably Aristotle), that the sounds of language bear a particular proximity to intelligible meaning (11). Logocentrism seems to be what Charles Taylor has explained as "ontic logos" – that compatibility of reality, thinking, and language that makes intelligible discourse possible. Derrida predicts the "historical closure" of the logocentric mentality after 2,500 years of domination.

Derrida does ask about the causes of this logocentrism and the "transcendentality" that it implies (23). He does not pause to pursue the matter, but his answer seems to be that this hypostatized view of language has resulted from the heritage of Western metaphysical and religious thought – what he terms "onto-theologism." He accordingly condemns logocentrism as "ethnocentric" and seeks to purge his rigorous analysis of any lingering "sediment" of this inheritance. All nostalgia for the old certainties, all "securities" to which we might be tempted to cling by persisting in outmoded views of language, we must "forbid ourselves" (9) in the name of neutral, unbiased investigation.

If Derrida were to have answered the question that he raises, he might have considered the problems to which logocentrism seemed a reasonable solution. He might, for example, have considered Augustine's reflections on his experience of language in *De magistro*, particularly his ponderings on how it can be that our minds do pick out from all the aspects of walking something distinct and intelligible that we would call "walking" itself. But Derrida does not admit experience into his analysis; he discounts it as ethnocentric, unavoidably tainted by Western onto-theologism (60). We are left wholly dependent on the pure, brilliant, but somewhat slippery reasoning of which perhaps only Derrida himself is fully capable.

Derrida condemns Saussure for logocentrism simply because he distinguishes the signifier and the signified; Derrida denies that the signified is in any way a separable entity (11, 43, 73). He does not clearly articulate Saussure's dyadicism and perhaps for this reason seems to attribute to him, pressing very hard on the word "natural," the view that there is a natural link between the referent, the third term in the semiotic triangle, and the signifier (35 – but he denies this a few pages on, at 44 and 46). This accusation is not consistent with Saussure's insistence on the arbitrariness of the sign, with the artificiality of his system. What Derrida's attack on him seems ultimately to consist of is a denial of the claim that language is able to convey the intelligible distinctness of ideas at all. To maintain otherwise is to assert a metaphysics of presence, which Derrida rejects (12).

And yet his own theory of "arche-writing" owes much to Saussure's notion of *langue*, the system of linguistic values that stands behind language's capability of articulation. Derrida's arche-writing is similarly a network of differences, but further abstracted or etherealized, for here the network is deprived of any placeholders at its intersections; instead, there is only pure relationship. Within this pluri-dimensional pattern (87), signified meanings have no determined position but slip around without being caught at any permanently fixed point where a discernible significance could be revealed. And so "the self-identity of the signified conceals itself unceasingly and is always on the move" (49). Discourse loses the rationality of logos (10).

In arche-writing, Derrida has come up with a linguistic principle that is completely insubstantial, devoid of presence, nothing but multiple tissues of relationships of difference – untainted certainly by ethnocentric logocentrism (65). He achieves this by unsparing exclusion of our experiences of language and by ever-more-rarefied abstraction – a process that Saussure had already begun. Derrida takes this process to an extreme.

Baudrillard does not often explicitly acknowledge his sources, but in *Simulations*, for instance, he brings together something of the early Barthes with something of Derrida, within the overall paradigm, as Norris remarks (188), of Saussure. Like Barthes, Baudrillard addresses "cultural texts," particularly those circulated in the form of images: TV programming, Watergate, Disneyland. At the same time, the theory of language that underlies his readings of events and representations seems to be the extremely reductive one of Derrida; accordingly, very much in the idiom of Derrida's poststructuralism, he reproaches us for harbouring a "nostalgic for a natural referent of the sign" (86).

In particular, Baudrillard seems to assume something similar to "arche-writing." Like Derrida, he deprives Saussure's system of *langue* of its placeholders: he pronounces "the radical negation of the sign as value" (11). Once onto-theologism has collapsed under critical attack and can no longer seem to ground stable meaning, "then the whole system becomes weightless, it is no longer anything but a gigantic simulacrum – not unreal, but a simulacrum, never again exchanging for what is real, but exchanging in itself, in an uninterrupted circuit without reference or circumference" (10–11). This sounds like the self-contained, insubstantial patterns of difference through which meanings endlessly circulate as Derrida proposed. A discourse sustained only by a "gigantic simulacrum" can no longer be logical or make sense of the world. We are left with a "vertigo of interpretation" (31) as Baudrillard says, a "centrifugalism" in Harland's terms (136), in which meaning recedes, spinning out from a non-existent centre.

Both Barthes and Derrida had regarded whatever sort of texts they took up for consideration as autonomous structures. Baudrillard, however, brings into his analysis the larger context of the social processes of producing and consuming the mass media, appropriating some key concepts from Marx and other social theorists. He takes reproduction as the limitless duplication of signifiers made possible by industrial capitalism. So many copies are produced, in the print or broadcast media, that the sheer quantity of identical representations overwhelms their meaning – one confronts "a vertigo of duplication" (136 – see also 99–100). The capitalist market reduces all values to exchange values, which circulate as equivalencies through commercial networks, much as signs that lack any significance circulate in the networks of difference. Although Baudrillard has less to say about consumption, his analysis seems to imply an apathetic mass-media audience that takes in an endless flow of messages without comprehending their meaning. Drenched by a shower of signifiers, engulfed by a flood of ever-fluctuating surface images, the consumer of mass media surrenders to the onslaught of simulation and is not able even to expect the media's version of the world to make sense. This seems to be one reason, in Baudrillard's thinking, for the breakdown of the sign.

Baudrillard returns to McLuhan's dictum, "the medium is the message," and understands by it that there is only the medium; the message is eclipsed (54, 99). What carried meaning has displaced meaning; the signifier and the signified collapse into each other. There results a hybrid in which reality and image meld into an indistinguishable and meaningless unity. The outcome of Derrida's analysis is the invalidation of discourse, where the system of representation deconstructed is that of natural language, which is arbitrary. But when Baudrillard brings a similar deconstructive analysis to bear on iconic representations, depriving even photographs of any connection to reality, this ungrounding of our experience of the world is even more dismaying. No longer is it a matter of at least partial motivation, as for Barthes. The media image, lacking any connection to things by reference to them, has penetrated reality itself and made it insubstantial.

Clearly the postmodernist theorists would not be inclined to dream Plato's dream at the end of the *Cratylus* that things "do not leak like a pot." Plato's not-so-very-successful reasoning was an attempt to prevent that dribbling away of the intelligibility of things by proposing some basis for "the correctness of names." On the contrary, postmodernists such as Derrida and Baudrillard, spurning such nostalgic reveries, would insist on the pot's inevitable inability to contain any meaningful presence. They seem to have arrived at this position by carrying to an extreme Saussure's exclusions of certain experiences of language from consideration in the name of a rigorous formalistic analysis and by further reducing Saussure's dyadicism to some sort of a dynamic monadic system that cannot represent or hold stable meaning. On this account, the pot is forever emptying. But perhaps a coherent theory of ambiguity could allow for some slippage or play of meaning and yet be compatible with an ontology of language that could stem the dribble.

Taylor, and other philosophers like Marcuse and Schaff who share such an ontology, shed contemporary light on twelfth-century ideas about what resources language can offer for understanding the world and on the poetic practices, Langland's in particular, that follow from those ideas. Postmodernist theories are also illuminating, by way of contrast to these earlier views. Implied in Langland's poetic is a theory of language that would enable words to help people deal with the world and strive to understand God's revelation in all its manifestations – in Creation and in Scripture. Langland frequently collocates "word" and "work" and investigates words-as-words to explore the practicalities of the world that the self works on in its quest for greater understanding and greater love of neighbour.

LINKING THE TWELFTH-CENTURY ARTS OF DISCOURSE AND LANGLAND

Any sketch of the traditions of discourse doctrines that could inform a reading of *Piers Plowman* can offer only likely or representative lines of transmission. We can only speculate on how Langland might have learned of twelfth-century ideas about the role of the liberal arts and about "grammatical platonism." Certainly there were many scholars who went to England or returned there, after study in the Paris schools, to high positions at centres of learning. Langland shared interests with the Paris Masters, which suggests contact with this legacy of twelfth-century arts doctrines.

The vigour of collegiate intellectual life at the English cathedrals about 1200 was the result largely of the traffic across the Channel to the schools of northern France. English and Norman scholars went to England to run both secular and monastic institutions. William de Montibus and Thomas of Chobham (as we saw above) were among those who came back to put their learning to use in the practical matters of preaching and pastoral ministry, William at Lincoln, Thomas at Salisbury. The great monasteries also received some of England's sons on their return after an education in France: the famous Abbot Samson of Bury is an example. His biographer, Jocelin of Brakelond, records that Samson had been to the schools at Paris and that he was learned in the liberal arts and the Scriptures (*Chronicle*, 33, 44).

John of Salisbury was the most eminent Englishman of the time to be educated at the Paris schools; he was prominent in government and church and in the archepiscopal circle of Thomas à Becket at Canterbury. Although his *Policraticus* was much read in the later Middle Ages, his *Metalogicon*, an extended treatment of the verbal arts, was probably not (Linder, 884). John's version of twelfth-century humanism seems to have had no sequel in England (Hunt, "English Learning," 26).

Englishmen schooled in France returned to church institutions in Worcester and environs, where Langland would have been able to benefit later from their learning. Paris-educated and reform-minded Norman nobleman Roger, bishop of Worcester, served from 1164 to 1179; he probably had studied for a time at St Victor (Cheney, 10, 64). The new bishop called a learned monk from the priory to assist in diocesan responsibilities; this man, Senatus, also may have had theological training on the Continent (Cheney, 64). Thomas of Marlborough, monk, later abbot, at the neighbouring Benedictine house of Evesham in the early thirteenth century, had been to the Paris schools and returned with books that became part of the monastery's library (Hunt, "English Learning," 27–8). There was certainly contact among the neighbouring Benedictine houses at Worcester, Evesham, and Pershore during this time and later.

In the course of the twelfth century, many Englishmen came to be associated with the community of canons at St Victor (Châtillon, "La culture de l'École," 150). The legacy of Hugh lies not only in his writings, which continued to be read, but also in the influence of his achievement on the preaching at St Victor (Baron, "L'influence," 59). Some sermons by Richard of St Victor on the New Testament had exceptionally wide distribution as part of *Allegoriae in Vetus et Novum Testamentum*, a section of Richard's *Liber exceptionum* (Châtillon's "Introduction" to his edition of Richard, *Liber,* 71, 86). Copies of *Allegoriae* were numerous in England and appeared especially in monastic libraries; we know that there was a copy at Pershore, near Worcester (Châtillon, "Introduction," 37, no. 93).

The priory cathedral library at Worcester held manuscripts during the Middle Ages that contained numerous treatises on the art of grammar. Two manuscripts in particular attest to the wealth of resources on grammar to be found there. Worcester Cathedral Ms. F.61 is, according to R.W. Hunt, "a splendid folio which contains first a collection of works on the study of words and meanings in the Bible, and then a collection of grammatical tracts. The format and scale of the volume is very unusual for such works, and the History of grammar, probability is that it was put together at the instance of someone in authority in the monastic community at Worcester" (Hunt, "Oxford Grammar Masters," in his *History of Grammar,* 168). Another manuscript, F.123, is of similar make-up, containing selections from the grammarians on the parts of speech, extracts from Peter the Chanter's *De tropis* (Hunt, *History,* 39), lexical articles on certain words, and so on (see Hunt, *History,* Appendix, 194–5). The first item in the manuscript is an anonymous commentary on the first chapter of Petrus de Isolela's grammatical *Summa*, which incorporates Victorine ideas about the purposes of the arts of discourse and the role of grammar among the arts. Like Hugh of St Victor, the commentator mentions the mechanical arts and offers as an etymology for the word "trivium" that it is derived from "tres viae" (f. 11v). Two copies of Peter Helias's *Summa* were at Worcester, with at least one (Ms. F.137) there when Langland could have come across it. The ideas of Peter Helias gained circulation also by being incorporated into various later compilations that were widely available.

The pursuit of knowledge by etymological investigation – a notable part of grammar since antiquity, used in theorizing the art's own subject matter – was a productive interpretive strategy in the *enarratio* of the Paris Masters. At the end of the twelfth century Hugutio of Pisa made a systematic compendium of such etymologies, drawing also on Peter Helias's *Summa* in his compiling (Hunt, "Hugutio and P.H.," in *History*, 146, ˈ149). Later in the thirteenth century, the Dominican friar Johannes Balbus augmented and recast this compendium as the *Catholicon*, greatest of the medieval encyclopaedic dictionaries. It was, as Wallis says, "an ubiquitous reference work," readily available for consultation by any who could use it (Wallis, iii). Its voluminous glossary and the grammatical treatise that accompanied it were much used by English grammarians (Thomson, *Descriptive Catalogue*, 35). The prefatory exposition of grammar is oriented to the descriptive and etymological focus of the entries in the lexicon section, but it remains theoretical in a way that does not entail the assimilation of grammar by logic.

Whether through intermediary sources or directly, Balbus's *Catholicon* borrows the formulations for his definitions, both in the grammatical Preface and in the lexical entries of the dictionary, not only from Priscian, as we would expect, but also from Peter Helias. Balbus expounds the parts of speech in the Preface, not in a section of their own, but in a section under the heading "*Ethimologia.*" Odd as this may seem, it recalls Isidore's dictum that the pursuit of knowledge in every learned subject is advanced by investigation of the derivations of its key terms, and Balbus organizes his material accordingly. For the noun and the infinitive, Balbus simply repeats passages from Priscian. For the entry under "*ethimologia*" in the lexicon section, however, he excerpts the definition given by Peter Helias (through Hugutio as intermediary – Hunt, "The 'Lost' Preface," in *History*, 155 n. 2): etymology gives an account of a word by means of other well-known words according to some common property of the meaning and a likeness in the words themselves (*Summa*, 70). This fairly precise definition clearly states the assumption that the development of the word's composition as a word matches the development of its meaning from origin to outcome. This assumption then warrants speculations in reverse; that is, analysis of the make-up of the word as word facilitates a search for better-known words which are rather like the constituents that result from the analysis and can be presumed to be antecedent. It is expected that the meaning of the words discovered in this way will help explicate the meaning of the analysed word. Thus the grammarian's analysis of the word's make-up yields knowledge about the thing designated by the word. By analysing "*rex*" into its elements *regere* and *recte*, the grammarian learns about how kings should act. The great reference works, such as *Catholicon*, gave such grammatical theory and etymologizing procedures considerable currency in the practices of later medieval literary culture.

Several routes – links between English collegiate institutions and the Paris schools; collections of Victorine sermons; standard texts and reference works (such as those of Peter Helias and Johannes Balbus); and commentaries in the arts of discourse (such as those in various Worcester manuscripts) – may have permitted Langland to learn, in Worcester or London, about twelfth-century grammar and theories of language. We saw above that Langland, like some of the twelfth-century Latin poets, sometimes introduces elaborate metaphors taken from the technicalities of the art of grammar: notably, the Mede and Mercede passage in the C text (iii.332–405), which compares the two kinds of reward to various syntactic relations (see Amassian and Sadowsky); and in the B text, Passus xiii, Clergy's similitude comparing Dowel and Dobet to two infinities (ll. 126–30) (see Middleton), followed closely by Patience's riddle (ll. 148–73a) about the box of transitivity (see Bland). Also, Langland uses certain terms that would have been commonplace in the grammar-school classroom: examples include, in the C text, "*hic et haec*" (e.g., iii.404), and in the B text, Passus xv, 608–11, "*spelle*," "*rendren*," and "*recorden*."

In fact, as we see below, Passus xv can be regarded as a grammar lesson, with Will as the attentive pupil. The passus begins with Anima reciting the various names by which he is identified, a list taken ultimately from Isidore, as we saw above. And later in the passus, Anima states emphatically that "grammar is the ground of all," the basis of all other subjects, the starting point in the progress to higher knowledge – a familiar doctrine in the liberal arts tradition. Anima is complaining that the weather is getting harder to predict and that there has been a decline in the teaching of grammar: "Grammar, the ground of al, bigileth now children: / For is noon of thise newe clerkes – whoso nymeth hede – / That kan versifie faire ne formaliche enditen, / Ne naught oon among an hundred that an auctor kan construwe, / Ne rede a lettre in any language but in Latyn or in Englissh" (xv.371–5). The list of what constitutes instruction in grammar ("versifye ... enditen ... construwe ... rede" (i.e., read in some language other than Latin or English – undoubtedly, French) follows exactly the requirements set out in the Oxford statutes of the time: masters should be prepared to offer instruction in how to versify and compose, perhaps particularly a letter in prose ("*de modo versificandi et dictandi*"), as well as instruction in the set texts of the authors and in identifying words in those texts according to parts of speech ("*de auctoribus et partibus*") (Strickland Gibson, ed., *Statua*, 20, ll. 18–22). Masters should also insist on facility in French as well (171, ll. 4–10).

There are thus numerous indications that Langland may actually have been associated in some way with grammar teaching. At any rate, his inclination to develop his poem by exploring the resources of language, to investigate words-as-words, seems often to imply just the ideas about the nature of language that were set forth in the art of grammar, particularly as it was formulated in the twelfth century.

CHAPTER EIGHT

Piers Plowman
and the Ambiguity of Words-as-Words

Langland does have characters in his poem commend the discourse arts and put into practice their doctrines in the exploration of the resources of language, even if he hedges this affirmation of the usefulness of the arts with warnings of their limitations and of how they can go wrong in ways that betray their ultimate purposes. Grammar is the art that has the potential to draw out the surplus meaning that words may have as words and to initiate the inward journey that leads to the realization of the human creature's association with the Creator's articulation of the world. Like John of Salisbury, Langland seems to have thought that the poet would do well to pay attention to the affinities between language and nature. It is Anima in B.xv especially who puts grammatical doctrines to use in a poetical way as he/she teaches the Dreamer about names and the importance of language for the clergy's discharging of its responsibilities to teach, preach, and convert. Carefully, artfully, considered, *words* reveal that certain *work* follows on their meaning as they do – just as the word "*feith*" contains in its make-up the essential element, "feet," i.e., contains right action that follows on a commitment to belief. The word, its sense, and the thing for which it stands coalesce with each other and together warrant a response of judgment and action from the one who studies their interrelation.

It is then not surprising that a network of words, formed especially by different kinds of repetition, is what carries the poem along, more than the story of Will's quest. Langland's readers have found the progression of his narrative line to be indirect and fractured. I suggest that the poem's overall progression (B text) might best be regarded thematically as a zigzag within a frame: once we set aside the Prologue and Passus i as constituting an introduction to the whole poem, the sections at either end (vision 1, B Passus ii–iv and visions 6, 7, and 8, B Passus xviii–xx), generally historical in orientation, frame Langland's thematic interests, which alternate back and forth between two topics. The poem deals first with matters of sin and restitution; then with the interrelation between love and knowledge, then sin again, then back to love and knowledge, to return at the end to the last visions, which, like the first, are historical.

Thus, after the poem situates itself initially (vision 1) in the historical and worldly circumstances of the Mede Episode, it moves towards penitential themes (the Seven Sins and Piers' Pardon, vision 2), then turns with the third vision to explore issues of the value of knowledge in the encounter with Clergy and others, the Dream-within-a-Dream (including Trajan's speech praising love), and Ymaginatif's exposition of that dream. Returning to the topic of sin and restitution in the fourth vision, the poem recounts the pilgrimage of Patience and Conscience and their conversation with Hawkyn, in which the seven sins are again expounded; but then in the fifth vision the poem addresses questions of knowledge and love in the talk with Anima, the dream of the Tree of Charity tended by Piers, and the episodes involving Abraham, Moses, and the Samaritan. In the final three visions, the poem again places its action in history, this time amid the events of salvation history and the fate of the church as an institution.

These successive zigzags are not strictly exclusive of each other – certainly there are lines of continuity – but these dominant moments identify a pattern more in keeping with my experience of how the poem moves than does a straight, linear scheme defined by the search for Truth, followed by the search for Dowell, Dobetter, and Dobest.

LOVE AND "CLERGIE": THE USES OF WRITTEN LANGUAGE

It is in those sections of the poem that deal with the interrelation between knowledge and love – i.e., visions 3 and 5 in B text (Passus viii–xii, xv–xvii) – that Langland most extensively uses the art of grammar to explore the resources of language. Two metaphors of writing that appear in the first of these sections, the third vision, suggest, by what they imply about how language is grounded in reality, ways in which knowledge might be brought into the active love of "Doing well." One metaphor is Ymaginatif's interpretation in Passus xii of Christ's writing in the dust when he confronts those who accuse the woman taken in adultery; the other is Wit's similitude in Passus ix of how writing on parchment is like the Creator's inscribing of the divine image in the human person as part of bringing the world into existence. Both metaphors depend on a view of language in which words play an essential role both in the articulation of Creation according to "ontic *logos*" and in bringing the created order to fulfilment. The one passage suggests that there is something sacramental about the purposes that language serves in salvation history; the other implies Augustinian and twelfth-century ideas regarding the interdependence of words and the forms of things as apprehensible by the human creature's special relationship to the Creator.

In Passus xii, Ymaginatif indicates to Will how he ought to understand his Dream-within-a-Dream of the previous passus. That Dream-within-a-Dream was evidently brought on by the Dreamer's outburst of exasperation – his response to having come to the conclusion that all learning ("*clergie*") is useless. In the course of Ymaginatif's explanation, the possibility emerges of knowledge that is useful and worthwhile because it is rooted in love: "Ac yet is clergie to comende, and kynde wit bothe, / And namely clergie for Cristes love, that of clergie is roote" (B.xii.70–1). Ymaginatif illustrates what learning rooted in love and in reality could be by explicating an episode in the Gospel of John that reveals the true purposes of written language.

In the story of the woman taken in adultery from John 8, Christ challenges those who accuse the woman and then bends down and mysteriously writes something in the dust. Ymaginatif finds the very writing itself to be significant, for it is a paradigm of book-learning and the discourse arts. In this story, learning serves as the vehicle of Jesus' loving regard for others: comfort to the woman, warning to her accusers: "For thorugh Cristes caractes, the Jewes knewe hemselve / Giltier as afore God and gretter in synne / Than the womman that there was, and wenten awey for shame. / The clergie that there was conforted the womman" (B.xii.78–81). Written discourse is thus shown to be crucial to the church's office of performing pastoral care, particularly of ministering appropriately to sinners. Only language can articulate what needs to be conveyed to each in the reality of his or her situation.

Ymaginatif next explains that reading and writing in service books and the unbroken tradition that the written word guarantees by tying the legacy back to apostolic authority make possible the Eucharist. Language, as it were, underwrites the sacrament itself: "For Goddes body myghte noght ben of breed withouten clergie, / The which body is bothe boote to the rightfulle, / And deeth and dampnacion to hem that deyeth yvele; / As Cristes caracte confort-ede and bothe coupable shewed / The womman that the Jewes broughte, that Jesus thoughte to save" (B.xii.85–9). The written "caractes" and the eucharistic sacrament seem to merge here, both serving the same ultimate purpose of comforting or warning.

Written language itself has something sacramental about it, for without it the sacraments of penance and of the Eucharist could not be accomplished. An appropriate art, the art of grammar, is presumably necessary to interpret the mysterious written characters in a way that reveals their sacramental meaning for the spiritual condition of each person. Discourse accomplishes the divine purpose of fulfilling the Old Law, the vindictive code of retribution, in the New, bringing about the restoration of Creation that the law of love begins to achieve. Understood this way, the arts can be the means to a higher truth, reconceived according to the vision of a higher knowledge that would include love.

Ymaginatif thus explains to the Dreamer that written language has a sacramental function, rooted in Christ's love, serving to convey both comfort and warning for the renewing of Creation. Writing had already been spoken of back in Passus ix by Wit as part of an elaborate metaphor representing the creation of human-kind in the image of God. There Wit's answer to the Dreamer's question about Dowell begins by his comparing the Creator's making of the human person to writing. Wit makes the grammat-ical observation that the verbs that tell of the creation of everything else in the world are in the singular, but the author of Genesis uses a plural verb to tell of the creation of human beings – *Faciamus hominem* (9:35, 42). It is in developing this point that Wit elabo-rates another metaphor of writing.

In this metaphor, Wit makes use of the traditional interpretation of the persons of the Trinity that characterize the Father as divine power and the Son as the divine Word. In explaining that the Creator had to express the multiplicity of the Godhead in making humankind in the divine image, Wit shows that this had to be so by making the point that writing, like the creation of the human person, requires several items for its accomplishment: parchment (underlying substance), language itself (the Word), and a pen (power): "As who seith, 'Moore moot herto than my word oone: / My myght moot helpe now with my speche.' / Right as a lord sholde make lettres, and hym [ne] lakked parchemyn, / Though he koude write never so wel, if he [wel]de no penne, / The lettre, for al the lordshipe, I leve were nevere ymaked!" (B.ix.36–40). The pen is the divine power of the Father; the words to be written are the Son. Perhaps we are to understand the parchment to be the spiritual stuff needed to receive the activity of the Father in manifesting the expression of the Son – i.e., the parchment is the soul, "a goost, of the godhede of hevene" (l. 46).

Because we as God's creatures are the written characters so produced, humankind too bears the image of this multiplicity of the divine persons: power, language, spirit: "And so it semeth by him, as the Bible telleth, there he seide – / [Dixit, 'Faciamus'] – / He moste werche with his word and wit shew. / And in this manere was man maad thorugh myght of God almyghty, / With his word and werkmanshipe and with lif to laste" (B.ix.41–5). If we take the pronoun in line 43 to refer to the human creature, "*homo*" ("*hominem*" comes right after "*Faciamus*" in Gen. 1:26), then the point seems to be that, because we are endowed with the image of the triune God in us, we are therefore meant to realize the Word's inscription in ourselves by our own doing in word and work: "He moste werche with his word." "Word and work" is a frequent collocation in the poem used to express some of humankind's fundamental obligations.

Murtaugh has suggested that this metaphor of Creation as writing on parchment implies a "Christian version of Platonic exemplarism" (17) – the image of God in humankind is but a special instance of the Creator's articulation of all things in the world according to the ideas in the divine mind. The created order brought into existence in this way manifests an "ontic *logos*."

Furthermore, Wit's metaphorical exposition of *"Faciamus"* implies that the image of God in humankind consists particularly in our having inscribed in us the capability of language, according to which we can apprehend what everything is. Words and entities rely on each other for their distinct articulations, and reflection on the human capacity for language leads to our realization of our special relationship to the Creator. We share with God the intelligible language by which Creation was accomplished; the Word made us and thereby wrote into us our capacity for understanding words and things. For Augustine and the twelfth-century masters, pursuing this line of thought is how the study of the art of grammar can lead to a higher understanding of the human condition.

A bit later in his talk with the Dreamer, after the metaphor of writing on parchment, Wit remarks that speech, language itself, is a particularly valuable gift of grace, a source of delight, like music, shared with the saints, and as such must not be squandered or abused in idle chatter and misconduct. Wit says to the Dreamer: "'[Tyn]ynge of tyme, Truthe woot the sothe, / Is moost yhated upon erthe of hem that ben in hevene; / And siththe to spille speche, that spire is of grace, / And Goddes gleman and a game of hevene. / Wolde nevere the feithful fader his fithele were untempred, / Ne his gleman a gedelyng, a goere to tavernes.'" (B.ix.99–104). Again, Langland gives a moral dimension to his understanding of language. He is judgmental, but not dourly so: speech should be a source of joy.

Here the language user's obligation stems not only from a sense of gratitude to the Creator for the gift of speech, but also from a sense of community with the saints in heaven. In the two metaphors of writing, that obligation to use language in the right way follows rather from love of neighbours here in this world, of our *"evencristens"* in the church: language has a special sacramental function in the loving ministry to sinners; we human creatures, made capable of articulating the intelligibility of the world, should "werche the worde" that is inscribed in us by acting lovingly to others. The wrong use of words involves a kind of misworking and is but another version of actions done out of covetousness that betray God's image written in us at Creation (Davlin, *Game*, 58–9; Murtaugh, 22–3).

In this way, then, one comes to the realization that language has a certain natural ecology, a sort of integrity or rightness that lays some claim on the creature that has been endowed with this wonderful capacity. The language that articulates what the Creator, the human creature, and created Nature together manifest in expressing themselves and which makes for their mutual communicability should not be misappropriated. The obligation to be true to oneself as a child of God made in the divine image thus involves the obligation to treat with respect the intrinsic integrity of "lele words," language grounded in reality. To regard language in such a way and to pursue its study accordingly is surely to root "*clergie*" in love – for Langland, perhaps not so much in a love of God aimed at achieving an inward otherworldy ascent to the divine presence, as in love of neighbour.

THE ARTS AND GRAMMAR

Several passages in the third vision – and over into the fourth vision in the transition episode of Clergy's banquet – explicitly mention the seven arts, grammar in particular. These passages raise the issue of the limitations to which the arts are subject if not rooted in love. And yet despite this qualification, as we see also in Passus xv, grammatical doctrine used in the analysis of words-as-words is clearly shown to produce helpful insights. In Passus x, at the beginning of the third vision, the Dreamer is browbeaten by the rather imperious Dame Study; in the end she mitigates her speech, however, by offering to provide a letter of introduction to her relatives, Clergy and his wife, Scripture, "sib to the sevene arts": "'For thi mekenesse, man,' quod she, 'and for thi mylde speche, / I shal kenne thee to my cosyn that Clergie is hoten. / He hath wedded a wif withinne thise six monthes, / Is sib to the sevene arts – Scripture is hir name.'" (B.x.149–52). This suggests that the traditional subjects of the liberal arts are related to the study of Scripture as a propaedeutic, a relation that recalls Hugh of St Victor's *Didascalicon*, which precedes three books on Scripture with three books on the arts. Augustine, too, at least at the time of the Cassiacum dialogues, regarded the arts as useful preliminaries to the pursuit of theology and scriptural interpretation. Hugh argues (as we saw above) that the progress through intellectual pursuits constitutes an ascent to the subjects dealt with by the higher understanding. Dame Study associates herself further with *Didascalicon* by including the practical artisan crafts among the disciplines for which she takes some credit

(B.x.179–81), an unusual inclusion that Hugh also makes (*Didas-calicon*, Bk. II, chaps. 20ff.; see Murtaugh, 68).

In commending the Dreamer to her cousins, Study reviews at length her claim of all that Clergy and Scripture are beholden to her for: she taught them the essentials. She mentions three of the seven arts by name, including grammar. Study seems to stress the value of two of her arts of discourse, grammar and logic, to the pursuits of philosophical and biblical learning. "'Plato the poete, I putte hym first to boke; / Aristotle and othere mo to argue I taughte. / Grammer for girles I garte first write, / And bette hem with a baleys but if thei wolde lerne.'" (B.x.175–8). Study has taught both how to write and how to argue, abilities essential to her cousin, Clergy, but also, as she suggests, to the transmission and interpretation of Scripture.

But these arts, essential to the higher subjects, have limitations if not guided by concern for others. Study admits that she is baffled by Theology and explains that this is because Theology somehow incorporates love in its understanding, something all too often ignored in the arts themselves. (B.x.182–90). That the arts can have this lack is illustrated by an aphorism, which Study quotes, from the standard text used in the teaching of grammar, (pseudo-) Cato's *Distichs* – it is an art to give back as good as you get – certainly an unloving sentiment, as Study remarks. (ll. 191–201). All the same, despite what they may omit, the arts of discourse here have a fundamental place in the pursuit of knowledge.

Like Study, her cousin Clergy alludes to the seven arts when the Dreamer's question about Dowel is put to him during the banquet scene at the beginning of Passus xiii. When asked the inevitable question, "What is Dowel?," Clergy demurs in his answer and says that he is unable to reply until his seven sons (the seven arts) return from their educational training and he has been able to confer with them. "'Now thow, Clergie,' quod Conscience, 'carpest what is Dowel?' / 'I have sevene sones,' he seide, 'serven in a castel / Ther the lord of lif wonyeth, to leren hym what is Dowel. / Til I se tho sevene and myself acorden / I am unhardy,' quod he, 'to any wight to preven it.'" (B.xiii.119–23). Even though the seven arts are said to dwell with the Lord of life, Clergy expresses his suspicion that even an answer based on what they had learned might be inadequate, for the same reason that Study had thought the arts deficient in themselves: an answer by the seven sons might

well leave love out of the account. But Piers the Plowman is one
who does know about love and understands how to bring knowledge into love's realm.

Piers then would have an answer regarding Dowel's identity, says
Clergy, and it incorporates knowledge about language and sees
grammatical doctrine as leading to theological insight. Already a
way seems to open for the reconciliation of knowledge and love.
Piers's reply would be that Dowel and Dobet are "two infinites."
Clergie continues: "Piers the Plowman ... / ... no text ne taketh to
mayntene his cause / But *Dilige Deum* and *Domine quis
habitabit* ... / And seith that Dowel and Dobet arn two infinites, /
Whiche infinites with a feith fynden out Dobest, / Which shal save
mannes soule – thus seith Piers the Plowman" (B.xiii.126–30). But
certainly Anne Middleton is right in suggesting that Langland is
punning on "*infinite*" and the reader is to understand that besides
being said to be limitless things "Dowel" and "Dobet" are said also
by Clergy to be infinitives, verbal substantives, so that we are to
take them as "to do well" and "to do better." As we saw above,
Langland is remarkable for his innovation in translating grammatical terms into the vernacular, and here is just such an instance.
To find surplus meaning in the very form of the word as analysed
by the art of grammar is to explore the ambiguity of the word-as-
word. Clergy states that when faith is added to the infinitives, Dowel
and Dobet, they are perfected to a superlative state, Dobest, and
become unique, no longer limitless.

Peter Helias follows Priscian, as we saw above, in regarding the
infinitive as part verb, part noun. In so far as it is a noun, the
infinitive *legere*, "to read" (for example) is much like the noun,
lectio. As a substance *a substando*, Helias would say, something can
be predicated of *legere*, that is, the action can serve as a subject,
even though the infinitive does carry some indication of tense and
agency (as opposed to passivity) that the noun *lectio* does not. The
infinitive thus conveys a heightened sense of activity in the temporal world in contrast to the comparable but static nominative form.
As a substance *a subsistendo*, the infinitive takes on the particular
quality of the action denoted by the word – in this instance, "to
do," "the essential transitive verb," as Middleton says (175). The
quality of the verb is itself a rather abstract concept of action *per
se*, signifying "to operate upon," "to bring about," and within the
moral world of the poem assimilating the sense of the word "to

work." Adding "well" and "better" does qualify the action as being at least in a particular direction of valuation. In so far as it is a verb, while sharing some dimensions of time and agency, the infinitive lacks the specificity of the finite verb forms, so that "Do well" and "Do bet" are not limited by specific circumstances of time or person. They are thus sort of open radicals, presenting the opportunity for an agent-subject to enter the action. The infinitive form extends an open invitation for a person to assume the task of achieving the quality that the word conveys – to do, to work, well and better. Should the invitation be accepted, the infinitive becomes finite, specific actions done for others. If faith completes these actions, then the doing is perfected into its uniquely super-lative form.

This is an instance not so much of a grammatical detail turned into a metaphor as of making the assumption that Peter Helias makes in supposing that any noun, as an existing something, as idea, and as word, is all one and that all three aspects are mutually illuminating; all three factors in the triadic semiotic are mediated together. Dowel and Dobet are at once certain active roles in the world (existing somethings), actions that work out to some result (concepts), evaluated the one positively and the other compara-tively, and word forms (infinitives) that are not constrained by context. If grammar is in some sense the paradigm of all knowl-edge, as Augustine and Hugh of St Victor held, then to use gram-matical doctrine in this way, to explain how love in action might be realized, is to suggest that there may be ways to redeem knowl-edge from selfishness, to root it in love (Simpson, "Scientia," 63). Investigating words-as-words, the infinitives as infinitives, is what has revealed this to be so. As Middleton says, the meaning of these terms "lies in the words themselves" (170).

ANIMA'S GRAMMAR LESSON

The investigation of words-as-words is a pursuit also in B.xv. Much of that passus is in effect a grammar lesson conducted by Anima. The lesson begins with the list of names for the several aspects of the soul taken from Isidore, ends by commending the *enarratio* of the creed, and throughout emphasizes the importance of language to the various responsibilities of the clergy. It is in this passus as well that Anima refers to the art of grammar as "the ground of al."

At the beginning of Passus xv, the Dreamer encounters a strange creature who, on being asked his name, replies that he is called "*Anima*" – but in addition he is called by any of a series of other names that designate powers of the soul, a series that goes back ultimately to Isidore's etymological encyclopaedia, *Origines* (as we saw above; B.xv.22–39ᵉ). The Dreamer admits to an interest in knowing all the names of things, for by that means, as Isidore had held, one can gain knowledge about everything. Anima comments on Will's interest in the names of bishops: "'Thow woldest knowe and konne the cause of alle hire names, / And of myne, if thow myghtest, me thynketh by thi speche!' / 'Ye, sire,' I seide, 'by so no man were greved, / Alle the sciences under sonne and alle the sotile craftes / I wolde I knewe and kouthe kyndely in myn herte!'" (B.xv.45–9).

But Anima denounces this excessive curiosity and, arguing that to accumulate knowledge about the world by investigating the names of things obliges one all the more to live virtuously, cites a quotation attributed to St Bernard – probably the locus of the word/work collocation in the poem: "'*Beautus est*' seith Seint Bernard, '*qui scripturas legit / Et verba vertit in opera* fulliche to his power. ... '" (B.xv.60–1). "Blessed is the one," so St Bernard says, "who reads the Scriptures and turns its words into works to the extent possible." This quotation underlies a main theme in this passus – the betrayal of names by neglect or by misdoing. The Dreamer jokes about Anima's multiple nominations and compares them to the many possible names of a bishop – "*presul*," "*pontifex*," "*metropolitanus*," "*episcopus*," and "*pastor*" (ll. 40–4).

Later Anima argues that many of the bishops who bear these names of office and other titles have betrayed their appellations both by their misdeeds and also by the obligations that they have neglected. This is one way in which the passus develops the theme of hypocrisy – prelates bear "beles paroles" outwardly but belie the fine words of their titles with unworthy deeds, which disfigure not only their official titles but also the uniquely human character of the word imprinted in the soul: "For [in Latyn ypocrisie] is likned to a dongehill / That were bisnewed with snow, and snakes withinne, / Or to a wal that were whitlymed and were foul withinne. / Right so manye preestes, prechours and prelates – / Ye [b]en enblaunched with *bele paroles* and with clothes, / Ac youre werkes and wordes therunder aren ful w[o]lveliche" (B.xv.111–16).

Balbus's etymology (s.v. "Ipocrita") has it that the word is derived from the word for gold; a gold, rather than a white, exterior covers over worthless contents. But the article does give a cross-reference to "*sacerdos*," priest, which sets out the bad effects that follow from the ignorance and immorality of hypocritical priests. Balbus thus suggests associations for the word similar to Anima's.

When the Dreamer asks about love, Anima's teaching takes on a different dimension. Just as Clergy spoke in B.xiii of how Piers valued love over knowledge, so here Anima says that it is Piers Plowman who understands love best and that his perception of love extends beyond words, even beyond works as the intelligence and judgment understand them, to the will: "'Clerkes have no knowyng,' quod he, 'but by werkes and by wordes. / Ac Piers the Plowman parceyveth moore depper / What is the wille, and wherfore that many wight suffreth': / ... / 'Therfore by colour ne by clergie knowe shaltow hym nevere, / Neither thorugh wordes ne werkes, but thorugh wil oone, / And that knoweth no clerk ne creature on erthe / But Piers the Plowman – *Petrus, id est, Christus.*'" (B.xv.198–200, 209–12). Again, the name of Piers appears in a context in which distrust of superficial knowledge is expressed.

And yet, the very same passage that insists on the limitations of learning says that love finds its expression above all in language. For love, Anima goes on, is perhaps finally a matter of a certain disposition of the spirit, an outgoing sense of joy and good will, which shows itself especially in cheerful conversation: "For Charite is Goddes champion, and as a good child hende, / And the murieste of mouth at mete where he sitteth. / The love that lith in his herte maketh hym light of speche ... " (B.xv.216–8). These lines remind the reader of the passage (discussed above) in which Wit had insisted that language was not to be abused because it was a gift of grace, a source of delight, God's "*gleman*" (B.ix.104). Music and mealtime conversation seem to be expressions of the use of language at its best, for communing in fellowship and for taking joy with others in God's gifts. The study of words follows from an appreciation of the central role of language in people's lives.

But language is abused, the gifts of creation are sinned against, and people do not act in accordance with love. It is for this reason that the very nature of things and the arts that give an account of the phenomena of nature in systems of knowledge are now so disordered and unreliable (B.xv.354). Astronomers can no longer predict the weather (ll. 358–9), and grammarians fail to master reading and writing (ll. 370–4). If it were somehow possible to infuse the disciplines with love, then knowledge could be refounded and become efficacious again in explaining a reordered world. All the same, even now, when the motif of the names of bishops is resumed, associations within the system of language as analysed by the art of grammar enable Anima to make his point, just as it had allowed Clergie to make his point about the identity of Dowell and Dobet by recourse to grammatical doctrine about infinitives.

Much of the rest of Anima's speech deals with the theme of the clergy's obligation to teach; uninstructed Christians are, remarkably enough, grouped with unbelievers, Muslims, and Jews, as those for whose sake the clergy have the duty to be knowledgeable themselves and to impart knowledge of the faith to others (B.xv.387–8). As Anima says later, those bishops who bear the name of "pastour" (ll. 494, 495[a] – see 43) and are called "bishops" of sees *in partibus infidelium* (Of Nazareth ... of Bethleem; ll. 492, 508) must live up to their names by working to convert the Saracen, just as bishops in Christendom also must instruct the faithful in their care. Not to do so is another instance of failure to fulfil the word by the work that would accomplish it.

Anima makes his argument that bishops should teach by offering what amounts to two etymologies, one for *"fullynge"* (or *"folwing"*) (meaning baptism) and one for *"hethen"* (meaning un-Christianized people). He then intertwines these two words around two words similar to *"folwing,"* – *"fowel"* (meaning bird) and *"folwen"* (meaning to follow) – near-homonyms to *"folwing."* It becomes apparent that to investigate the etymology of words is but another way of exploring the surplus of lexical meaning. The self-consciously learned pursuit of etymologies blends easily here with plays on words; exploring the ambiguity of words-as-words comes close to exploring the ambiguity that results from the repetition of homonyms.

Anima's etymologizing suggests that knowledge can be pursued by tracing words back to their origins, for the lines of descent in the networks of language express the derivational interrelationships among things. This was the assumption of the Stoics in antiquity, subsequently incorporated into the doctrine of the art of grammar, carried over into the pursuit of other realms of knowledge by Isidore, and taken as the basis of the great encyclopaedic dictionary of the later Middle Ages, *Catholicon.* As Balbus assumes in his definition of etymology, the development of the word's composition as a word matches the development of its meaning from origin to outcome. The art of grammar is a source of knowledge about the world because the system of language relates to the created order, sharing in its distinctiveness and apprehensibility.

When missionaries first came to England, Anima tells the Dreamer, clerics converted the heathens ("*hethynesse*," B.xv.441) by the *word* of their preaching, but also by the *work* of their miracles and their baptizings ("*fullynge*"): "Austyn at Caunterbury cristnede the kyng there, / And thorugh miracles, as men mow rede, al that marche he tornede / To Crist and to Cristendom, and cros to honoure, / And follede <=*fullede*> folk faste, and the feith taughte / Moore thorugh miracles than thorugh muche prechyng, / As wel thorugh hise werkes as with hise holy wordes, / And [fourmed] what *fullynge* and feith was to mene" (B.xv.444–50).

Anima then proceeds to give his own explanation of what "*fullynge*" means by offering its derivation. Part of the significance of baptism in the context is as an act of the receiving into the faith of those otherwise lost, receiving them not just by sacrament, but also by instruction. To show that baptism in some sense means a completing or finishing of the process of bringing to faith, Anima implies the etymology that "*fullynge*" (baptism) (MED "*fulwen*") is derived from "*fullynge*" (MED "*fullen*," v. 2) – i.e., the word for baptism is related to the word for the finishing of woolen cloth by washing it in a bath of water and a special clay while treading on it or beating it in a mill: "Clooth that cometh fro the wevyng is noght comly to were / Til it is fulled underfoot or in fullyng stokkes, / Wasshen wel with water and with taseles cracched, / Ytouked and yteynted and under taillours hande; / And so it fareth by a barn that born is of wombe: / Til it be cristned in Cristes name and confermed of the bisshop, / It is hethene as to heveneward, and helplees to the soule" (B.xv.451–7). The words for "baptising" and "fulling" are connected; both convey the idea of bringing a process to its final achievement by washing.

By such a process of instruction and baptism, the unchristian "heathen" – or uninstructed Christians – is tamed and brought into the household of the church. It is quite in keeping with the truth of this statement, Anima explains, sounding just like a grammar master in his use of the phrase "to mene," that "*heathen*" is derived from "*heeth*," wilderness, where wild animals run about lost:

"Hethen" is to mene after heeth and untiled erthe – / As in wilde wildernesse wexeth wilde beestes, / Rude and unresonable, rennynge withouten keperes" (B.xv.458–60). This is Anima's second etymology – this time explicitly in the manner of the grammarians. While the etymology for the Latin equivalent to "heathen," viz., "*paganus*," may lie behind the English derivation offered here, as N.F. Blake has suggested (94), the etymology for the English word does stand on its own, as does the explanation offered for "*fullynge.*"

By *fullynge/folwing*, the heathen enter into the king's hall to be present at the eschatological wedding feast there. (The allusion is to Matthew 22.) The Gospel makes no mention of preparing domestic fowls for this banquet, but Anima, carried by the identity or near-identity of words, associates *fowls* (who *follow* the one who tends them) with the previously lost and untamed (heathen) who are brought into the household of faith by instruction and baptism (*fullynge/folwing*) (the guests served and the fare served up have perhaps gotten rather confused here – both are "foweles folwed," fowls that followed, followers baptized; see B.xv.462–3): "And by the hond-fedde foweles [i]s folk understonde / That looth ben to lovye withouten lernynge of ensaumples. / Right as capons in a court cometh to mennes whistlynge – / In menynge after mete folweth men that whistlen – / Right so rude men that litel reson konneth / Loven and bileven by lettred mennes doynges, / And by hire wordes and werkes wenen and trowen" (B.xv.471–7).

The implication of the passage seems to be that the network and association of words-as-words as discerned by grammatical anaylsis condemn the negligent clergy who betray language by not fulfilling their names because they do not teach, do not baptize, do not finish out their task of bringing the lost and ignorant to an informed faith. That this lexical concatenation can have this force of argument depends on the way of thinking about words that Clergy's comments about "the two infinites" also depended on – i.e., that words, ideas, and things themselves are somehow the same (as Peter Helias claimed) and mutually inform each other according to a theory of "semiologizing ontology."

At the end of the passus, Anima offers some advice on pedagogy to bishops should they take up their task of instructing the heathen; the teaching methods that he commends are from the grammar classroom, proving again the importance of the art of reading and writing to the church's accomplishing its tasks. The clerics should proceed in teaching the credo "litlum and litlum," (l. 609) not only by a progression from simpler to more difficult, but by going through the text clause by clause, word by word, incrementally, according to the time-honoured, "compositional," procedure of grammatical commentary (*enarratio*). Those being instructed in the faith should be called on to "speke and spelle," (B.xv.610) – i.e, to read out loud (the *lectio* of the art of grammar) – and even to spell words out in letters (for "spellen," see MED, v. 2, c.) and then to "rendren it and recorden it" (B.xv.611) – i.e., to recite (MED "rendren" c.; "recorden" 6) or perhaps to commit to memory (MED "recorden" 1). Anima may have early on faulted the Dreamer's excessive interest in names but by the end of the passus admits that knowing about names and other such grammatical matters can have its uses after all.

Anima commends to the clergy the proselytizing work of the apostles and martyrs, their lives serving as a "forbisene" and "myrour" to bishops (B.xv.526); in this regard he commends also Christ himself, to whom he attributes the archepiscopal title "metropolitanus" (l. 515). Some of the manuscripts of the C text add that Jesus during his ministry was "bisshopid" (where Schmidt's B text reads "bishined," B.xv.516; see Pearsall's edition of C.xvii.268, apparatus), thus suggesting that Christ carried the title also of bishop.

In ascribing these names to Christ, Anima anticipates a passage in the next-to-last vision (B.xix) in which again attention to names and to the essential meanings they express generates the poem's development. The last three visions (B.xviii, xix, and xx) in some sense return to the first vision's concern with the particulars of history. In these last visions, it is sacred history that seems to be the poet's preoccupation, and at the beginning of passus xix the economy of Christ's redemptive acts during the course of his life is defined in three successive accounts of the two pairs of names and titles that Christ bears: Jesus/king, Christ/conqueror.

When the Dreamer asks in B.xix who it is that appears like Piers Plowman in the midst of the Mass, Conscience replies that it is Christ. But the Dreamer (apparently with Phil. 2:10 in mind, "at the name of Jesus every knee should bow" – see l. 80a) is puzzled that the Lord's name should be Christ rather than Jesus: "'Why calle ye hym Crist?' quod I, 'sithen Jewes called hym Jesus? / Patriarkes and prophetes prophecied bifore / That alle kynne creatures sholden knelen and bowen / Anoon as men nempned the name of God Jesu.'" (B.xix.15–18). It is in showing the essential correctness of *both* names that Conscience offers in turn three versions of the soteriological significance of events in Christ's life. In the first account (ll. 26–68), the Son's actions in his human capacity as teacher and prophet receive meaning from the name "Jesus" and from the title King of the Jews, while his actions as God in triumphing over Death and Hell are defined in the scheme of salvation history by the name "Christ" and by the title Conqueror. In the second account (ll. 69–107) it is another two events that are singled out and identified by the paired names and titles: the Epiphany, when as "Jesus," the King, he received gifts of honour from other kings; and the Ministry, when as "Christ," the Conqueror, he gathered and consolidated a redeemed people.

Conscience's third explanation (ll. 108–99) distributes the two roles of king and conqueror among the last two of that elusive threesome, the search for whom has sporadically driven the Dreamer's rambling quest in the last part of the poem – Dowell, Dobetter, and Dobest: Dobetter is again "Jesus" the king of Israel, son of David (ll. 133, 136); Dobest is the "Christ" of the triumph over death, *Christus resurgens* (ll. 152, 160). But Dowell is identified with the doubly named "Christ Jesus," who, by only saying the word, turned the water into wine at Cana, a miracle that is understood to show that its performer was the person who had come to fulfil the law by transforming it into the law of love (ll. 108–14). This role is also that which Jesus plays in the story of the woman taken in adultery that Ymaginatif recounts in B.xii (as we have seen), where writing, rather than speech, is the vehicle of the transformation of the law. Conscience, in referring in B.xix to the miracle at Cana, emphasizes again that the means of bringing into existence this new commandment to love one another is language: "So at the feeste first, as I bifore tolde, / Bigan God of his grace and goodnesse to do wel; / And tho was he cleped and called noght oonly Crist but Jesu – / A fauntekyn ful of wit, *filius Marie*. / For bifore his moder Marie made he that wonder, / That she first and formest sholde ferme bileve / That he thorugh Grace was gete, and of no gome ellis. / He wroghte that by no wit but *thorugh word one*, / After the kynde that he cam of; there comsede he Dowel" (B.xix.115–23). As Schmidt notes, "After the kynde that he cam of" (l. 123) suggests "In accord with the nature of God his Father [who *created* by his word]." Thus the restoration of Creation in history according to the new dispensation of love begins with the uttering of the word, just as Creation did. Again, it is language, because it plays a role in the articulation of Creation and in bringing the created order to fulfilment in history, that joins knowledge to the active love of "Doing well," as Jesus did in acting according to his double name, "Christ Jesus," and as bishops should do in living up to their names as well.

The variety and distribution of Christ's names reveal his roles in redemption in something of the way in which the titles of bishops identify their essential tasks. Names bestow essential being on things, as Thierry of Chartres had said, and so they are reliable expressions of what things most truly are and impose roles on what they designate. Overall, Langland seems to suggest in these passages that language plays a part in the restoration of creation just as it had in Creation itself. God brought the world forth by speech, articulated the distinctiveness of things by the designation of words. On the expressive side, humankind among the creatures most fully manifests the divinity, for people bear the image of their Creator, which makes them uniquely capable of language and gives them the means to express in their actions what is inscribed in them – or not to do so – whether by loving or by coveting. Language is itself a manifestation of Creation, a resource for exploring knowledge about the world and for acting in accord with Creation's intentions, as the twelfth-century arts-of-discourse doctrines in particular held. Knowledge and love can come together when learning begins with the study of language and proceeds inward and then outward to discover a common, utterable, intelligibility between the mind and the world, an "ontic *logos*." This is the destination of the pursuit of knowledge about words also for both Augustine and the Paris Masters, although Langland is exceptional in the emphasis that he gives to understanding love as love of neighbour.

The arts of discourse thus have a crucial role to play in bringing together the language that designates nature and the language immanent in the human soul from Creation. Grammar, in particular, can work against the betrayal of language, not so much by insisting on standards of correctness as by showing the intelligibility of language in its interconnectedness and differentiation and by holding together the dimensions of language, designative and expressive both, in order to keep it true to the actual experience of it and by maintaining it for the purposes God has for it in this world. Grammar is truly "the grounde of al," as Anima says.

Conclusion

Looking into ambiguity, as we have in this book, reveals that any one instance of a word's use leaves unrealized a surplus of meaning there to be explored. It is repetition that brings out these additional potentials of meaning – repetition of the same word in a somewhat different context to give a polysemous variation in meaning, repetition to bring out metaphorically associated significances, repetition by homonym or polysemy to stretch out the associations of meaning to the unexpected and witty. The repetition may be explicit in the text or only a reverberation set going in the reader's mind. Often in *Piers Plowman* it is the intertextual echoes from Scripture that make possible these resonances. As these patterns of sameness in difference ramify and spread, they elaborate a network that, by its very extension and coherence, seems to confirm itself and to bear out language's capacity to disclose truth about the world. Exploring the ambiguity of words seems to allow them to realize themselves in fuller and fuller meaning.

Drawing out the full potential of significance from ambiguous words by means of various kinds of repetition is but one way of pursuing the resources inherent in language for coming to know more about the world. If Creation presents itself in terms to which natural language is adequate, and there is indeed some sort of reciprocity between verbal expression and the reality that it both discloses and somehow permeates, then the art of grammar can prove an entry point for reason's investigation of reality, even ontological and theological reality. Various topics within the purview of the grammarian come to have relevance to understanding the structure and make-up of Creation: the system of word classes, what word items exhaust a class, etymologies and other patterns of derivation and make-up of words, the meanings of names.

Langland finds much here that serves his purpose of struggling to comprehend how knowledge and love can be joined together in the historical circumstances in which he and those he writes for must work out their salvation and practice the faith to which they are committed. Will's zigzag journey keeps criss-crossing the arts of discourse because it is a part of human experience particularly felt by medieval writers that language seems not only to represent the world but also to enter into the reality that it represents. We, as creatures who speak and write and so have this affinity with the Word that spoke Creation into existence, have a sense of participating in language's founding relationship with the world. Thus, for Langland, the exploration of the excess meaning of words-as-words as discovered by the art of grammar can lead both to self-understanding and to knowledge of the world.

We may think that Saussure set aside too much that is integral to our experience of language when he separated "langue" from "langage" (trans., 9, and C. Bally et al., eds., 25). "Langue" is what can be regarded scientistically as an artificial code for communication transmission, but this leaves out of account the experience (by both the self and the community) of the richness of the relationship between natural language and the world. Viewed in such a way, Saussure's achievement may seem a very successful treatment of what is only a part of the total phenomena of language, and the structuralist and poststructuralist revolution in the human sciences that he did so much to bring about may seem to need some rethinking. Such rethinking would mean returning to re-examine what was a crucial juncture in the philosophy of language as in so much else, the point at which the paths that have led to present positions initially diverged in their several directions – viz., a return to the Romantics. It is for some such reason that Charles Taylor has proposed a rereading of Herder and von Humboldt on the origins of language ("Language," 227ff.; "Theories," 255ff.) and that Habermas has directed attention back to the reception of Hegel (53). Romantic and medieval authors speak to each other in most interesting ways.

George Steiner, in *Real Presences*, similarly attributes to a positivist, scientistic view of language (84–5) the breaking of the covenant between word and world (93; see Rudd, xii). He perhaps states the dichotomy between poststructuralist nominalism and logocentric realism too sharply, not allowing for the ways in which language enters into the realities it is about. Steiner's view has a creationist side to it (201), but largely an aesthetic creationism rather than the scriptural one of medieval authors.

Steiner's remedy for this covenant-breaking is a moral education of the sensibility in a return to the "excellence" of high art as defined by the cultural tradition (64). Marcuse, in *One-Dimensional Man*, also challenges the positivist view of language and sees in poetic art one means of restoring the fully significative dimensions of discourse flattened out in highly technologized societies, but Marcuse's arguments lead to a rather more radically subversive conclusion than do Steiner's. For Marcuse, a word conveys a cognitive concept that has the power to signify beyond its function in a particular context, beyond the given facts to which it refers. This excess of meaning makes the word "transitive" – i.e., able to mediate out of the particular instance to a wider significance (95, 106). As one of my epigraphs, quoting Marcuse, states, poetry releases this transcendent potential in language and in so doing "breaks the spell of the things that are." Marcuse has the poet reply to the positivist philosopher of language: "My language can be learned like any other language (in point of fact, it is also your own language); then it will appear that my symbols, metaphors, etc., are *not* symbols, metaphors, etc., but mean exactly what they say" (192). This is the very position that Levin also maintains: the surplus signification of words is not deviant or merely supplemental, but rather their hypersemiosis is integral to language and essential to its power to change the given present. Justice must be done to our experience of language: the concept must be allowed the full extent of its range of reference; ambiguities and metaphorical associations must be dwelt on seriously, allowing the full richness of their reverberations. To regard these transcendental dimensions of language as merely a way of speaking is to undermine its power to "express the other order." Only by letting ourselves be addressed by words in all their wealth of meaning can we let words do their work. Only thereby do knowledge and love come together in Will's pursuit of truth and goodness.

Langland, it seems to me, by the arts-of-discourse procedures to which he has recourse in developing his poem, affirms the idea that language is a resource for learning about the world and for transforming it. Language, thought of in this way, is a sort of medieval commons, Ivan Illich has suggested – "People called commons that part of the environment which lay beyond their own thresholds and outside of their own possessions, to which, however, they had recognized claims of usage, not to produce commodities, but to provide for the subsistence of their households" (49). So understood, language is both a part of the natural environment, with its own ecology beyond the realm of private property, and the rules for its customary usage in the interests of everyone. It is a commons that needs to be reclaimed as a resource for the community's benefit and to be used in ways true to its nature: to envision a different order of things as well as to meet practical challenges that face the community. Rethinking medieval views of language as a resource and rereading Langland's poetry in light of that rethinking can perhaps help us in that work of reclamation.

Works Cited

ABBREVIATIONS

CCCM *Corpus Christianorum, continuatio medievalis.* Turnholt: Brepols, 1971.

CCSL *Corpus Christianorum, series latina.* Turnholt: Brepols, 1953– .

CSEL *Corpus scriptorum ecclesiasticorum latinorum.* Vienna: Hoelder-Pichler-Tempsky, 1866– .

Keil *Grammatici latini,* ed. H. Keil. 7 vols. Leipzig: Teubner, 1855–80.

Loeb Loeb Classical Library, Boston and London: Harvard University Press and William Heinemann.

OCT [Oxford Classical Texts] *Scriptorum classicorum bibliotheca Oxoniensis.* Oxford: Clarendon Press.

PL *Patrologiae cursus completus,* series latina. Ed. Abbé Migne. Paris: Garnier Fratres, 1878–90.

PRIMARY SOURCES

Abelard, Peter. *Sic et non.* Ed. B.B. Boyer and R. McKeon. Chicago: University of Chicago Press, 1976.

Aristotle *The "Art" of Rhetoric.* Text with trans. by J.H. Freese. Loeb, 1926.

– *Categories, On Interpretation.* Text with trans. by H.P. Cook. Loeb, 1938.

– *On Sophistical Refutations.* Text with trans. by E.S. Forster. Loeb, 1955.

– *Topics.* Text with trans. by E.S. Forster. Loeb, 1960.

Augustine. *Confessions.* CCSL 27. (Trans. R.S. Pine-Coffin. Harmondsworth: Penguin, 1961.)

– *De catechizandis rudibus.* CCSL 46. (Trans. J.P. Christopher. Westminster, Md.: Newman Bookshop, 1946.)

– *De civitate Dei.* CCSL 47–8. (Trans. H. Bettenson. Harmondsworth: Penguin, 1984.)

– *De dialectica.* Ed. J. Pinborg and trans. B.D. Jackson. Dordrecht: D. Reidel, 1975.

– *De doctrina christiana.* CCSL 32. (Trans. D.W. Robertson. Indianapolis: Bobbs-Merrill, 1958.)

– *De genesi ad litteram, imperfectus liber.* CSEL 28. (Trans. J.H. Taylor. Ancient Christian Writers, 41–2. New York: Newman Press, 1982.)

– *De magistro.* CCSL, 29. (Trans. J.H.S. Burleigh, Library of Christian Classics, 6; Philadelphia: Westminster Press, 1953.)

– *De ordine.* CCSL 29. (Trans. R.P. Russell. New York: Cima, 1948.)

– *De Trinitate.* CCSL 50–50A. (Trans. J. Burnaby [partial], Library of Christian Classics, 8; Philadelphia: Westminster Press, 1955.)

– *De utilitate credendi.* CSEL 25. (Trans. J.H.S. Burleigh, Library of Christian Classics, 6; Philadelphia: Westminster Press, 1953.)

– *Retractationes.* CSEL 36. (Trans. M.I. Bogan, The Fathers of the Church, 60; Washington, DC: Catholic University of America Press, 1968.)

Balbus, Joannes. *Catholicon.* Mainz, 1460. Reprinted, Ridgewood, NJ: Gregg International, 1971.

Boethius. *De divisione.* PL 64.

– *De Trinitate,* in *Theological Tractates.* Text and trans. H.F. Stewart et al. Loeb, 1973.

– *In librum "De interpretatione".* PL 64.

Diogenes Laertius. *Lives of Eminent Philosophers.* Text with trans. by R.D. Hicks. Loeb, 1925.

Donatus. *Ars grammatica.* In Keil, 4.

– *Commentum Terenti,* ed. P. Wessner. Stuttgart: Teubner, 1962–63.

Herder, Johann Gottfried. "Essay on the Origin of Language." In *On the Origin of Language.* Trans. J.H. Moran and A. Gode. New York: Frederick Ungar, 1967.

Hugh of St Victor. *De grammatica.* Ed. R. Baron, in *Opera propaedeutica.* Notre Dame, Ind.: University of Notre Dame Press, 1966.

– *De sacramentis.* PL 176. (Trans. R.J. Deferrari. Cambridge, Mass.: Medieval Academy, 1951.)

– *Didascalicon,* ed. C.H. Buttimer. Washington, DC: Catholic University of America, 1939. (Trans. and intro. J. Taylor. New York: Columbia University Press, 1961.)

– *Epitome.* Ed. R. Baron, in *Opera propraedeutica.* Notre Dame, Ind.: University of Notre Dame Press, 1966.

Humboldt, Wilhelm von. *On Language*. Trans. P. Heath. Cambridge: Cambridge University Press, 1988.

Isidore of Seville. *De differentiis*. PL 83.

– *Etymologiarum sive originum libri XX* ["Origines"]. OCT, ed. W.M. Lindsay, 1911.

Jocelin of Brakelond. *The Chronicle of Jocelin of Brakelond, Concerning the Acts of Samson, Abbot of the Monastery of St. Edmund*. Trans. H.E. Butler. London: Nelson, 1949.

John of Garland. *Multorum vocabulorum equivocorum interpretatio*. London: W. de Worde, 1505.

– *Synonima cum expositione magistri Galfridi anglici*. London: W. de Worde, 1505.

John of Salisbury. *Metalogicon*. CCCM 163. (Trans. D.D. McGarry. Berkeley, Calif.: University of California Press, 1955.)

– *Policraticus*. Ed. C.C.I. Webb. Oxford, 1929; [Books I–IV]. CCCM 118. (Books I–III, VII–VIII. Trans J.B. Pike as *Frivolities of Courtiers and Footprints of Philosophers*. New York: Octagon Books, 1972.)

Langland, William. *Piers Plowman: C–Text*, ed. D. Pearsall. Berkeley: University of California Press, 1978.

– *Piers the Ploughman*. Trans. into modern English with intro. by J.F. Goodridge. Harmondsworth: Penguin, 1966.

– *The Vision of Piers Plowman: B-Text*. Ed. A.V.C. Schmidt. London: Dent, 1978.

– *The Vision of William* … . Part IV, Section 1. Notes to texts A, B, and C. London: Published for the Early English Text Society by the Oxford University Press, 1877.

– *The Vision of William Concerning Piers the Plowman, Together with Vita de Dowel, Dobet, et Dobest*. Ed. W.W. Skeat. Part II, Text B. London: Published for the Early English Text Society by the Oxford University Press, 1869.

Peter Helias. *Summa super Priscianum*. Ed. L. Reilly. Toronto: Pontifical Institute of Medieval Studies, 1993.

Peter Lombard. *Sententiarum libri IV*. Grottaferrata: Editiones Collegii S. Bonaventurae ad Claras Aquas, 1971–81.

Peter the Chanter. *De tropis loquendi. Prologue*. In F. Giusberti, *Materials for the Study of Twelfth-Century Scholasticism*. Naples: Bibliopolis, 1982.

– *Summa "Abel"*. Corpus Christi College, Cambridge (CCCC), Ms. 47.

– *Summa de sacramentis et animae consiliis*. Ed. J.-A. Dugauquier. Louvain: Editions Nauwelaerts, 1954–62.

– *Verbum abbreviatum*. PL 205.

Plato. *Cratylus.* OCT: *Platonis Opera*, 1. Ed. I. Burnet (Trans. B. Jowett. In *Collected Dialogues.* Ed. E. Hamilton and H. Cairns. Princeton, NJ: Princeton University Press, 1971.)

– *Meno.* OCT: *Platonis Opera*, 5. (Trans. W.K.C. Guthrie. In *Collected Dialogues.*)

– *Phaedrus.* OCT: *Platonis Opera*, 2. (Trans. R. Hackforth. In *Collected Dialogues.*)

– *Protagoras.* OCT: *Platonis Opera*, 3. (Trans. W.K.C. Guthrie. In *Collected Dialogues.*)

– *Timaeus.* OCT: *Platonis Opera*, 4. (Trans. B. Jowett. In *Collected Dialogues.*)

Priscian. *Institutiones.* In Keil, 3, 4.

Proclus. *Commentary on the First Book of Euclid's Elements.* Trans. G.R. Morrow. Princeton, NJ: Princeton University Press, 1970.

– *On the Cratylus of Plato.* Ed. G. Pasquali. Leipzig: Teubner, 1908.

Remigius of Auxerre. *In artem Donati minorem commentum.* Ed. W. Fox. Leipzig: Teubner, 1902.

Richard of St Victor. *Liber exceptionum.* Ed. J. Châtillon. Paris: Vrin, 1958.

Richard of Thetford. *Octo modi.* Printed as Part III of Pseudo–Bonaventure's *Ars concionandi* in Bonaventure, *Opera Omnia*, vol. IX, 8–21. Ad Clara Aquas (Quaracchi): ex typographia Collegii S. Bonaventurae, 1882–1902.

Servius. *In Vergilii Aeneidos libros XI commentarius.* Ed. G. Thilo and H. Hagen, 3 vols. Leipzig: Teubner, 1878–81.

Smaragdus of St Mihiel. *Expositio super Donatum.* CCCM 68.

Thierry of Chartres. *Commentaries on Boethius.* Ed. N.M. Häring. Toronto: PIMS, 1971.

– *The Latin Rhetorical Commentaries.* Ed. K.M. Fredborg. Toronto: PIMS, 1988.

Thomas of Chobham. *Summa de arte praedicandi.* CCCM 82.

Victorinus, C. Marius. "Commentary on Cicero's 'De inventione.'" In *Rhetores latini minores.* Ed. C Halm. Leipzing: Teubner, 1863; Reprint, Dubuque, Iowa: W.C. Brown, n.d.

SECONDARY SOURCES

Aers, David. "Christ's Humanity and Piers Plowman: Contexts and Political Implications." *Yearbook of Langland Studies* 8 (1994): 107–25.

Alford, John A. The Grammatical Metaphor: A Survey of Its Use in the Middle Ages." *Speculum* 57 no. 4 (1982): 728–60.

– *Piers Plowman: A Guide to the Quotations.* Binghamton, NY: Medieval and Renaissance Texts and Studies, 1992.

– "The Role of the Quotations in *Piers Plowman.*" *Speculum* 52 (1977): 80–99.

Alford, John A., ed. *A Companion to Piers Plowman*. Berkeley: University of California Press, 1988.

Allen, Judson Boyce. *The Ethical Poetic of the Later Middle Ages*. Toronto: University of Toronto Press, 1982.

– "Langland's Reading and Writing: Detractor and the Pardon Passus." *Speculum* 59 (1984): 342–62.

Allen, W.S. "Ancient Ideas on the Origin and Development of Language." *Transactions of the Philological Society* (1948; appeared 1949): 35–60.

Amassian, Margaret, and Sadowsky, James. "Mede and Mercede: A Study of the Grammatical Metaphor in 'Piers Plowman' C:IV:335–409." *Neuphilologische Mitteilungen* 72 (1971): 457–76.

Amsler, Mark. *Etymology and Grammatical Discourse in Late Antiquity and the Early Middle Ages*. Studies in the History of the Language Sciences, 44, gen. ed. E.F. Konrad Koerner. Amsterdam: John Benjamins, 1989.

Anagnostopoulos, Georgios. "The Significance of Plato's *Cratylus*." *Review of Metaphysics* 27 (1973–74): 318–45.

Apel, Karl-Otto. "The Transcendental Conception of Language: Communication and the Idea of a First Philosophy." In Herman Parret, ed., *History of Linguistic Thought and Contemporary Linguistics*, 32–61. Berlin: De Gruyter, 1976.

Atherton, Catherine. *The Stoics on Ambiguity*. Cambridge Classical Series. Cambridge: Cambridge University Press, 1993.

Bahti, Timothy. "Ambiguity and Indeterminacy: The Juncture." *Comparative Literature* 38 (1980): 207–23.

Baldwin, John W. *Masters, Princes, and Merchants: The Social Views of Peter the Chanter and His Circle*. 2 vols. Princeton, NJ: Princeton University Press, 1970.

Barney, Stephen. "The Plowshare of the Tongue: The Progress of a Symbol from the Bible to Piers Plowman." *Medieval Studies* 35 (1973): 261–93.

Baron, Roger. "L'influence de Hugues de Saint-Victor." *Recherches de Théologie ancienne et médiévale* 22 (1955), 56–71.

– *Science et sagesse chez Hugues de Saint-Victor*. Paris: P. Lethielleux, 1957.

Barthes, Roland. *Criticism and Truth*. French original, 1966. Trans. and ed. Katrine Pilcher Keuneman. Minneapolis: University of Minnesota Press, 1987.

– "From Work to Text." In *Image – Music – Text*, trans. Stephen Heath, 155–64. New York: Gill and Wang, 1977.

– *Mythologies*. Trans. and selected A. Lauers. Frogmore: Paladin, 1973.

– "The Photographic Message." In *Image – Music – Text*. Trans. and selected S. Heath, 15–31. New York: Hill and Wong, 1977.

– "Rhetoric of the Image." In *Image – Music – Text*. Trans. and selected S. Heath, 32–51. New York: Hill and Wong, 1977.

Bastid, Paul. *Proclus et le crépuscule de la pensée grecque*. Paris: J. Vrin, 1969.

Baudrillard, Jean. *Simulations*. Trans. P. Foss, P. Patton, and P. Beitchman. New York: Semiotext(e), 1983.

Bertoff, Ann E. "Problem-Dissolving by Triadic Means." *College English* 58 no 1 (Jan. 1996): 9–21.

Biggs, Frederick M. "'For God Is After an Hand': *Piers Plowman* B.17.138–205." *Yearbook of Langland Studies* 5 (1991): 17–30.

Blake, N.F. *The English Language in Medieval Literature*. London: Methuen, 1979.

Bland, Cynthia. "Langland's Use of the Term Ex vi transicionis." *Yearbook of Langland Studies* 2 (1988): 125–35.

Bloch, R. Howard. *Etymologies and Genealogies*. Chicago: University of Chicago Press, 1983.

Bloomfield, Morton W. *Piers Plowman as a Fourteenth-Century Apocalypse*. New Brunswick, NJ: Rutgers University Press, 1961.

Bloomfield, Morton W., et al. *Incipits of Latin Works on the Virtues and Vices, 1100–1500 A.D. Including a Section of Incipits of Works on the Pater noster*. Mediaeval Academy of America Publication No. 88. Cambridge, Mass.: Mediaeval Academy of America, 1979.

Bowers, John M. *The Crisis of Will in "Piers Plowman"*. Washington, DC: Catholic University of America Press, 1986.

Boyer, Ernest L. *Scholarship Reconsidered*. Princeton, NJ: Carnegie Foundation, 1990.

Burrow, John. "Words, Works, and Will: Theme and Structure in *Piers Plowman*." In Hussey, ed., *Piers Plowman: Critical Approaches*, 111–24. London: Methuen, 1969.

Carlson, Paula Jean. "The Grammar of God: Grammatical Metaphor in 'Piers Plowman' and 'Pearl.'" PhD dissertation, Columbia University, 1983.

Carruthers, Mary. *The Search for St. Truth*. Evanston, Ill.: Northwestern University Press, 1973.

Cerquiglini, Jacqueline. "Polysémie, ambiguité, et équivoque dans la théorie et la pratique poétiques du Moyen Age français." In Irène Rosier, ed., *L'ambiguité: Cinq études historiques*, 167–80. Lille: Presses Universitaires de Lille, [1988].

Chamberlin, John S. *Increase and Multiply: Arts of Discourse Procedure in the Preaching of Donne*. Chapel Hill: University of North Carolina Press, 1976.

– "What Makes *Piers Plowman* So Hard to Read?" *Style* 23 (1989): 32–48.

Charland, Th. M. *Artes praedicandi*. Publications de l'institut d'études médiévales d'Ottawa, no. 8. Paris: Vrin, 1936.

Châtillon, Jean. "La Culture de l'École de Saint-Victor au 12ᵉ Siècle." In Maurice de Gandillac and Édouard Jeauneau, eds., *Entretiens sur la Renaissance du 12ᵉ Siècle*, 147–60. Decades du Centre Culturel International de Cerisy-la-Salle, nouvelle série 9. Paris: Mouton, 1968.

– "Le *Didascalicon* de Hugues de Saint-Victor." In *La pensée encyclopédique au Moyen Age*, 63–75. Neuchatel: Éditions de la Baconnière, 1966.

– "Les Écoles de Chartres et de Saint-Victor." In *La Scuola nell'Occidente Latino dell'Alto Medioevo*, Settimane di Studio del Centro Italiano di Studi sull'alto medioevo, 19, 795–839. Spoleto: Presso la Sede del Centro, 1972.

Cheney, Mary G. *Roger, Bishop of Worcester 1164–1179*. Oxford: Clarendon Press, 1980.

Chenu, M.-D. "Un cas de Platonisme grammatical au XIIᵉ siècle." *Revue des sciences philosophiques et théologiques* 51 (1967): 666–8.

– "Imaginatio: Note de lexicographie philosophique médiévale." *Studi e testi* (Biblioteca apostolica vaticana) 122 (1946). Miscellanea Giovanni Mercati II.

– *La théologie au douzième siècle*. Paris: J. Vrin, 1957.

Clerval, A. *Les Écoles de Chartres au Moyen-Age*. Paris, 1895. Reprinted Frankfurt am Main: Minerva, 1965.

Coleman, Janet. *Piers Plowman and the "Moderni."* Rome: Edizioni di storia e letteratura, 1981.

Collart, Jean. "Saint Augustin grammairien dans le *De Magistro*." *Revue des Études Augustiniennes* 17 (1971): 279–92.

Copeland, Rita. *Rhetorical Hermeneutics and Translation in the Middle Ages*. Cambridge Studies in Medieval Literature. Cambridge: Cambridge University Press, 1991.

Cruse, D.A. *Lexical Semantics*. Cambridge Textbooks in Linguistics. Cambridge: Cambridge University Press, 1986.

Culler, Jonathan. "The Call of the Phoeneme." Intro. to Jonathan Culler, ed., *On Puns*. Oxford: Basil Blackwell, 1988.

Curtius, Ernest. *European Literature and the Latin Middle Ages*, trans. Willard R. Trask. London: Routledge and K. Paul, 1953.

Davlin, Mary Clemente. *A Game of Heuene: Word Play and the Meaning of "Piers Plowman" B*. Piers Plowman Studies Series. Cambridge: D.S. Brewer, 1989.

– "Kynde Knowyng as a Middle English Equivalent for 'Wisdom' in *Piers Plowman B*." *Medium Ævum* 50 no. 1 (1981): 5–17.

d'Avray, D.L. *The Preachng of the Friars: Sermons Diffused from Paris before 1300.* Oxford: Clarendon Press, 1985.

Della Casa, Adriana. "Les glossaires et les traites de grammaire du Moyen-Age." In *La lexicographie du latin médiéval et ses rapports avec les recherches actuelles sur la civilisation du moyen-age,* 35–46. Paris: Éditions du centre national de la recherche scientifique, 1981.

de Rijk, L.M. *Logica Modernorum I.* Assen: van Gorcum, 1962.

– *Logica Modernorum II – Part I: The Origin and Early Development of the Theory of Supposition.* Assen: van Gorcum, 1967.

Derrida, Jacques. *Of Grammatology.* Trans. G.C. Spivzak. Baltimore: Johns Hopkins University Press, 1976.

Desbordes, Françoise. "Homonymie et synonymie d'après les textes théoriques latins." In Irène Rosier, ed., *L'ambiguité: Cinq études historiques,* 51–102. Lille: Presses Universitaires de Lille, [1988].

Dronke, Peter, ed. *A History of Twelfth-Century Western Philosophy.* Cambridge: Cambridge University Press, 1988.

Ducrot, Oswald, and Todorov, Tzvetzan. *Encyclopedic Dictionary of the Sciences of Language.* Trans. Catherine Porter. Baltimore: Johns Hopkins University Press, 1979 (French 1972).

Ebbesen, Sten. "Les Grecs et l'ambiguité." In Irène Rosier, ed., *L'ambiguité: Cinq études historiques,* 15–32. Lille: Presses Universitaires de Lille, [1988].

Eco, Umberto. *The Limits of Interpretation.* Bloomington: Indiana University Press, 1990.

– *The Role of the Reader.* Bloomington: Indiana University Press, 1979.

– *Semiotics and the Philosophy of Language.* Bloomington: Indiana University Press, 1984.

Eichenbaum, Boris. "The Structure of 'Gogol's Overcoat'" [= "How Gogol's Overcoat Is Made"]. Trans. Beth Paul and Muriel Nesbitt. *Russian Review* 22 (1963): 377–99.

Empson, William. *Seven Types of Ambiguity.* First pub. 1930. London: Hogarth Press, 1984.

English, Edward D., ed. *Reading and Wisdom: The De doctrina christiana of Augustine in the Middle Ages.* Notre Dame Conferences in Medieval Studies 6. Notre Dame, Ind.: University of Notre Dame Press, 1995.

Erlich, Victor. *Russian Formalism: History–Doctrine,* 3rd ed. New Haven, Conn.: Yale University Press, 1981.

Evans, G.R. *Alan of Lille: The Frontiers of Theology in the Later Twelfth Century.* Cambridge: Cambridge University Press, 1983.

– *The Language and Logic of the Bible: The Earlier Middle Ages.* Cambridge: Cambridge University Press, 1984.

– *The Language and Logic of the Bible: The Road to Reformation.* Cambridge: Cambridge University Press, 1985.

– "The Place of Peter the Chanter's *De tropis loquendi.*" *Analecta Cisterciensia* 39 (1983): 231–53.

– "Ponendo theologica exempla: Peter the Chanter's *De tropis loquendi.*" *History of Universities* 2 (1982): 1–14.

– "A Work of 'Terminist Theology': Peter the Chanter's *De Tropis loquendi* and Some *Fallacie.*" *Vivarium* 20 (1982): 40–58.

Floyer, John Kestell, and Hamilton, Sidney Graves, eds. *Catalogue of Manuscripts Preserved in the Cathedral Library of Worcester Cathedral.* Oxford: James Parker, for the Worcestershire Historical Society, 1906.

Fontaine, Jacques. *Isidore de Seville et la culture classique dans l'espagne Wisigothique,* 2 vols. Paris: Études Augustiniennes, 1959.

Fontanier, Pierre. *Les figures de discours.* Paris: Flammarion, 1977.

Fredborg, Karin M. "The Dependence of Petrus Helias' 'Summa super Priscianum' on William of Conches' 'Glose super Priscianum.'" In *Cahiers de l'Institut des études grecques et latines* 11 (1973): 1–57.

Friend, Albert C. "Master Ode of Cheriton." *Speculum* 23 (1948): 641–58.

Gabriel, Astrik L. *Garlandia: Studies in the History of the Mediaeval University.* Mediaeval Institute, University of Notre Dame. Frankfurt am Main: Josef Knecht, 1969.

Gellrich, Jesse M. *The Idea of the Book in the Middle Ages.* Ithaca, NY: Cornell University Press, 1985.

Genette, Gérard. *Mimologiques: Voyage en Cratylie.* Paris: Éditions du Seuil, 1976.

Gersh, Stephen. *Middle Platonism and Neoplatonism: The Latin Tradition.* Publications in Medieval Studies 23.1–2. Notre Dame, Ind.: University of Notre Dame Press, 1986.

Gibson, Margaret T. "The *De doctrina christiana* in the School of St. Victor." In English, ed., *Reading and Wisdom,* 41–7.

Gibson, Strickland, ed. *Statuta Antiqua Universitatis Oxoniensis.* Oxford: Clarendon Press, 1931.

Giusberti, Franco. "A Twelfth-Century Theological Grammar [Peter the Chanter's De tropis loquendi]." In his *Materials for a Study on Twelfth-Century Scholasticism: History of Logic,* vol. II, 87–109. Naples: Bibliopolis, 1982.

Goering, Joseph. "The Summa '*Qui bene presunt*' and Its Author." In Newhauser and Alford, eds., *Literature and Religion in the Later Middle Ages,* 143–59. Binghamton, NY: Medieval and Renaissance Texts and Studies, 1994.

- *William de Montibus (c. 1140–1213): The Schools and the Literature of Pastoral Care.* Studies and Texts 108. Toronto: PIMS, 1992.

Guiraud, Pierre. "Étymologie et ethymologia." *Poétique* 11 (1972): 405–13.

Habermas, Jürgen. *The Philosophical Discourse of Modernity.* Trans. Frederick Lawrence. Cambridge, Mass.: MIT Press, 1987.

Hadot, Ilsetraut. *Arts libéraux et philosophie dans la pensée antique.* Paris: Études Augustiniennes, 1984.

Hadot, Pierre. *Marius Victorinus: Recherches sur sa vie et ses œuvres.* Paris: Études Augustiniennes, 1971.

Halm, James Paul Patrick. "The Word Made Flesh: Word-Play in 'Piers Plowman B.'" PhD thesis, University of Michigan, 1984.

Häring, Nikolaus. "Chartres and Paris Revisited." In J. Reginald O'Donnell, ed., *Essays in Honour of Anton Charles Pegis*, 268–329. Toronto: PIMS, 1984.

Harland, Richard. *Superstructuralism: The Philosophy of Structuralism and Post-structuralism.* New Accents Series. London: Methuen, 1987.

Harris, Roy. *Reading Saussure.* La Salle, Ill.: Open Court, 1987.

Hinton, Nichols, and Ohala, eds. *Sound Symbolism.* Cambridge: Cambridge University Press, 1994.

Holdcroft, David. *Saussure: Signs, System, and Arbitrariness.* Cambridge: Campbridge University Press, 1991.

Holtz, Louis. *Donat et la tradition de l'enseignement grammatical.* Paris: Centre national de la Recherche Scientifique, 1981.

Hunt, R.W. "English Learning in the Late Twelfth Century." *Translations of the Royal Historical Society,* 4th Series, 19 (1936): 19–42.

- *The History of Grammar in the Middle Ages: Collected Papers.* Ed. G.L. Bursill-Hall. Amsterdam: John Benjamins, 1980.

- *The Schools and the Cloister: The Life and Writings of Alexander Nequam (1157–1217).* Ed. and revised by Margaret Gibson. Oxford: Clarendon Press, 1984.

- "Studies in Priscian in the Eleventh and Twelfth Centuries." *Medieval and Renaissance Studies* 1 (1941–43): 194–231.

Huppé, Bernard F. "'Petrus id est Christus': Word Play in *Piers Plowman,* the B-Text." *ELH* 17 (1950): 163–90.

Husserl, Edmund. *Logical Investigations,* 2 vols. Trans. J.N. Findlay. London: Routledge and Kegan Paul, 1970.

Hussey, S.S., ed. *Piers Plowman: Critical Approaches.* London: Methuen, 1969.

Illich, Ivan. *In the Mirror of the Past.* New York: M. Boyars, 1992.

Irvine, Martin. "Interpretation and the Semiotics of Allegory in Clement of Alexandria, Origen, and Augustine." *Semiotica* 63 (1987): 33–71.

– *The Making of Textual Culture: "Grammatica" and Literary Theory, 350–1100*. Cambridge Studies in Medieval Literature, 19. Cambridge: Cambridge University Press, 1994.

Jackson, B. Darrell. "The Theory of Signs in St. Augustine's 'De doctrina christiana.'" In R.A. Markus, ed., *Augustine: A Collection of Critical Essays*, 92–147. Garden City, NY: Doubleday, 1972.

Jolivet, Jean. "Éléments pour une étude des rapports entre la grammaire et l'ontologie au moyen age." In Jan P. Bechman, ed., *Sprache und Erkenntnis im Mittelalter*, Miscellanea Mediaevalia, Bd. 13, 135–64. Berlin: de Gruyter, 1981.

– "Quelques cas de 'platonisme grammatical' du VIIᵉ au XIIᵉ siècle." In Pierre Gallais and Yves-Jean Riou, eds., *Mélanges offerts à René Crozet*, vol. I, 93–9. Poitiers: Société d'Études Médiévales, 1966.

Kaplan, Abraham, and Kris, Ernst. "Esthetic Ambiguity." *Philosophy and Phenomenological Research*, 8 (1947–48): 415–35.

Katz, J.J. *Language and Other Abstract Objects*. Totowa, NJ: Rowman and Littlefield, 1981.

Kaulbach, Ernest. *Imaginative Prophecy in the B-Text of "Piers Plowman."* Piers Plowman Studies VIII. Cambridge: D.S. Brewer, 1993.

Kretzmann, Norman. "Semantics, History of." In *The Encyclopedia of Philosophy*, vol. 7.

Lawton, David. "Alliterative Style." In Alford, ed., *Companion*, 223–49.

Leclerq, Jean. *The Love of Learning and the Desire for God*. Trans. Catharine Misrahi. New York: New American Library (Mentor), 1961.

– "Smaragde et la grammaire chrétienne." *Revue du moyen age latin* (1948): 15–22.

LeGoff, Jacques. *Intellectuals in the Middle Ages*. Oxford: Basil Blackwell, 1993.

Levin, Samuel R. *Metaphoric Worlds: Conceptions of a Romantic Nature*. New Haven, Conn.: Yale University Press, 1988.

Linder, Amnon. "The Knowledge of John of Salisbury in the Late Middle Ages." *Studi Medievali* 18 (1977): 881–932.

Longère, Jean. *La prédication médiévale*. Paris: Études Augustiniennes, 1983.

McKeon, Richard. "Aristotle's Conception of Language and the Arts of Language." *Classical Philology* 41 and 42 (1946 and 1947): 193–206; 21–50.

Mann, Jill. "Satiric Subject and Satiric Object in Goliardic Literature." *Mittellateinisches Jahrbuch* 15 (1980): 63–86.

Marcuse, Herbert. *One-Dimensional Man*. Boston: Beacon Press, 1964.

Marrou, H.I. *The History of Education in Antiquity*. Trans. George Lamb. Toronto: Mentor Books, 1964.

– *Saint Augustin et la fin de la culture antique*. Paris: Éditions E. de Boccard, 1958.

Middleton, Anne. "Two Infinites: Grammatical Metaphor in *Piers Plowman*." *ELH* 39 no. 2 (1972): 169–88.

Miner, John N. *The Grammar Schools of Medieval England*. Kingston: McGill-Queen's University Press, 1990.

Minnis, Alistair. *Medieval Theory of Authorship*. 2nd ed. Philadelphia: University of Pennsylvania Press, 1988.

Murphy, J.J. *Rhetoric in the Middle Ages*. Berkeley: University of California Press, 1974.

Murtaugh, Daniel Maher. *Piers Plowman and the Image of God*. Gainesville, Fla.: University Presses of Florida, 1978.

Norris, Christopher. *What's Wrong with Postmodernism: Critical Theory and the Ends of Philosophy*. Baltimore: Johns Hopkins University Press, 1990.

Nöth, Winfried. *Handbook of Semiotics*. Advances in Semiotics. Bloomington: Indiana University Press, 1990.

Ogden, C.K., and Richards, I.A. *The Meaning of Meaning*. New York: Harcourt Brace Jovanovich, 1923.

Ong, Walter J. "Wit and Mystery: A Revaluation in Medieval Latin Hymnody." *Speculum* 22 (1947): 310–41.

Orme, Nicholas. *English Schools in the Middle Ages*. London: Methuen, 1973.

Owst, G.R. *Literature and Pulpit in Medieval England*. Cambridge: Cambridge University Press, 1933.

Paré, Gérard Marie, Brunet, Adrien Marie, and Tremblay, Pierre. *La renaissance du XIIᵉ siècle: Les écoles et l'enseignement*. Publications de l'institut d'études medievales d'Ottawa, no. 3. Paris: Vrin, 1933.

Pavel, Thomas G. *The Feud of Language: A History of Structuralist Thought*. Oxford: Basil Blackwell, 1989.

Pfeiffer, Rudolf. *History of Classical Scholarship From the Beginnings to the End of the Hellenistic Age*. Oxford: Clarendon Press, 1968.

Pinborg, Jan. "Classical Antiquity: Greece." *Historiography of Linguistics*, vol. 13 of *Current Trends in Linguistics*, ed. Thomas A. Sebeok. 69–126. The Hague: Mouton, 1975.

Quick, Anne Wenley. "The Sources of the Quotations in Piers Plowman." PhD thesis, University of Toronto, 1982.

Quilligan, Maureen. *The Language of Allegory*. Ithaca, NY: Cornell University Press, 1979.

Raw, Barbara. "Piers and the Image of God in Man." In Hussey, ed., *Piers Plowman: Critical Approaches*, 141–79.

Reynolds, Suzanne. *Medieval Reading: Grammar, Rhetoric, and the Classical Text.* Cambridge Studies in Medieval Literature. Cambridge: Cambridge University Press, 1996.

Richards, I.A. *The Philosophy of Rhetoric.* New York: Oxford University Press, 1936.

Rist, John M. *Augustine: Ancient Thought Baptized.* Cambridge: Cambridge University Press, 1994.

Rist, John M., ed. *The Stoics.* Berkeley: University of California Press, 1978.

Robertson, D.W., and Huppé, B.F. *Piers Plowman and Striptural Tradition.* Princeton, NJ: Princeton University Press, 1951.

Robins, R.H. *Ancient and Medieval Grammatical Theory in Europe.* London: G. Bell, 1951.

Rosier, Irène. "Les acceptions du terme 'substantia' chez Pierre Helie." In Jean Jolinet et Alain de Libra, eds., *Gilbert de Poitiers et ses contemporains.* History of Logic 5. Naples: Bibliopolis, 1987.

Rosier, Irène, and Stefanini, Jean. "Théories médiévales du pronom et du nom général." In G.L. Bursill-Hall et al., eds., *De Ortu grammaticae: Studies in Medieval Grammar and Linguistic Theory in Memory of Jean Pinborg*, 285–303. Amsterdam Studies in the Theory and History of Lingusitic Science. Amsterdam: J. Benjamins, 1990.

Rosier, Irène, ed. and intro. *L'Ambiguité: Cinq études historiques.* Histoire de la linguistique, gen. ed. Anne Nicolas. Lille: Presses Universitaires de Lille, [1988].

Rouse, Richard H., and Rouse, Mary A. "Biblical Distinctions in the Thirteenth Century." *Archives d'histoire doctrinale et littéraire du moyen age* 41 (1974): 27–37.

– *Preachers, Florilegia, and Sermons: Studies on the "Manipulus florum" of Thomas of Ireland.* Toronto: PIMS, 1979.

– "Statim invenire: Schools, Preachers, and New Attitudes to the Page." In Robert L. Benson and Giles Constable, eds., *Renaissance and Renewal in the Twelfth Century*, 201–25. Cambridge, Mass.: Harvard University Press, 1982.

Rudd, Gillian. *Managing Language in Piers Plowman.* Piers Plowman Studies IX. Cambridge: D.S. Brewer, 1994.

Salter, Elizabeth. *Piers Plowman: An Introduction.* Oxford: Basil Blackwell, 1962.

Saussure, Ferdinand de. *Cours de linguistique générale.* Ed. with notes by C. Bally, A. Sechehaye, A. Reidlinger, and T. de Mauro. Paris: Payot, 1982. (Trans. as *Course in General Linguistics* by W. Baskin. New York: McGraw-Hill, 1959.)

Schaff, Adam. *Introduction to Semantics.* Trans. from Polish by O. Wojtasiewicz. New York: Macmillan and Pergamon Press, 1962.

– *Language and Cognition.* Ed. Robert S. Cohen; trans. from original 1964 Polish version by O. Wojtasiewicz. New York: McGraw-Hill, 1973.

Schmidt, A.V.C. *The Clerkly Maker: Langland's Poetic Art.* Piers Plowman Studies, No. 4. Cambridge: D.S. Brewer, 1987.

– "Langland and Scholastic Philosophy." *Medium Ævum* 38 (1969): 134–56.

– "Langland's 'Book of Conscience' and Alanus de Insulis." *Notes and Queries* 29 no. 227 (Dec. 1982).

– "Lele Wordes and Bele Paroles: Some Aspects of Langland's Word-Play." *RES* n.s. 34 (1983): 137–50.

Simpson, Greg B. "Varieties of Ambiguity: What Are We Seeking?" In David S. Gorfein, ed., *Resolving Semantic Ambiguity*, 13–21. Series: Cognitive Science. New York: Springer–Verlag, 1989.

Simpson, James. "The Role of Scientia in Piers Plowman." In Gregory Kratzmann and James Simpson, eds., *Medieval English Religious and Ethical Literature*, 49–65. Cambridge: D.S. Bewer, 1986.

Smalley, Beryl. *The Gospels in the Schools (c. 1100–c. 1280).* London: Hambledon Press, 1985.

– *The Study of the Bible in the Middle Ages.* Notre Dame, Ind.: University of Notre Dame Press, 1964.

Southern, R.W. "The Schools of Paris and the School of Chartres." In Robert L. Benson and Giles Constable, eds., *Renaissance and Renewal in the Twelfth Century*, 113–37. Cambridge, Mass.: Harvard University Press, 1982.

Spearing, A.C. "The Art of Preaching in Piers Plowman." In his *Criticism and Medieval Poetry*, 107–34. London: Edward Arnold, 1972.

– "Verbal Repetition in Piers Plowman B and C." *Journal of English and Germanic Philology* 62 (1963): 722–37.

Spencer, H. Leith. *English Preachng in the Late Middle Ages.* Oxford: Clarendon Press, 1993.

Steiner, George. *Real Presences.* Chicago: University of Chicago Press, 1989.

Stock, Brian. *Augustine the Reader: Meditation, Self-Knowledge, and the Ethics of Interpretation.* Cambridge, Mass.: Harvard University Press, 1996.

Su, Soon Peng. *Lexical Ambiguity in Poetry.* Studies in Language and Linguistics Series. London: Longman, 1994.

Sweeney, Eileen C. "Hugh of St. Victor: The Augustinian Tradition of Sacred and Secular Reading Revised." In English, ed., *Reading and Wisdom*, 61–83.

Taylor, Charles. "Language and Human Nature." In his *Human Agency and Language, Philosophical Papers I*, 215–47. Cambridge: Cambridge University Press, 1985.

– *Sources of the Self.* Cambridge, Mass.: Harvard University Press, 1989.

– "Theories of Meaning." In his *Human Agency and Language, Philosophical Papers I*, 248–92. Cambridge: Cambridge University Press, 1985.

Taylor, Daniel B. "Rethinking the History of Language Science in Classical Antiquity." In Daniel J. Taylor, ed., *The History of Linguistics in the Classical Period*, 1–16. Amsterdam: John Benjamins Publishing Co., 1987.

Thomson, David. *A Descriptive Catalogue of Middle English Grammatical Texts.* New York: Garland Publishing, 1979.

– *An Edition of the Middle English Grammatical Texts.* New York: Garland, 1984.

Todorov, Tzvetan. *Symbolism and Interpretation.* French, 1978. Trans. Catherine Porter. Ithaca, NY: Cornell University Press, 1982.

– *Theories of the Symbol.* French, 1977. Trans. Catherine Porter. Ithaca, NY: Cornell University Press, 1982.

Turner, C.H. *Early Worcester MSS.* Oxford: Clarendon Press, 1916.

Tynianov, Yuri. *The Problem of Verse Language.* Russian, 1924. Trans. and ed. Michael Sosa and Brent Harvey. Ann Arbor, Mich.: Ardis, 1981.

Ullmann, Stephen. *Semantics.* Oxford: Basic Blackwell, 1962.

Vance, Eugene. *Marvelous Signals: Poetics and Sign Theory in the Middle Ages.* Lincoln: University of Nebraska Press, 1986.

Voloshinov, V.N. *Marxism and the Philosophy of Language.* Trans. Ladislav Matejha and I.R. Titunik. New York: Seminar Press, 1973.

von Nolcken, Christina. "Some Alphabetical Compendia and How Preachers Used Them in Fourteenth–Century England." *Viator* 12 (1981), 27–88.

Wagner, David, ed. *The Seven Liberal Arts in the Middle Ages.* Bloomington: Indiana University Press, 1983.

Wallis, Faith E. "Communis et universalis: The Catholicon of Giovanni Balbi of Genoa, O.P." Licentiate paper in Medieval Studies, PIMS, Toronto, Aug. 1981.

Waswo, Richard. *Language and Meaning in the Renaissance.* Princeton, NJ: Princeton University Press, 1987.

Wenzel, Siegfried. "Medieval Sermons." In Alford, ed., *Companion*, 155–72.

Wilmart, André. "Un répertoire d'exégèse." In H. Vincent, ed., *Memorial Lagrange*, 307–46. Paris: Librairie Lecoffre, 1940.

Zinn, Grover A., Jr. "The Influence of Augustine's *De doctrina christiana* upon the Writings of Hugh of St. Victor." In English, ed., *Reading and Wisdom*, 48–60.

Ziolkowski, Jan. *Alan of Lille's Grammar of Sex: The Meaning of Grammar to a Twelfth–Century Intellectual.* Cambridge, Mass.: Medieval Academy of America, 1985.

Zumthor, Paul. *Langue, texte, énigme.* Paris: du Seuil, 1975.

Index

Abelard, Peter, 46, 117

Adelard of Bath, 22; *De eodem et verso*, 22

Alanus de Insulis: *De planctu naturae*, 82; *Distinctiones dictionum theologica-lium*, 16

Alford, John, 7, 16, 69, 82, 84, 85, 100

allegory, allegorical, 16; Carolingian commentators, 39; Goethe on, 43; interpretation of medieval litera-ture, 75; interpretation of the Bible in Augustine, 40; not a central con-cept in this book, 4 (*see also* Alanus de Insulis)

Allen, Judson, 16, 54

Allen, W.S., 95

alliteration, in *Piers Plowman*, 15, 21, 69

Amassian, Margaret, and Sadowsky, James, 82, 137

ambiguity, 5; in arts-of-discourse doc-trine, 16, 17, 23, 31, 41, 46, 51, 73; in classical period, 9; figurative, 37, 39, 43; metaphorical, 55; in *Piers Plowman*, 6–7, 13, 38, 60, 67, 70, 74; in poetic language, 20, 58; as resource for meditative richness, 30, 73; syntactical, 56; versus vagueness, 41–2; of various kinds of signs: in Augustine, 32, 34, 76, in John of Salisbury, 22, 46; of words, 54, 65, 76

– lexical: in classical period, 24, 25, 29, Stoic doctrine on, 26–7; com-pound, 34, 43, 74; conjunctive, 19,

30–1, 33, 37, 51, 69, 72, 74; defined, 4–5, 8–9; disjunctive, 19, in Aristotle, 25, 26, 31, in Augustine, 32, 46, 47, 51, 58, 67, 74, in Latin grammar, 28, 30; figurative, 37, 39; as result of excess of meaning, 17–18; sacred power of, 37; of scrip-tural words, 34, 36, 38; as source of experience among Christians, 33–4; univocals and equivocals (August-ine), 32

– words-as-words, 8–9, 27, 32, 73, 77, 78, 89, 112, 128; in Augustine, 100–7; in Barthes, 128; in classical philos-ophers, 92; defined, 4–5; in John of Salisbury, 122; in Langland, 82, 139–57; as source of knowledge about reality and Creation, 81

ambiguous-equivocals-in-art (August-ine), 32, 36; -in-use (Augustine), 32, 76

amphibolia, 26, 28, 29. *See also* ambiguity

Amsler, Mark, 96, 99, 100, 108, 111

Anagnostopoulos, Georgios, 96–7

analogue, 128. *See also* Barthes

analogy, as expanding fullness of mean-ing, 15

Anselm of Laon, 23; *Glossa ordinaria*, 22

antanaclasis, defined, 19

Antisthenes, 24

Apel, K.O., 87–8

Aristotelian: dialectic, 32; philoso-phers, 25, 27; sense of quality, 120

Aristotle, 25–6, 27, 30, 46, 85, 129;
Categories, 26, 32, 119; De interpretatione, 26, 46; Organon, 118; On
Sophistical Refutations, 25, 26, 46;
three sorts of fallacy, 26; Topics, 26
ars praedicandi: doctrines, 14; in late
twelfth century, 57; Richard of
Thetford on, 56; Thomas of
Chobham's treatise on, 54–5
art of grammar: analysis of words, 76;
in classical period and Augustine,
25, 69, 92, 102, 103, 106 (see also
ambiguous-equivocals-in-art); in John
of Salisbury, 122; in Langland, used
to explore resources of knowledge,
140, 144–5, 152; and meaning, 44;
medieval, 3, 7, 78, 81; Neoplatonic
elements in, 112; parts of speech,
99, 108, 109, 110, 117 (see also
Diogenes the Babylonian); in pedagogical methods of Masters of Paris,
92, of Sophists, 27; pedagogical tradition in, 108 (see also compendia);
relevant to all learning, 110 (see also
Isidore; Priscian); role in poetry and
in Piers Plowman, 81–2; surveyed by
Irvine, 41; treatises on, 28, 135
arts-of-discourse doctrines: ambiguity
in, 19, 31, 70 (see also Langland,
William: analysed); in ancient and
medieval grammarians, 78; classical,
for Christian uses (Augustine), 8,
24, 31, 37, 38, 102; in Derrida, 132;
in Hellenistic and Roman period,
94; in Hugh of St Victor, 91, 113; a
main subject of this book, 4, 6, 7; in
Peter the Chanter, 45, 47, 51, 53; in
preaching, 44, 55, 81; procedures,
60–1; in Thomas of Chobham, 55;
in town grammar schools, 57; in
twelfth century, 9, 13, 16, 17, 23,
53; Victorine ideas about, 135; in
William de Montibus, 54
arts of theology, 54
arts of the trivium (grammar, logic,
rhetoric), 23; in Augustine, 38; to
discern the truth of discourse, 114–
15; etymology of, 135; in Hugh of
St Victor, 91; in Isidore, 108; for
reading Scripture, 31; reformulated
by Paris Masters, 122; in Thierry of
Chartres, 118

arts tradition, 5, 19, 21, 46, 52–3, 56;
classical, 25; renewed interest in,
113; three-point interrelationship
(Creation, philosophy, language),
90–1; twelfth-century reformulation
of, 30, 53, 90–2
Atherton, Catherine, 26, 27, 29, 32
Augustine, 4, 7–8, 9, 24, 31–9, 49, 51,
55, 57, 72–4, 91, 98, 111, 113, 116,
118–19, 122, 125, 128, 141, 144,
148, 156; art of grammar in, 25, 92;
discourse arts in, 26, 81; exposition
of scriptural multivocity, 17, 28, 29,
30–49, 89; on language, 13, 16, 23,
29, 38, 86, 92, 100–7; principles for
a "new method," 101, 105, 115, 121;
theory of ambiguity in, 21, 31, 32,
36, 76; word-as-word, 27
– WORKS: Confessions, 38, 101, 105–6,
109; De catechizandis rudibus, 106; De
civitate Dei, 100; De dialectica, 23, 31,
33, 34, 36; De doctrina christiana, 4,
23, 29, 30–4, 36, 38, 40–3, 47–51,
53, 55–6, 59, 61, 76, 91, 100, 113;
De genesi ad litteram, 104; De magistro,
92, 101, 104–5, 130; De musica, 23;
De ordine, 101–4, 109, 115, 121; De
Trinitate, 106; De utilitate credendi, 33;
Retractiones, 104
Aulus Gellius, 27

Bahti, Timothy, 42
Balbus, Johannes: Catholicon, 136–7,
151–2
Baldwin, John W., 23, 45, 51, 53, 57
Barney, Stephen, 14
Baron, Roger, 114, 115, 135
Barthes, Roland, 21, 41, 43–4, 51, 127;
mythic sign, 128–9, 131, 132
Bastid, Paul, 97
Baudrillard, Jean, 127–8; "simula-
tions," 131–2; "vertigo of interpreta-
tion and duplication," 133
Becket, Thomas à, 134
Bernard, St, 102
Bernard of Chartres, 92, 117, 122
Bertoft, Ann, 87
Bible, 15, 22, 34–6, 40–2, 44–7, 49,
55, 61–2, 64, 67, 70–1
Blake, N.F., 7
Bland, Cynthia, 82, 137
Bloch, R. Howard, 85, 112

Bloomfield, Morton W., 8, 54, 85
Bodleian Library, 47
Boethius, 46, 115, 116; *De divisione*, 56;
    De Trinitate, 118; *On Aristotle's "De*
    interpretatione" (*see also* semiotics: tri-
    adic), 86, 87, 118
Bowers, John M., 8
Boyer, Ernest, v, 5
Buttimer, C.H., 114, 115

Cambridge University Library, xi
Canterbury, 120, 134
Carlson, Paula, 82, 91
Carruthers, Mary, 74
Carolingians, 30, 48, 109, 110, 112. *See*
    also Remigius; Smaragdus
Cassiodorus, 108
cathedrals, 57; cathedral school of
    Canterbury, 120; cathedral schools,
    91; intellectual life in English, 134
Cerquiglini, Jacqueline, 5
Charland, Th.M., 56
Chartres, 91; masters at, 116
Châtillon, Jean, 91, 135
Chaucer, Geoffrey, 8
Cheney, Mary, 134
Chenu, M.-D., 22, 91, 115, 117, 118
Chomsky, Noam, 85
Chrysippus, 26, 27, 32, 76
Cicero, 116, 119; *De inventione*, 118
classical antiquity, 5, 9; in Augustine,
    23; classical culture, 38, 48; classical
    learning, 40; glossaries, 29; gram-
    mar in, 39, 126; use of poetic text,
    24, 36; view of language (in rela-
    tion to reality), 86, 92–9, 108–9,
    116, 119
Clerval, A., 118
Coleman, Janet, 8
Collart, Jean, 101
"combinatorial explosion," 6, 44, 69
compendia (commentaries), 72, 108;
    anonymous, on Petrus de Isolela's
    Summa, 135; *Catholicon* (Johannes
    Balbus), 136; on Donatus, 109–11;
    on Euclid, 103, 117; on Hugutio of
    Pisa, 136; Peter Helias: on Pris-
    cian's *Institutiones*, 119; Proclus: on
    Cratylus, 97; on Euclid, 103, Thi-
    erry: on Aristotle, 118, on Boethius,
    118, on Cicero, 118, *Eptateuchon*,
    118

"compositionality" (approach to lan-
    guage), defined, 33
Condillac, Étienne Bonnot de, 125
Copeland, Rita, 33
Corpus Christi College, Cambridge
    (cccc), xi, 48, 50
"crisis of sign," 5, 132
Cruse, D.A., 17, 19, 67; "reversive
    pairs," 77–8, 88
Culler, Jonathan, 9, 20, 69, 88, 112

Davlin, Sister Mary Clemente, 8, 15,
    16, 84, 89–90, 144
d'Avray, D.I., 45, 51, 53
deconstructionists, 5
Della Casa, Adriana, 30
de Rijk, L.M., 46, 120
Derrida, Jacques: "arche-writing," 131;
    invalidation of discourse, 132; *Of*
    Grammatology, 129–30
Desbordes, Françoise, 28
Deuteronomy, 35, 36
Diogenes Laertius, 26, 27, 99, 101
Diogenes the Babylonian, 101; *On*
    Voice, 99
disputatio (*quaestiones*), 45, 46, 49, 51;
    see also *lectio; praedicatio*
dissonantia, 46
distinctiones dictionaries: *distinctiones*
    collections, 57, 58, 62, 64, 70; *Dis-*
    tinctiones dictionum theologicalium (*see*
    also Alanus de Insulis), 16; etymolog-
    ical encyclopaedic dictionaries in
    twelfth century, 111–12; *Origines* (*see*
    also Isidore of Seville), 111; *Summa*
    "Abel" (*see also* Peter the Chanter),
    30, 46, 48, 50, 51; William de
    Montibus, 54
Donatus, 28, 29, 30, 33, 82, 92; *Ars*
    grammatica, 28, 99, 109–11; in Hugh
    of St Victor, 116; in Peter Helias,
    119–20; in Thierry of Chartres,
    118
Dronke, Peter, 118
Ducrot, Oswald, 20

Ebbesen, Sten, 24, 25, 27, 32
Eco, Umberto, 39–44, 51, 55
Eichenbaum, Boris, 7
Empson, William, 20
enarratio: for interpretation of the
    Bible, 99; in *Piers Plowman*, 82; in

poetry, 98; scriptural interpretation
by Augustine, 31, 34; strategy of
Paris Masters, 136
Enlightenment, 125
Erlich, Victor, 21
Evans, G.R., 22, 45, 47, 91
etymology: etymological dictionaries
(Isidore of Seville), 111–12, 116;
etymological investigation, 135; as
expanding fullness of meaning, 15,
78, 83; of grammatical terms in
Augustine, 101
Eucherius, bishop of Lyons: *Formulae
spiritualis intelligentiae*, 30, 48
Evesham (Benedictine house), 134, 135
exegesis, 4; biblical 85, 99; exegetes in
Renaissance, 39, 40; exegetical
preaching, 13, 16, 17, 23, 55, 59,
81; exegetical procedures in Augustine, 33, 40, 100, in Eucherus, 30;
exegetical writing, 22; figurative, 71;
medieval, 41; patristic, 44

focal points of meaning, 17–18, 55
Fontaine, Jacques, 99, 111
Fontanier, Pierre, 19
Fourth Lateran Council (1215), 57

Galen, 26
Gellrich, Jesse, 84–5, 88
Genesis, 125
Genette, Gerard, 95, 96; *Mimologiques*,
123
Gersh, Stephen, 111
Gibson, Margaret T., 91
Giusberti, Franco, 51
gloss, 51, 75
Glossa ordinaria, 22
glossaries, 29, 30, 45; *differentiae*
glossaries, 48–9; *Glose* (William of
Conches), 119; *Glosule* (William of
Champeaux), 119; Joseph Goering,
53, 54, 61, 66; Johann Wolfgang von
Goethe, 43; Nikolai Gogol (similar-
ity to Langland), 7; in verse: *Syn-
onyma* and *Aequivoca* (*see also* John of
Garland), 57
glossing, 116; Victorines on glossing
Cicero, 119
goliardic satire (substantive relation
between words and things), 82–4,
126

Goodridge, J.F., 67
Gorgias, 93
Gower, John, 8
grammar (*see also enarratio*): classes of
words (*Protagoras*), 25; definition of,
in Hugh of St Victor, 115; grammar
masters, 103; grammar textbooks
(*see also* glossaries), 30; grammatical
art versus speculative grammar, 8;
grammatical doctrine of ambiguity,
28–9; Latin grammarians, 27, 37; as
a legislator of language, 98; as one
of arts of trivium, 25; and richness
of implication in poetry, 20–1; role
in medieval literature, 7–8; as a subject, 27, 93; town grammar schools,
57, 82, 90
grammarians, 31, 38, 76, 78; role of,
33; treatment of rhetorical figures,
33
grammatical Platonism, 77, 83–4, 87,
92, 112, 116, 134
Greek, 25; Bible, 34
Groarke, Leo, xi
Guiraud, Pierre, 88–9

Habermas, Jurgen, 158
Hadot, Ilsetrant, 102, 103
Halm, James Paul Patrick, 15–16, 165
Häring, Nikolaus, 119
Harland, Richard, 127, 128; centrifu-
galism, 132
Harris, Roy, 123–5
Hebrew, 34; Bible, 34
Hegel, G.W.F., 158
Heraclitus, 93; view of language, 96
Herder, Johann Gottfried: triadic semi-
otic, 125, 158
Hinton, Nichols, and Ohala, 77
Holdcroft, David, 124
Holtz, Louis, 96, 99, 109
Homer, 24, 27
homonyms, 19–20, 22, 25, 29, 32–3,
35–7, 159; glossary of, 30–1
homonymy, 5, 75–6; in Aristotle, 26,
38, 46; in glossaries, 57; in Lang-
land, 59; in Latin grammarians, 28;
metaphor, 18; scriptural dictionary
of, 16; in Stoic doctrine, 27; in
Summa "Abel", 48–9; in Thomas
of Chobham, 55; in wordplay, 14–
15, 43

Horace, 75
Hugh of Avalon, Bishop, 53
Hugh of St Victor, 22, 89, 113, 116,
    120–1, 148; *De grammatica*, 115–16;
    Didascalion, 91, 113–16, 145–6;
    Epitome, 113–15; legacy of, 135
Hugutio of Pisa, 136
Humboldt, Wilhelm von: *On Language*,
    125–6, 158
Hunt, R.W., 45, 48, 134, 135
Huppé, Bernard F., 14–16, 20, 60
Husserl, Edmund, 85; triadic semiot-
    ics, 124–5
hypersemiosis, hypersemiotic, 17–18,
    21, 31, 33, 38, 42, 69, 81; defined,
    4; potential of language, 76; signifi-
    cation, 51

icon, 128; iconic representation, 132
improprietas, 47
interdisciplinary approach, v, 5, 6, 9
Irvine, Martin, 4, 7–8, 31, 38, 41, 74,
    96, 99, 108–9, 111
Isidore of Seville, 50, 57–8, 84, 136; *De
    differentiis*, 50; *Origines* (*Etymologia-
    rum*), 58, 83, 108, 110–12, 115–16
isomorphism, 76; isomorphic reason-
    ing in Augustine, 100, 102, in
    Stoics, 96, 98–9

Jackson, B. Darrell, 31, 32, 115
Jerome, 28, 99, 109
Jocelin of Brakelond, 134
John of Garland, 57; *Synonyma* and
    Aequivoca, 57
John of Salisbury, 22, 46–7, 116–17,
    119, 121–3; in Langland, 139; *Meta-
    logicon*, 92, 116–17, 119, 121, 134;
    Policraticus, 46, 83, 134
Jolivet, Jean, 83, 112–13, 116–17

Kaplan, Abraham, 19
Katz, J.J., 85
Kretzmann, Norman, 26
Kris, Ernst, 19

Langland, William, 3, 5, 7, 8, 13, 31,
    38, 39, 44, 45, 52, 53, 54, 56, 57,
    58, 60–7, 71–2, 73, 74, 78, 81, 90,
    92; affinity with *distinctiones*, 51;
    ambiguity in, 17; analysed, 13–16,
    19–21, 60–72, 81–6, 139–56;

criticism about, 13–16, 67, 73–5,
    81–6, 89–90, 91; and discourse of
    preaching, 13; grammatical con-
    cepts in, 82; homiletic idiom of, 14;
    interest in liberal arts, 103; Latin
    quotations in, 22; *Piers Plowman*, 4–9,
    42, 44, 46, 53–4, 57, 60–72, 74, 81,
    85, 91, 94, 102, 106, 123, 134, 137–
    8; relations between sign and reality,
    83–4, 86, 89; repetition-alliteration,
    21; repetitions in, 19–20; "word" and
    "work" unity, 107, 110, 112, 133–5,
    137; wordplay in, 14–16, 30, 42
language: in Augustine, 100–10; gram-
    matical Platonism, 77, 83–4, 86, 90;
    language and reality, 5, 22, 26;
    logological view of, 16, 22; philoso-
    phy of language, 85, 133; poetic lan-
    guage, 5; as resource for knowledge,
    4, 6, 19, 20, 21, 28, 31, 33, 39, 44,
    71, 73; as source of experience of
    the Word among Christians, 33–4;
    theories of language, 84–6. *See also*
    significance; signification
"langue" (*see* Saussure), 124, 127, 131,
    158
Latin, 7; grammar book, 82; grammari-
    ans, 27; preaching in, 57; quota-
    tions in Langland, 22; twelfth-
    century poets, 137; wordplay in
    medieval Latin hymns, 14
Lawton, David, 15, 21, 69, 81
Leclerq, Jean, 30, 108
lectio (commenting), 45, 51; William de
    Montibus's, 54. *See also disputatio*;
    praedicatio
Le Goff, 91
Levin, Samuel, 4, 36, 159
liberal arts, 102–3, 121; role in
    Langland, 134
Lincoln Cathedral, 134
literary criticism, linked to philosophy
    of language, 5
Locke, John, 125
logical fallacies, 26, 46
logocentrism, 5; versus phonocentrism,
    129, 130, 159. *See also* language
London, 56, 137
Longère, Jean, 45, 51, 56

McGarry, D.D., 116–17, 119, 121–2
Mackenzie, Canon Iain, xi

McKeon, Richard, 26
McLuhan, Marshall, 132
Mallarmé, Stéphane, 39, 43
Mann, Jill, 82, 83–4, 92, 112,
   126
Marcuse, Herbert, v, 3, 9; contrast
   with Saussure's ideas, 123; language
   as resource, 133; *One-Dimensional
   Man*, 159
Marius Victorinus, 109
Marrou, H.I., 23, 24, 27, 31, 33, 39,
   40, 44, 100
Marx, Karl, 132
meaning: excess of, 36, 41, 44, 127–
   8, 159; literal, 75–7; multiple, 31,
   38, 39, 46, 75; multiplication of,
   56; richness of, 73; surface, 4, 58,
   75; surplus of, 4, 13–14, 17–21, 34,
   42, 54, 73, 94, 100, 106, 122, 139
medieval English poetry, relevance of
   arts doctrines to, 7
mendicant study centres, 57
metaphor (*see also* homonymy), 55, 64–
   5, 69–71, 137; as clue to medieval
   mind, 7; as conceptual association,
   28; grammatical, 82, 117; in Langland, 141, 143–4, 148; metaphorical ambiguity, 55; metaphorical
   meaning, 31, 33, 37, 44, 75; metaphoric signification, 41, 49, 157; in
   Scripture, 34–6; surplus connota-
   tion of, 43
metonymy, defined, 18
Middleton, Ann, 84, 137, 147–8
Miner, John N., 57
Minnis, Alistair, 8
monastic education, 108, 134
monastic philosophy, and *Piers
   Plowman*, 8
motivation: retromotivation, 88–9; of
   sign, 92; of words, 90
Murphy, J.J., 45, 55
Murtaugh, Daniel Maher, 53, 91, 113,
   143, 144

Neoplatonists, 92, 94, 96, 102, 106,
   109, 111
"new method." *See* Augustine: *De
   dialectica*
nominalism, 5, 8; modern, 123; poststructuralist, 159
Norris, Christopher, 127, 131

Noth, Winfried, 86

obscurity (*obscuritas*), 32–4, 74
Odo of Cheriton, 57
Ogden, C.K., and Richards, I.A.: *The
   Meaning of Meaning*, 86–8. *See also*
   semiotics: triadic
Old English poetry, 8
Old Testament, 35
Ong, Walter, 14
onomatopoeia, 5, 77
ontic logos, 86–90, 93, 96, 102, 105,
   112, 126, 129; in Langland, 141, 143
ontology, of language, 9, 81; ontologiz-
   ing semiology, 126; opacity, 43; semi-
   ologizing ontology, 98–9, 123; in
   Stoics, 94; of words, 85
Orme, Nicholas, 57
Owst, G.R., 13–14
Oxford, 138

panmetaphoricism, 40–1. *See also*
   allegory
Paré, Gérard Marie, 120
Paris Masters, 8–9, 21–2, 29, 31, 39,
   54, 72, 91–2, 116, 119–20, 122,
   134–5, 156
Paris schools, 53, 57, 113, 134
past mediating present (Marcuse), 9
Paul, St, 35–6
Pearsall, Derek, xi, 66, 82
Pershore, 135
Peter Helias: contrast with Saussure,
   124, 126, 127; source for Balbus's
   Catholicon, 136; *Summa super Priscianum*, 119, 120, 135, 136; words
   versus reality, 119–21, 135–7
Peter Lombard, 62–3; *magna glosatura*,
   45; *Sententiae*, 62–3
Peter of Cornwall, 48
Peter the Chanter, 22, 45, 53–5, 57,
   61–3, 65, 70; on ambiguity, 46–7; *De
   tropis loquendi*, 45–7, 51, 54–5, 135;
   scientia rerum, 55; sets up gloss tradition, 45; *Summa "Abel"*, 46, 48–53,
   55, 57, 63; *Summa de sacramentis*, 45;
   Verbum abbreviatum, 22, 45, 51–3, 61
   (*see also distinctiones*)
Petrus de Isolela: *Summa*, 135
Pfeiffer, Rudolf, 24, 25
philosophy of language: linked to
   literary criticism, 5

Piers Plowman. See under Langland, William

Pinborg, Jan, 31, 96

Plato, 24, 93, 100, 109, 117, 118, 120; *Cratylus*, 93–6, 101, 103, 117, 133; *Meno*, 97, 102; "Platonic experimentation," 143. *See also* ontic logic; ontology: semiologizing ontology

poetic language: in classical period, 24, 27; medieval, 5, 17; in nineteenth-century poets, 42; shift from naturalist referentialism to conventionalist relationalism, 85; similitudes in, 28

polixenus. *See* polysemy: = polixenus

polysemic ambiguity, 76

polysemy, polysemous, 4, 18, 32–3, 37, 50–1, 75, 157; in Aristotle, 26, 46; in Barthes, 129; in grammar, 28; meaning, 59, 157; metaphoric meaning, 41, 43; multiplication of ambiguous words, 70, 72; = polixenus, 47; senses of words, 55, 57, 61; in Servius, 29; signification, 58; in Stoic doctrine, 27; words, 19, 30, 35, 36, 65

postmodernism, 5, 127–8, 133

poststructuralists, 41–2, 127, 128, 134–5; revolution, 158

praedicatio (preaching), 45. *See also disputatio, lectio*

preaching: arts-of-discourse in, 44, 47, 52; in Augustine, 33, 34, 38; exegetical, 13; in Latin 57; medieval, 3, 7, 13, 14, 17, 56; in *Piers Plowman*, 30; *praedicatio*, 45; "*praedicatio suspenditur*," 52; public discourse of, in *Piers Plowman*, 71; richness of signification in, 21; role in Christian society, 91; "summa" of, 54; twelfth-century, 8, 22, 23, 45; urban revival, 8, 91

primary words, 101

Priscian, 108, 110–11, 116, 118–19, 120, 124, 127, 136, 147; *Institutiones*, 108, 111, 118, 119, 120

Proclus, 97, 103, 117

Prodicus, 25, 27, 29

Protagoras, 24–5, 27, 93–4, 96

Psalms, 4, 45, 54

pun, 15; "historicized," 112; in Latin, 147. *See also* goliardic satire

Quick, Anne Wenley, 22

Quilligan, Maureen, 38

Rawlinson Ms., 47

realism, 5

Remigius of Auxurre: *In artem Donati*, 109–10

Reynolds, Suzanne, 7, 75, 82

rhetorical language: in Langland, 21; in poetic verse, 17; rhetorical figures, 33; rhetorical ingenuity, 18; rhetoric of concealment, 75; in sermons, 17

rhetoric of texts, 3

Richard of St Victor, 135; *Liber exceptionum*, 135

Richard of Wetheringsett: "*Qui bene presunt*", 54, 66

Rist, John M., 23, 99, 106

Robertson, D.W., 16

Robins, R.H., 85

Roger, bishop of Worcester, 134

romantic, 4, 39, 42, 127, 158; philosophers, 126; poetic theory, 42; symbolism, 41; view of language, 40

Rosier, Irene, 119, 120

Rudd, Gillian, 74, 158

Russian formalists, 5, 7. *See also* Eichenbaum, Boris

sacramentalism. *See* grammatical Platonism

St Victor, Abbey of, 91, 134, 135

Salisbury, 54, 134

Salter, Elizabeth, 14, 19

Samson of Bury, Abbot, 134

Sapir-Whorf hypothesis, 87

Saussure, Ferdinand de, 76, 85, 128, 131, 133, 158; concept of sign, 123–5; dyadic model of language, 87, 123, 127, 129, 130; synchronic linguistics, 86

Schaff, Adam, 123, 125; language as resource for understanding world, 133; process of cognition, 127

Schmidt, A.V.C., 8, 15, 16, 67, 78, 83, 155

"scholarship of integration," v, 5. *See also* Boyer, Ernest

scholasticism: nominalistic, 8; versus twelfth-century thought, 8; at universities, 8

School of St Victor, 121

Scripture: ambiguous words in, 13, 46, 48; coherence of scriptural meaning, 35, 47, 55; implication in *Piers*

Plowman, 15–16, 20; interpretation of, in Middle Ages, 41, 99; lecturing on, 23, 31; metaphor in, 14, 65; in Peter the Chanter, 45, 47, 49; reading of, by Augustine, 28–30, 33–4, 37–9, 42, 49, 71; richness of language, 34, 40, 44, 48, 55; self-reflective reading of, 113; system of significations in, 21, 22, 40; theological study of, 52, 54–5
semantic: analysis, 43; field, 37; nebula, 42
semanticist critics, 20–1
semantics, revolution in, 84–5
semiotic, semiotics, 41; designative and expressive ways of thinking about language, 88–9, 100, 102–3, 112–13, 123, 125; semiotic supplementarity, 75; triadic versus dyadic, 86–8, 90, 97–8, 123, 125–7, 133
semiotical ontologies, 89, 90
Senatus, 134
sermons, 13; anthologies of preaching, 53–4, 56–7; rhetorical language of, 17, 34; of Richard of St Victor, 135; Samaritan's sermon, 44, 60–72; "school sermon," 51; verbally oriented versus theological school sermon, 8
Servius, 29, 37, 47, 50
sign, signs, 5, 46, 49; arbitrariness of, 129–30; in Barthes, 128–9; motivation of (*see also* Saussure), 76–8, 81; signification of, 46; system of, in Saussure, 124
significance: abundant, 20; moral, in Bible, 22, 33, 34, 39; symbolic, 39, 75; wealth of, disclosed, 15
signification, 34–5, 55–6, 59, 69, 76, 128; abundance of, 21–2; ambiguous, 47; in classical and modern theories, 87; differentiation of, 60; excess, 4, 21, 27, 31, 72; figurative, 37, 43; hypersemiotic, 51; indirect (in Goethe), 43; of language in Augustine, 105; literal, 75; metaphoric, 41; multiplication of, 60; multiplicity of, 40, 46, 48–51; polysemous, 58; richness of, as source of knowledge, 73–4; surplus, 157; of symbol, 40–1; system of, in Scripture, 40

signifier, 34, 74; in Augustine, 105; in Barthes, 128; in Baudrillard, 132; in Saussure, 87, 128, 130
similitudes, 34, 55–7, 60, 64–6, 69, 71–2
Simonides, 24–5, 27
Simpson, Greg B., 17
Simpson, James, 16, 91, 148
Skeat, W.W., 22, 61, 83
Smalley, Beryl, 23, 91
Smaragdus of St Mihiel: *Expositio super Donatum*, 30, 109–10
Socrates, 24, 25; on correctness of names in *Cratylus*, 94–6; on knowledge about things in *Meno*, 97. *See also* ontic logos
Sophists, 24–5, 27, 92; arts-of-discourse, 98; on correctness of names, 93–5, 118; education, 38, 57
Southern, R.W., 119
Spearing, A.C., 14, 19
Spencer, H. Leith, 8, 57
Stefanini, Jean, 119
Steiner, George, 158–9
Stock, Brian, 101
Stoics, 25–8, 30, 76, 106, 109–10, 115, 128, 151; etymological research, 98; influence on Augustine, 101–2; logic, 31; mythology of cosmogenesis, 99; notions about language, 94, 96; semantics, 32
structuralism, 87, 127, 158
structuralists, 41–2
Su, Soon Peng, 19, 35, 41–3, 67
summae. *See under* Peter Helias; Peter the Chanter; Petrus de Isolela; Richard of Wetheringsett; Thomas of Chobham
superstructuralist notion of language, 127
Sweeney, Eileen C., 91, 113
"symbolic density," 22
symbolist: aesthetic, 39; in *Summa "Abel"*, 48; symbol in Goethe, 43; view of language, 40
syncategoremata = function words, 47
synonyms: in Augustine, 31, 35, 38, 40; in Donatus, 28; in Peter the Chanter, 49–50; in *Piers Plowman*, 62; a scriptural dictionary of, 15; in Sophists, 25; in Thomas of Chobham, 55; in twelfth century, 22
synonymy, 57, 59

Taylor, Charles, 86–9, 93, 106, 112, 123, 125, 126, 129, 133, 158
Taylor, Daniel J., 27, 113–15
Terence, 28, 29, 33
Theon of Alexandria, 26
theory, contemporary, 6
"theory wars," 3
Thierry of Chartres, 83, 113, 117–20, 156
Thomas of Chobham, 53–6, 66, 71, 134; *Summa de arte praedicandi*, 54–5
Thomas of Marlborough, 134–5
Thomson, David, 136
Todorov, Tzvetan, 20, 39, 42–4, 51, 69
Tremblay, Pierre, 120
Trinity: analogues to faculties of mind, 105; in Augustine, 104; in Langland, 143
tropes (theory of), 34
Tweedale, Martin, 118
Tynianov, Yuri, 20–1

vagueness, as opposed to ambiguity, 42, 43
Valéry, Paul, 89
Vance, Eugene, 7, 84–5, 88
vernacular, 7–8, 61, 72–3; in English poetry: Langland, 82
Victorine, Victorines, 22, 91, 118–19; ideas, 135; sermons, 137
Virgil, 27, 29, 33, 50, 74, 108
von Nolcken, Christina, 51

Wallis, Faith E., 136
Waswo, Richard, 85
Wenzel, Siegfried, 13
William de Montibus, 53–4, 66, 71; *Numerale*, 61, 66; preaching and pastoral ministry, 134; *Similitudinarium*, 66; *Tropi*, 54; *Versarius*, 66, 71
William of Champeaux (founder of Abbey of St Victor), 119
William of Conches, 116–17, 119
Wilmart, André, 49, 51
Worcester Cathedral, xi; lectures and manuscripts, 8, 54, 56, 135, 137; Peter Helias's *Summa*, 119; work of Englishmen schooled in France, 134
wordplay: defined, 13, 16; homonymous, 43; in *Piers Plowman*, 14–15, 17, 30, 42, 60; in Scripture, 30, 37; in sermons, 57; in Terence's plays, 29
words: as ambiguous tools of thought, 74; categories of, in Scripture (Augustine), 34–7; classes of, 81, 100; force of, 31; primary (*see also* "new method"), 101; relation with things, 82–4, 86–7; retromotivation, 88; superfluous excess of, 51; unique power to reveal reality, 6; "word" and "work" in Langland, 107, 133; the Word in Augustine, 104–6

Zinn, Grover A., Jr, 91
Zumthar, Paul, 111